D0722328

Mapping Extreme Right Ideology

Mapping Extreme Right Ideology

An Empirical Geography of the European Extreme Right

Sarah Harrison
Research Officer, London School of Economics and Political Science, UK

and

Michael Bruter
Senior Lecturer in European Political Science, London School of Economics and Political Science, UK

First published 2011 by
PALGRAVE MACMILLAN

Palgrave Macmillan in the UK is an imprint of Macmillan Publishers Limited, registered in England, company number 785998, of Houndmills, Basingstoke, Hampshire RG21 6XS.

Palgrave Macmillan in the US is a division of St Martin's Press LLC, 175 Fifth Avenue, New York, NY 10010.

Palgrave Macmillan is the global academic imprint of the above companies and has companies and representatives throughout the world.

Palgrave® and Macmillan® are registered trademarks in the United States, the United Kingdom, Europe and other countries.

ISBN: 978–0–230–58101–2

This book is printed on paper suitable for recycling and made from fully managed and sustained forest sources. Logging, pulping and manufacturing processes are expected to conform to the environmental regulations of the country of origin.

A catalogue record for this book is available from the British Library.

Library of Congress Cataloging-in-Publication Data

Harrison, Sarah, 1982–
    Mapping extreme right ideology : an empirical geography of the European extreme right / Sarah Harrison, Michael Bruter.
        p. cm.
    Includes index.
    ISBN 978–0–230–58101–2 (hardback)
        1. Political parties – Europe. 2. Right-wing extremists – Europe.
    3. Radicalism – Europe. 4. Europe – Politics and government – 1989– I. Bruter, Michael, 1975– II. Title.
JN94.A979H37 2011
324.2′13094—dc23   2011018682

10 9 8 7 6 5 4 3 2 1
20 19 18 17 16 15 14 13 12 11

Printed and bound in Great Britain by
CPI Antony Rowe, Chippenham and Eastbourne

Contents

List of Tables	vi
List of Figures	viii
List of Plates	ix
List of Abbreviations	x
Acknowledgements	xii
Preface	xiii

1	Introduction and Research Question	1
2	Theoretical Framework and Conceptual Map	25
3	Case Selection and Methodology	49
4	The Conceptual Map and Extreme Right Elites	68
5	Capturing the Ideological Identities of Extreme Right Parties	94
6	Exploring the Extreme Right Universe: Patterns of Internal Party Competition	113
7	How Stable Is the Discourse of Extreme Right Parties over Time? Analysis of the Press Releases of Five European Extreme Right Parties	134
8	Match or Mismatch? Investigating the Match between Extreme Right Parties' Ideological Positions and the Ideological Preferences of Voters	149
9	Summary of Findings, Conclusions, and Discussion	194

Appendix A: Word Lists for the Four Pillars (British Sample)	207
Appendix B: Interviews of Extreme Right Party Elites: Interview Template	210
Appendix C: Selected Questions from Mass Survey (see Chapter 3): Version United Kingdom-Great Britain	211
Notes	213
References	218
Index	235

Tables

1.1	Notable electoral successes of extreme right parties in Europe	7
5.1	References to the two ideological dimensions in the twenty-five extreme right party manifestos	105
8.1	Distribution of likeliness to vote for the extreme right by country	151
8.2	Actual vote for extreme right parties	152
8.3	Increase in actual extreme right vote as propensity to vote for extreme right parties gets higher	154
8.4	Gender and vote for the extreme right	157
8.5	Age and vote for the extreme right	160
8.6	Education and vote for the extreme right	162
8.7	Income and vote for the extreme right	163
8.8	A comparison of extreme right support in six European democracies	164
8.9	Relative support for the extreme right ideological pillars	167
8.10	Correlations between four fundamental pillars of extreme right ideology	168
8.11	Correlates of the four cardinal pillars of extreme right ideology	169
8.12	Correlations between extreme right ideology pillars, propensity to vote, and effective vote for extreme right parties	169
8.13	Evolution of extreme right ideological pillars scores as the propensity to vote for extreme right parties increases	171
8.14	Evolution of extreme right ideological pillar scores with actual and projected effective vote	172
8.15	Regression of propensity to vote for extreme right parties	174
8.16	Explanatory power of individual-level multivariate predictions of propensity to vote for the extreme right by country	176
8.17	Regression of actual vote for extreme right parties	177
8.18	Extreme right parties' scores in national elections	180
8.19	Average electoral score of extreme right party by quadrant	182
8.20	Evolution of the aggregate level success of European extreme right parties by strategic-discursive quadrant	183
8.21	Election results of French extreme right parties in general elections since 1978	184
8.22	Evolution of French extreme right parties' electoral success in European Parliament elections	186
8.23	Election results of German extreme right parties in federal elections since 1949	188

8.24 Evolution of German extreme right parties' electoral
     success in European Parliament elections   188
8.25 Election Results of British extreme right parties in
     general elections since 1964   190
8.26 Evolution of British extreme right parties' electoral success
     in European Parliament elections   191

Figures

2.1 A conceptual map of the extreme right ideological space   35
3.1 Methodological integration of the project   51
5.1 The distribution of discourse across the four ideological pillars   107
6.1 A strategic dilemma? The dynamics of internal party family competition   116
6.2 Patterns of competition within the French extreme right party family   121
6.3 Patterns of competition within the British extreme right party family   124
6.4 Patterns of competition within the German extreme right party family   127
7.1 Evolution of the discourse of the Front National from 1999 to 2008   136
7.2 Evolution of the discourse of the Vlaams Belang from 2002 to 2008   140
7.3 Evolution of the discourse of the BNP from 2004 to 2009   141
7.4 Evolution of the discourse of the SVP from 2002 to 2009   143
7.5 Evolution of the discourse of the DF from 2001 to 2008   145
8.1 Ideological pillars, propensity to vote, and actual vote for the extreme right   173
8.2 Evolution of extreme right parties over time by quadrant   182
8.3 Extreme right electoral success in France   185
8.4 German extreme right electoral success   189
8.5 Extreme right electoral success in Britain   190

Plates

1 The ideological identities of twenty-five extreme right parties
2 Europe's populist-repressive parties
3 Europe's xenophobic-repressive parties
4 Europe's populist-reactionary parties
5 Europe's xenophobic-reactionary parties
6 Distribution of likeliness to vote for the extreme right by country
7 Evolution of extreme right parties' scores in national elections

Abbreviations

Austria	FPÖ	Freiheitliche Partei Österreichs
	BZÖ	Bündnis Zukunft Österreich
Belgium	VB	Vlaams Blok/Vlaams Belang
	FNB	Front National Belge
Bulgaria	ATAKA	Национален съюз Атака, *Natsionalen Săyuz Ataka*
Denmark	FRPd	Fremskridtspartiet (Denmark)
	DF	Dansk Folkeparti
Finland	TF	Perussuomalaiset
France	FN	Front National
	MNR	Mouvement National Republicain
	MPF	Mouvement pour la France
Germany	REP	Die Republikaner
	DVU	Deutsche Volksunion
	NPD	Nationaldemokratische Partei Deutschlands
	NSDAP	Nationalsozialistische Deutsche Arbeiterpartei
	SRP	Sozialistische Reichspartei Deutschlands
Great Britain	BNP	British National Party
	UKIP	UK Independence Party
Greece	LAOS	Laikos Othodoxos Synagermos
Hungary	MIEP	Magyar Igazság és Elet Pártja
	Jobbik	Jobbik Magyarországért Mozgalom
Italy	MSI	Movimento Sociale Italiano
	AN	AlleanzaNazionale
	LN	Lega Nord
	MSFT	Movimento Sociale-Fiamma Tricolore
Latvia	TB/LNNK	Tēvzemei un Brīvībai/LNNK
Netherlands	CD	Centrumdemocraten
	LPF	Lijst Pim Fortuyn
	LD	Lijst Dedecker
	PVV	Partij voor de Vrijheid
Norway	FRPn	Fremskrittspartiet (Norway)
Poland	SD	SamoobronaRzeczypospolitej Polskiej
	LPR	Liga Polskich Rodzin
	PiS	Prawo i Sprawiedliwość
Romania	PRM	Partidul Romania Mare
Russia	LD	Liberal Democratic Party

Slovakia	SNS	Slovenska Nacionalna Stranka
Sweden	ND	Ny Demokrati
	SDk	Sverigedemokraterna
Switzerland	SVP	Schweizerische VolksPartei
Turkey	MHP	Milliyetçi Hareket Partisi

Acknowledgements

Co-authorship is a rare, stimulating, and unpredictable experience whereby two minds join forces to try and shape the conceptual, analytical, and empirical nature of a book. But conceiving is not the end of the road, and writing a comparative book also necessarily relies upon further contributions from colleagues who accept to embrace the design of the authors and the challenge of adapting it to specific contexts. In this particular case, we relied on such help for the coding of the manifestos and press releases of extreme right parties across Europe and must sincerely thank Peter Gazik, Peter Huisman, Irina Iordachescu, Alessandra Lacqua, Thanasos Manis, Julie Paquay, Julieta Peneva, Julie Vogt, Rebecca Wolffberg, and Valentina Zigante, who all did a wonderfully committed and careful job without which this book would not be the same.

Several parts of the project also relied on external funding from the LSE Seed Research Fund, the ESRC ('Feeling European? Citizens' European Identity and Parties' Vision on the Future of EU Citizenship' grant reference number RES-062-23-1838, as well as the Doctoral Scholarship of Sarah Harrison), and the STICERD Foundation.

We remain very grateful to all of those who accepted to give us their time in the context of long and thorough interviews, whether they acted within the framework of the party or out of their own individual will. Each and every interview was enriching and useful in making us understand a little bit better the choices and constraints we are trying to depict and analyse throughout this volume.

Lastly, we reiterate our sincere thanks to James Enderby, Paul Crooke, Sarah MacKinnon, Dan Foreman, and Matthew Webster, current or former members of the Opinium team which did a fabulous job conducting our multi-waved panel survey on our behalf.

Preface

The existing literature has long mused over the questions of what defines the extreme right ideology, as well as why some extreme right parties seem to be consistently – or occasionally – more successful than others. For decades, scholars have failed to reach a consensus regarding the nature of the extreme right, used a plethora of labels to describe it, and disagreed on the core characteristics of the party family. In order to progress from this conundrum, we define a model of the extreme right as a multi-dimensional ideology based on two strategic-discursive dimensions (negative identity and authoritarianism), and four resulting ideological pillars (xenophobic, populist, reactionary, and repressive). We also show that the location of each individual extreme right party affects the number and the nature of the voters whom they will attract. Our model is tested in 17 European political systems which comprise 25 extreme right parties. Using a variety of quantitative and qualitative methods, we text-analysed party manifestos and press releases, interviewed extreme right party elites, analysed an ad hoc survey, and interpreted time series electoral results. All in all, we show how the European extreme right is mapped by the different positions espoused by each party, and how parties' choices and the extent to which they match the preferences of potential extreme right voters have an impact on the dynamics of ideological discourse over time, intra-extreme right party competition, the voters each party attracts and ultimately, the level of electoral success it obtains.

1
Introduction and Research Question

1.1 The problem with words ...

> There are as many differences as there are similarities within the
> extreme right party family.
>
> Schain et al. (2002)

What is an extreme right party? How do we define the extreme right party
family? Who is a member and who is not? Is it a party family at all? These
definitional and conceptual questions have plagued the existing literature
for a long time. Even now we are not much closer to agreeing on what constitutes an extreme right party. Few party families seem to attract so many
contradictory emotions from parties, voters, and commentators alike, which
makes defining the term 'extreme right' extremely difficult.

None of the goals of the studies we have conducted and of the publications we have written is, in any way whatsoever, political. We are simply
not interested in figuring out whether the parties that fall into the category
of extreme right, their members, their leaders, and their voters, are good
or bad, commendable or criticisable, the sign of a healthy diversity within
democracies, or a danger to them. For us, the extreme right is neither more
nor less than an analytical category, which corresponds to a more or less
clearly perceived segment of the political spectrum. This segment is, however, often poorly defined, and the people and organisations that shape it
are often mistakenly perceived as a rather nebulous yet monolithic block.
Our goal is to understand better this increasingly important political party
family, to make sense of the differences between various parties and voters
using analytical categories. Every step of our analysis should be viewed under
such a light, as a purely analytical quest, and any attempt whatsoever to use
our results to legitimise or delegitimise any or all extreme right party(ies),
member(s), leader(s), or voter(s) would be incompatible with the spirit of our
work. All the categories, labels, and typologies that we use should be seen as
mere analytical categories used in an academic book and strictly directed at

1

an academic audience. Categories that have a fairly specific meaning in an academic context can often be transformed into vaguer and less safeguarded words in a more casual context. Analytical categories also have the beauty of being neutral almost in essence and certainly in purpose, although non-academic language can sometimes charge words with (often fluctuating and changing) connotations that can be positive or negative.

Our readers are researchers, but researchers also have a life, and they also think, discuss, and vote. The beauty of democracy is that researchers derive no further legitimacy from their research expertise in their non-professional life, and can therefore behave as rationally or irrationally, knowledgeably or ignorantly, cautiously or emotionally as any other voter. Some researchers run for extreme right parties and others against them; some vote for the extreme right and others wish extreme right politics would just disappear. There is no reason why these considerations should be either more or less relevant when reading this book than when reading any other political science volume on left, right, or extreme left politics, or for that matter on regulation, the reorganisation of public administration in Zambia, or the vote of suburban citizens in Paris, London, and Berlin. All colleagues, including younger researchers, are perfectly used to distinguishing between the academic meaning of a word that they use at the office and lighter meanings that same word may have when used at the dinner table or at the pub with their (thankfully non-academic) friends. All of us make this distinction daily, but we particularly ask our readers to bear this distinction in mind when reading our work. This is all the more important to remember than our model of text analysis is based on priming and evocation, not on connotation (Roskos Ewoldsen et al., 2002). In other words, the categories we use correspond to lexical fields expected to be referred to by extreme right parties and to evoke relevant questions from potential voters rather than actual connotations or judgements on the part of the parties (in the sense that a socialist party will simply need to refer often to social justice or a liberal party to freedom or a conservative party to tradition without any explicit connotation, in order to ring a bell in the minds of their potential voters). By nature, many of the words and categories one is bound to use when covering the subject of the extreme right academically (starting with extreme right itself, and continuing with such notions as populism, nationalism, xenophobia, repression, reaction, leadership, radicalism, tradition, pride, fear, and originality) could have an entirely different connotation (some positive and some negative) in everyday language than they do in an academic context. Short of avoiding using meaningful analytical categories academically if the words used have a different, more casual meaning in everyday language, thereby inventing some secret and exclusive language composed of words only a few cognoscenti would know and use from their ivory towers, there is simply no way to avoid this problem. As a result, and to avoid any risk of confusion, it is all the more essential that readers adhere to the strict scientific (academic and specific) meaning of everything we say and avoid transforming or extrapolating it into judgements or connotations that are neither intended nor relevant in the context of this strictly academic volume. Pro-extreme right readers will undoubtedly remain pro-extreme right and anti-extreme right readers will undoubtedly remain anti-extreme right after reading our volume; those who do not care will undoubtedly still not care. We hope all readers nonetheless find interesting elements of strictly academic debate in the following volume, which offers new analytical models and new data for fellow researchers who desire to go beyond some of the apparent contradictions, paradoxes, and uncertainties of the existing social science literature on the subject of the extreme right.

The debate we want to suscitate and the discussion and data we provide are academic, not political. Political systems have rules about what is or is not a legal and legitimate political party, and voters have their own individual perceptions regarding their voting choices. Across countries, commentators and opinion leaders are also concerned with trying to change these rules or affect these votes. Our academic work is simply not part of this. It is neither intended nor suitable as a substitute or addition to these rules, debates, and choices, which alone are interested in serving as a basis for democratic practice.

In this spirit, in the next few paragraphs we explore the existing literature to highlight some problems we will tackle within our framework of analysis. We first start by discussing the conception and definition of an extreme right party. Then we evaluate the various explanations in the existing literature as to why there is so much variation in the success of the extreme right party family across Europe.

1.2 A problem of definition: an analytical minefield

The double problem of defining the concept of extreme right and establishing its empirical scope is one of the great unsolved debates of the social sciences. Both theoretically and empirically, authors vibrantly disagree on where the demarcation line lies between the extreme right and potentially neighbouring party families (Mudde, 2007; Betz, 1994; Kitschelt, 1997; Betz & Immerfall, 1998). Stark discursive differences raise serious questions about the uniformity of the party family. From the Italian Alleanza Nazionale (AN), which claims Fascism was an absolute evil, to the Austrian Freiheitliche Partei Österreichs (FPÖ), which has defended some of the NSDAP's (Nationalsozialistische Deutsche Arbeiterpartei's) economic policies, and from the ultra-liberal stance of the Swiss Schweizerische Volkspartei (SVP) to the interventionist anti-globalisation preferences of the French Front National (FN), the similarities are few and far between. Indeed, although many authors agree to some extent on the core members of the party family, such as the FN, MSI-AN, VB, BNP, FPÖ, difficulties persist at the peripheries of the party family.[1] For example, the Lijst Pim Fortuyn (LPF) was not considered to be extreme right by Mudde; the AN is not a member of the extreme right for Ignazi; and the Danish and Norwegian neo-nationalist parties are extreme right or not, depending on the author assessing the case. As a result, scholars use a plethora of labels to describe parties of the extreme right. Cheles et al. (1991) talk of neo-fascist parties; Betz (1994) prefers the term radical right-wing parties.

To distinguish contemporary extreme right parties from their inter-war predecessors, Betz and Immerfall (1998) speak of new populist parties, Minkenberg (1994) of new right parties, and Kitschelt (2007) of new radical right parties. Consequently, some authors claim the extreme right is represented by two completely distinct party families rather than one. This argument often compares old style Fascism to modern-day right-wing extremism. Some authors argue that, in terms of racism, modern positions are more subtle than those in the past, and anti-Semitism is rather moderate in comparison to previous positions (von Beyme, 1988). Ignazi (2003) argues that 'the ideological and intellectual elaboration provided by the Italian neo-Fascist milieu and by some other [mainly German] groups accounts for the "master" extreme right ideology up to the 1980s', although later movements constitute the new extreme right with a lighter ideological core. Here again, the relevance of the fascist reference as a fundamental benchmark is questioned by large segments of the literature, and the criteria to differentiate old versus new extreme right parties are difficult to operationalise (Mudde, 2007).

Some authors question the very existence of an extreme right party family, although Schain et al. (2002) insist there are 'as many differences as there are similarities' within it. Attempts to determine empirically who belongs to this family are equally inconclusive, with persistent debate centred upon which parties should be included and which should be excluded from the party family. Defining the ideological space and boundaries of the extreme right party family is therefore important not only to delineate who should be included or excluded from it, but also to determine the real extent of the extreme right party family's success.

Several scholars have given up trying to define analytically the extreme right party family, relying instead on expert studies, secondary data analysis, or simply what the existing literature defines as extreme right. In light of these conceptual and definitional hazards, some authors propose a list of criteria a given party should meet in order to be included in the party family. We are then left with a multitude of competing lists, a lack of unanimity as to which criteria define an extreme right party, and elements that are not exclusive to the extreme right party family. Fundamental disagreements remain as scholars fail to agree on the common features and distinctive criteria that unify the members of the extreme right family. Few authors agree on a common definition that includes all of the supposedly obvious members of the party family but simultaneously respects their individual diversity and differences in radicalism. Similarly, some of these proposed party family characteristics are not exclusive to the extreme right but are in fact relevant to other party families. Features such as ethnocentrism and hyper-nationalism, for example, are common within the ideological core of some ethno-regionalist and separatist parties in Europe (e.g. Basque nationalists).

This lack of unanimity within the existing literature makes it impossible simply to rely on an accepted and relevant definition of an extreme right party. Mudde (1996) found an overwhelming 26 definitions of the extreme right currently used to distinguish this particular party family and counts no less than 58 different features of extreme right ideology. Adorno et al. (1950), for example, highlight the importance of a charismatic and strong leader combined with the classical elements of dogmatism, rigidity, exclusionism, authoritarianism, nationalism, anti-permissiveness, xenophobia, racism, and intolerance, among other features of right-wing extremism. Falter and Schumann (1988) also detail no less than ten characteristics of extreme right parties: extreme nationalism, ethnocentrism, anti-communism, anti-parliamentarism, anti-pluralism, militarism, emphasis on strong law and order, a demand for a strong political leader and/or executive, anti-Americanism, and cultural pessimism. Attempts to operationalise these characteristics empirically continue to be problematic, so the question remains: how can we define the extreme right empirically and analytically?

By and large, existing approaches are often contradictory, non-exhaustive, and inefficient at differentiating the specificity of the extreme right party family from all other types of partisan ideologies. There are numerous competing characteristics of extreme right ideology, a multitude of approaches (many excluding an extremely important empirical twist), and lingering doubts as to whether these parties are so different that they do not constitute a real party family. Our argument throughout this book is that the variation between the extreme right parties' ideological positions, which seems troubling when attempting to find points of commonality, is part of the essential nature of the extreme right; far from being disruptive and exceptional, that variation is systematic and symptomatic of the constrained ideological choices every extreme right party has to make. In other words, we should first try to understand and perhaps typologise the different sub-categories of extreme right parties based upon their discursive strategies before we compare their similarities and differences in other respects such as party competition, voter profiles, or electoral success.

In addition to this problem of definition, another puzzle deserves our attention: the variation in electoral success within the extreme right party family. In the next section, we discuss the nature of the inconsistency in electoral success and review some of the explanations proffered by the existing literature as to why some parties are significantly more successful than others.

1.3   The roller coaster of electoral success

During the late 1980s and early 1990s, shock waves reverberated within the institutional frameworks of several major European democracies. Extreme right parties, albeit in the context of coalitions, were obtaining representation in their national political arenas. By the turn of the millennium, parties of the extreme right party family, both old and new, have (re)emerged across all four corners of Europe and are now considered to be an established part of most European party systems. Several of these parties have obtained impressive scores in several local, regional, and European elections and have a relatively stable party history. This includes parties such as the Austrian Freiheitliche Partei Österreichs, the Vlaams Belang (VB) in Flanders, the Front National in France, and the Fremskrittspartiet (FRPn) in Norway. Elsewhere, other parties of the extreme right party family such as those in Germany or Britain struggle to surpass electoral thresholds of representation, existing merely as marginal parties at the peripheries of their respective party systems and having to be content with local or regional electoral successes. Moreover, some parties that gained occasional electoral success have had difficulty sustaining their momentum and have regularly faced competitors that have tried to capitalise upon the potential extreme right vote. Parties in Denmark and the Netherlands have enjoyed the occasional electoral success, but this success has often been short-lived and their support in elections can be volatile. Norris (2005) uses the label 'flash parties' to describe parties such as the Lijst Pim Fortuyn in the Netherlands. These parties seem to come from nowhere, often attracting large shares of the vote, and then disappear as quickly as they appeared. Additionally, in some situations multiple parties represent the extreme right party family within one party system. Competition for their share of the potential extreme right electorate adds a further dynamic to their electoral campaigns and success.. The distinctive variation in electoral success is arguably one of the most interesting puzzles that have emerged from the study of extreme right politics.

Over the past decade, extreme right parties across Europe have enjoyed relative success. Historically, many built their main electoral credentials in local or regional elections. The success of the Front National in French regional elections and its ability to control three city councils in the 1990s was an important breakthrough, as it allowed the FN not only to push other parties into a corner in proportionally elected regional assemblies but also to access (local) executive positions in city councils to achieve policy goals. Similarly, the FPÖ first emerged as a major party in Carinthia, and the

Vlaams Blok and then the Vlaams Belang managed historical successes in some city and regional elections in Antwerp and Flanders. National electoral success has been more important symbolically for many extreme right parties. In 1999, the FPÖ managed federal elections upsets in Austria and caused a European uproar by being invited to form a coalition government with the conservative ÖVP. In the 2001 Italian general elections, the Lega Nord (LN) and the Alleanza Nazionale (AN) were made junior coalition partners of the new Berlusconi government.[2] In Denmark, the Dansk Folkeparti (DF), headed by Pia Kjaersgaard, obtained a substantial 12 per cent of the vote in the 2001 general election. In Poland in 2005, the Law and Justice Party (PiS) won national elections and formed a government with the League of Polish Families (LPR). Similarly, the Norwegian Fremskrittspartiet won 14.7 per cent of the vote and consequently became the third largest party in the national parliament. In France, the leader of the FN, Jean-Marie Le Pen, obtained the second largest share of the vote in the first round of the 2002 presidential election, ushering him into the second ballot. (See Table 1.1.)

Beyond the national level, the majority of European extreme right parties have been particularly successful in consecutive European Parliament elections (see Chapter 8). These elections have been used by extreme right parties as a platform for their protest against the mainstream parties and

Table 1.1 Notable electoral successes of extreme right parties in Europe

Country	Party	% Vote & election year
Switzerland	SVP	28.9 (2007)
Austria	FPÖ	26.9 (1999)
Russia	LD	22.9 (1993)
Romania	PRM	19.4 (2000)
Turkey	MHP	18.0 (1999)
France	FN	17.9 (2002)
Belgium	VB	16.8 (2003)
Hungary	Jobbik	16.7 (2010)
Italy	AN	15.7 (1996)
Netherlands	PVV	15.5 (2010)
Denmark	DF	13.9 (2007)
Poland	LPR	8.0 (2005)

Note: Elections are general or presidential. Some parties have scored much higher results in specific regions.

their politicians as well as a useful arena to vent their Eurosceptic discourse. European Parliament elections offer an advantageous electoral setting. The combination of the 'second-order election' phenomenon and the use of proportional representation often provide electoral benefits for small parties such as the extreme right. As a result, these elections play an essential role in the electoral strategies of extreme right parties. The European elections are often a unique opportunity for the extreme right party family to build its bid for representation. We start with a look at the results of the extreme right party family in the June 2004 European Parliament elections, as this was the first time the recently established extreme right parties in the ten new member states competed on the European political stage.

We then move on to discuss the results of the 2009 European Parliament elections. In the 2004 European Parliament elections, most of the larger and more established extreme right parties consolidated their electoral success. For example, the Vlaams Belang in Belgium, and the majority of the Eastern European extreme right parties, made gains on their previous performances. Some core members of the party family were disappointed, however, with the underwhelming results: both the Austrian FPÖ and the French FN failed to consolidate previous electoral successes and were visibly dissatisfied with their performance in these key elections. Many of the smaller parties such as the British National Party (BNP) and the German Republikaner (REP) and NPD improved their electoral scores. Extreme right parties in Central and Eastern Europe also made gains. In Latvia, the TB/LNNK obtained almost 30 per cent of the vote. Similarly, in Poland, the LPR and PiS made a dramatic entrance onto the European stage. The overwhelming success of the extreme right party family across Europe prompted the formation of a new European parliamentary group, Identity, Tradition and Sovereignty. The group encompassed members from the French FN, the Greater Romania party, the Bulgarian Ataka party, the Italian Social Alternative and Tricolour Flame, and the FPÖ, among a few independent candidates.[3] These electoral successes at the European level have provided the extreme right party family with important visibility and leverage.

In the 2009 European Parliament elections, the extreme right party family gained an additional eight seats compared to the 2004 European elections results. In Austria, Denmark, Finland, Greece, Hungary, Italy, the Netherlands, Romania, and the United Kingdom, extreme right parties made moderate to significant advances on their previous electoral scores. In the Netherlands, Geert Wilders's party won four seats. In Austria, the FPÖ also performed well, winning two seats by obtaining 13.4 per cent of the vote. Splinter party BZÖ (Bündnis Zukunft Österreich) was denied any representation in the European Parliament, despite obtaining the support of 4.6 per cent of voters. In addition, successes were gained in the Eastern European member states. The Hungarian extreme right party, Jobbik, gained an impressive 15 per cent of the vote and the Greater Romania Party gained two seats. The Danish People's Party gained an additional seat, giving it two representatives in the European Parliament. The True Finns party, following several domestic electoral successes, gained an additional 8.9 per cent compared to its 2004 performance and was able to return its first European representative. The British National Party also secured its first two seats in the European Parliament. Similarly, UKIP (UK Independence Party) consolidated its 2004 European success, gaining 16.1 per cent and 13 seats. Greece's Popular Orthodox Rally, or LAOS grouping, led by right-wing journalist Georgios Karatzaferis, doubled its representation (from one to two MEPs) with around 7 per cent of the vote. Italy's Northern League also doubled its representation from four to eight MEPs. The two other Italian extreme right parties, the AN and the Social Alternative of Alessandra Mussolini, agreed to merge with Forza Italia to create the People of Freedom party in early 2009.

Although there were many reports of electoral success across Europe for the extreme right party family, several parties failed to capture the popular vote. The French Front National, for example, lost four seats in the European Parliament, down from seven; Philippe de Villiers's party, Movement for France, which ran under the Libertas umbrella, lost one seat, leaving it with a solitary representative in the Parliament. Libertas, founded on 24 October 2006, was originally a lobby group that campaigned against the Lisbon Treaty in the referendum held in Ireland on 12 June 2008. Following the success of the campaign, founder Declan Ganley established a pan-European political party of the same name, which took part in the 2009 European Parliament elections across several member states, including the United Kingdom, Germany, the Netherlands, and Poland.

The Flemish Vlaams Belang also lost one seat (leaving it with only two seats), although the Lijst Dedecker (LD) gained one. Poland saw the biggest drop in the extreme right vote. In 2004, the three extreme right parties combined returned 16 MEPs in 2004. Neither the League of Polish Families nor the Self-Defence party was able to gain any seats in 2009. Bulgaria's Ataka party also lost one seat and now only has two representatives. Finally, Latvia's LNNK lost three seats. On the whole, the 2009 European Parliament elections represented a successful campaign for the extreme right party family across the four corners of Europe. As a result, a new parliamentary group under the title of Europe of Freedom and Democracy (EFD) was created by some of the core members of the party family.

The emergence of extreme right parties across Europe has been debated because of inconsistencies in how such parties are defined, but equally vibrantly discussed in academic circles has been whether the extreme right's success has long-term sustainability. By no means has scholarly consensus been reached as to whether an extreme right party's electoral success is likely to be only momentary and key to its own failure or whether such success will lead to consolidation and legitimation.

In some cases, extreme right parties fail to repeat or consolidate their electoral success, resulting in largely inconsistent electoral records across the party family. For example, following the German Die Republikaner's success in the 1989 European Parliament elections, the party hoped to surpass the 5 per cent threshold for the Bundestag in the 1990 parliamentary elections yet received less than 2 per cent of the vote. Similarly, the French Front National has struggled to find a successful electoral strategy to build upon its local, regional, and national successes. Le Pen's triumph in the 2002 presidential election was followed by a disappointing result in the subsequent legislative elections. The FN received 11 per cent of the vote, four points lower than its score in the 1997 election, and its electoral appeal eroded further after that.

In other cases, however, while extreme right parties seemed to lose ground after some temporary success but managed significant comebacks after short-term declines. For instance, in Austria, although many had predicted the collapse of the FPÖ after its experience of government and the departure of its charismatic leader, Jörg Haider (who left to create the BZÖ before dying a few years later in a car accident), the party scored major successes in the Viennese 2010 local elections. Similarly, many had believed in the death of the Front National after its implosion in the late 1990s but, as explained, Jean-Marie Le Pen then achieved a major success in the presidential elections of 2002. The party suffered a major blow in 2007 with extremely poor results, but in the past few years it managed a few local successes. Current opinion polls suggest that in the forthcoming 2012 presidential elections, the fn's new leader, Jean-Marie le Pen's daughter marine, could break the electoral record set by her father in 2002. Although extreme right parties can apparently lose ground after a period of strong success, they can also clearly regain it after the legitimation achieved by this original breakthrough.

At the same time, the extreme right party family has failed to secure any real presence in party systems in such countries as Portugal, Finland, and Spain. As demonstrated in the preceding discussion, electoral success is far from homogeneous across the extreme right party family. In some countries, parties belonging to this family regularly obtain relatively large shares of the vote, whilst in other party systems they rarely manage an impact at the ballot box. The next section deals with this question of electoral variance: why some parties are more successful than others.

1.4 The state of current research

As seen in the preceding discussion, some extreme right parties are clearly more successful than others. The Austrian FPÖ's emergence and continued success during a period of relatively low unemployment and immigration and the absence of any fundamental crisis within the Austrian political system is still considered puzzling by the existing literature. The emergence of extreme right parties in Scandinavia has long defied its strong social democratic traditions and has beguiled observers into searching for a solution to this conundrum. The existing literature has widely debated some of the reasons behind the heterogeneous electoral success of different extreme right parties. Some publications investigate contextual elements (such as institutional explanations, socio-political context, levels of immigration and unemployment), comparing for example the various parties' electoral successes across several countries (e.g. Perrineau, 2002; Schain et al., 2002). Other scholars adopt a micro level of analysis, by studying voter characteristics (e.g. van der Brug & Fennema, 2003; Dülmer & Klein, 2005). After discussing the various approaches in the existing literature, we highlight the need for more party-centric approach in explaining how and why some extreme right parties achieve greater levels of electoral success across Europe than do other such parties.

Institutional explanations

The degree of proportionality within the electoral system can influence the chance of small parties of gaining representation. Single-member majoritarian districts tend to foster a two-party system, whereas proportional representation encourages multipartism (Duverger, 1951). The French Front National, for example, became a significant political actor on the national party stage after proportional representation rules were adopted for the 1986 general elections. As a result of this change in the electoral rules, the Front National returned 34 representatives to the National Assembly in 1986 with 9.9 per cent of the vote.

On the other hand, a more restrictive electoral framework such as the first-past-the post system in Britain hinders the success of smaller parties such as those of the extreme right. The likelihood of obtaining national-level representatives is slim, as small parties have few opportunities to gain national representation within this electoral system. Initially, the British National Party had to be satisfied with relatively small gains at the local level; however, in 2009 it managed to circumvent the restrictive framework of the national party system by gaining two representatives in the European Parliament. German extreme right parties are often victims of a mixed electoral system used for federal elections, a system also considered a relative impediment to the proliferation of extreme right parties. In addition, any party wishing to gain representation in the Bundestag is required to pass a 5 per cent electoral threshold, which has often foiled the relative electoral gains of the Republikaner and the NPD. Small parties, such as those belonging to the extreme right party family, often lose out to strategic voting: voters may not want to waste a vote on a party which has little chance of passing electoral thresholds or few opportunities to govern (Sartori, 1994). Jackman and Volpert (1996) conclude that support for the extreme right is a function of the electoral threshold and the effective number of parties; however, other scholars have failed to find supporting evidence and have sometimes provided evidence contrary to this argument (Knigge, 1998; Swank & Betz, 1996; Lewis-Beck & Mitchell, 1993). Carter (2002) concludes that the share of the vote won by right-wing extremist parties is unrelated to the type of electoral system involved. This suggests at the very least that although electoral systems using proportional representation can help facilitate the political representation of minor parties that would not have the same electoral opportunities in majoritarian systems, other factors undoubtedly influence the level of extreme right party success.

Some democracies have adopted restrictions against the proliferation of parties that are deemed to threaten or contravene the democratic process. These regulations often focus their attention on extremist groups, including those of the extreme right. The German *Verfassungsschutz* (Office for the Protection of the Constitution) monitors political parties and organisations, and those deemed anti-constitutional can be prohibited. This constitutional court has the jurisdiction to prohibit any party within the German political system if there is evidence that party contravenes the fundamental values of the constitution or conveys anti-democratic values. German authorities have used this constitutional tool to bring cases against several contemporary extreme right groups, including the NPD.

Scholars suggest that, in addition to electoral frameworks and constitutional arrangements, the degree of fragmentation within a given party system can help facilitate the success of extreme right parties (e.g. Bale, 2003; Poguntke, 2001; Ivaldi, 2001). The NSDAP's rise to power, the 1986 legislative victories of the FN, and more recently the electoral successes of the FPÖ, illustrate how the fragmentation of party systems can give extremist parties a foothold into national government. A high degree of decentralisation may foster the development of extreme right parties, as voters are perhaps more willing to support new or radical parties in second-order elections such as those for regional or local institutions (Reif & Schmitt, 1980). In countries such as Austria, Italy, and Belgium, decentralisation of the system has allowed extreme right parties to develop a stronghold in certain influential regions (Flanders for the Vlaams Blok, recently renamed Vlaams Belang, Carinthia for the FPÖ, and Lombardia for the Northern League), while remaining less influential in others. Multiple levels of governance (local, regional, national, European) increase the electoral opportunities for small parties, such as those of the extreme right, to claim an increasingly important political role. In this sense, the FN has traditionally compensated for its failure to have members elected to the National Assembly since 1993 by relatively good performances in regional and local elections. The Italian Lega Nord illustrated its political strength by achieving several electoral victories in regional and municipal elections throughout the mid-1990s and is readily expanding its appeal beyond its stronghold in the north. Although the electoral system, fragmentation, and additional levels of governance may increase an extreme right party's opportunities to gain representation, this does not explain fully why some parties are more successful than others. Continuing an aggregate level of analysis, we now discuss various factors related to the social and economic context within which extreme right parties reside.

The socio-economic context

Extreme right parties historically succeeded in times of economic recession or growing inequality. Socio-economic problems such as widespread unemployment, large-scale deindustrialisation, inflationary pressures, a widening gap between rich and poor all seem to build up frustration and anxiety about what the future may hold, providing a fertile ground for parties of the extreme right. This was of course the case in post-war France, Germany, and Italy, as well as some of the post-communist Eastern European countries. The relationship between a bad economy and the success of the extreme right has long been theorised. Relatively high unemployment rates among some groups of the population such as blue-collar workers or small business owners may contribute to the extreme right's electoral success when it emphasises issues of economic security. Extreme right parties often try to draw attention to the failings of the incumbent government and inability of the mainstream opposition parties to deal with hardships faced by the man on the street. Jackman and Volpert (1996) argue that electoral support for the extreme right increases directly with levels of unemployment.

Some contradictory findings within the literature concern the relationship between unemployment levels and the vote for parties of the extreme right. Rydgren (2005), for example, found that countries in which extreme right parties have not been particularly successful have also been post-industrial societies experiencing economic downturns and high levels of unemployment during the past 20 years. Similarly, Golder (2003) and Knigge (1998) argue that high unemployment stimulates support for extreme right parties only when immigration levels are also high. Some authors argue, however, that the relationship between the state of the economy and the electoral success of the extreme right is not as straightforward as it may appear. Betz and Immerfall (1998) argues that citizens' perceptions of the actual socio-economic context are rendered secondary to the predominant fear of what the future may hold. The fear of unemployment or social dislocation, rather than the actual experience of either, spurs people to vote for extreme right parties in times of recession and a bad economy. Rydgren (2005) finds that during the early and mid-1980s, years characterised by political protest, people voted more from feeling threatened by relative deprivation than from actual relative or absolute deprivation.

The socio-disintegration theory suggests that people alienated from society are more likely to vote for parties on the fringes of the political spectrum (Heitmeyer, 1994). Rydgren (2005) suggests that the extreme right party family emerged in the 1980s and 1990s because the post-industrialisation of western European countries both undermined the salience of the economic (class) cleavage and created new 'loser' groups susceptible to a political message combining cultural protectionism, xenophobic welfare chauvinism, a populist critique of the establishment, and a reactionary call to return to the good old values of yesterday (Betz, 1994). Most of the contemporary extreme right parties were formed in the late 1980s and the early 1990s, a period of undoubtedly important and consolidated social change. The theory of economic interests focuses on the competition brought about by the introduction of foreign labour into the job markets (Lubbers & Scheepers, 2001). Increased unemployment levels, combined with the perceived deprivation of their current or future situation, often spurs voters to consider the extreme right.

As a considerable section of the existing literature classifies extreme right parties based on their predominant anti-immigration discourse, it is logical that some studies have focused on the link between levels of immigration and the electoral success of the extreme right party family; however, these studies have cited contrasting findings. Anderson (1996) and Knigge (1998) suggest that high levels of immigration and the concentration of newcomers in specific areas or regions favour the likelihood of electoral success for extreme right parties. Some parties in the European extreme right party family emphasise the alleged correlation between the number of immigrants within a country and the number of unemployed citizens. Some of the electorate, such as less-skilled or less-educated people, are more likely to fall victim to market forces and will be more susceptible to the discourse of the extreme right because of their perceived insecurity and material concerns about their future employment (Falter, 1994). Extreme right leaders and their parties propose to defend the economic interests of the man on the street by restricting the number of immigrants, who are perceived as direct competitors in the workplace and in accessing social welfare and housing. Substantial country-specific differences exist, however. For example, Givens (2002) finds that support for extreme right parties is greater in Austrian and French regions with high levels of immigration, but this relationship does not hold within the context of the German Länder. Taking a polar opposite stance to Anderson's and Knigge's thesis, Perrineau (1985) asserts that the greater level of contact one has with immigrants, the higher the level of tolerance towards immigration; thus, areas with higher numbers of resident immigrants are more likely to understand the cultural differences than to fear them. Finally, Mudde (1999) finds no convincing evidence to suggest a link between immigration levels and electoral success, concluding that there is no clear-cut relationship between the number of immigrants and the electoral success of extreme right parties in certain territorial units.

Although an unfavourable socio-economic context can certainly help fuel the electoral success of extreme right parties as the fears and insecurities of the public are heightened and extreme right parties tend to feed off this atmosphere, not enough evidence suggests that this factor alone can explain the variation in electoral success. In the next section, we examine political opportunity structures to assess whether the perceived convergence of mainstream parties has helped boost the fortunes of extreme right parties in some countries but not in others or whether the various strategies adopted by the existing parties has indeed hampered their progress.

Political opportunity structures

The state of the economy or rather a perceived fear of future recession and unemployment may lead voters to consider a vote for an extreme right party, but additional factors such as political opportunity structures may play a part in the success or failure of an extreme right party. A political opportunity may arise at any time. For example, in October 1999 almost a third of Austrian citizens voted for the neo-populist Freedom Party (FPÖ), led by the charismatic leader Jörg Haider, toppling the conservative ÖVP from its position as main opposition party since 1945; the Social Democrat SPÖ received its worst-ever result in a general election. This shock result sent tremors throughout the political systems of Europe and even led the European Union to consider possible measures of isolation and the creation of a wiremen committee. The FPÖ's success was a clear sign that an extreme right party harnessing populist, anti-establishment discourse could connect with voters and send a message of discontent to the incumbent government and indeed disturb the existing status quo.

Koopmans et al. (2005) suggest that the vote for the radical right cannot be explained by most traditional sociological variables. Their analysis is based on publicly made political claims in national newspapers in France, Germany, the Netherlands, Great Britain, and Switzerland. The authors draw upon arguments within the theory of social movements in which political opportunity structures play a key role. They argue that discursive opportunities arise when these particular extreme right parties focus their discursive strategies on the topic of immigration.

In many European countries, citizens have become disenchanted by the perceived ideological convergence, reports of corruption scandals, and constant shifts in government leadership from one main moderate party to the next (Rydgren, 2005). Citizens who may not usually vote for the extreme right might consider this choice if they are disillusioned with the state of politics and effectively disenfranchised from the existing political system. This specific feeling of 'Politikverdrossenheit' is a form of political disenchantment negatively expressed by the electorate against the political system. Ignazi characterises the 'materialist versus post-materialist' debate that has marked the recent political climate as 'the emergence of new priorities and issues not treated by the established parties, a disillusionment towards parties in general, a growing lack of confidence in the political system and its institutions and a general pessimism about the future' (Ignazi, 1992). Extreme right parties across Europe soon realised electoral success might be achieved via a new ideological discourse emphasising populist criticism of incumbent governments for their many failures, for being out of touch with the common man and unresponsive to the needs of the nation. Parties belonging to the extreme right party family were able to capitalise upon a milieu of disillusionment and cynicism with the traditional parties of the Left and Right (Betz, 2002; Kitschelt, 1995). In this context, Schain et al. (2002:12) claim that 'weaknesses in the party system, marked by a decline of confidence by voters in existing parties may be exploited by far-right parties'.

Voters may express discontentment with the existing system by casting a protest vote to send a warning to the incumbent government. Indeed, van der Brug et al. (2000) conceptualise protest voting as a rational, goal-oriented activity. This maintains that the prime motive behind a protest vote is to show discontent with the political elite. As most extreme right parties are treated as pariahs by the elite within their respective party systems, votes for these parties are designed to send a message to the elite (van der Eijk, Franklin & Marsh, 1996). Givens (2002) claims that voters who might otherwise abstain may choose to vote for a radical right party as an alternative way to express discontent with the system.

Note, however, that a vote for an extreme right party cannot automatically and systematically be typified as a simple protest vote. Casting a protest vote in favour of a mainstream opposition party in order to send the incumbent government a message of dissatisfaction is undoubtedly different from voting for an extreme right party because of an ideological association with that party. In this respect, van der Brug and Fennema (2007) argue that support for radical right parties is just as much motivated by ideological and pragmatic considerations as is support for other parties, so calling support for these parties a protest vote is an inadequate explanation for such support.

Several authors have shown in multivariate analyses that the electoral fortunes of extreme right parties are affected significantly by the competition these parties face from mainstream competitors from the right (Kitschelt, 1995; Carter, 2005; Koopmans et al., 2005; Van der Brug et al., 2005). Norris (2005) finds, however that the correlation between the left/right position of the main competitor and the vote shares of 16 extreme right parties is not significant. In contrast to this finding, van der Brug et al. (2005) find that two supply-side factors and one demand-side variable explain 83 per cent of the variation in the electoral fortunes of the 25 parties included in their study. The supply-side variables include:

1. The degree to which the party is seen to be a normal democratic party; and
2. The ideological position of its mainstream competitors.

The first variable has a positive effect: the more a party is perceived as normal, the higher the likelihood of greater electoral success. The second variable has a negative effect: when the largest mainstream right-wing party moves to the right on the ideological spectrum, the extreme right party is less likely to succeed at the ballot box.

In the preceding discussion a vast majority of authors have tried to understand the extreme right phenomenon with reference to contextual factors at the aggregate level. We now move on to examine the demand-side explanations at the individual level. These explanations try to isolate the various socio-demographic groups that are most likely to vote for the extreme right in order to shed light upon why some parties are more successful than others. The existing literature shows inconsistent conclusions, as no single social group has been highlighted as the main reservoir of support for extreme right parties.

Variation in voter profiles

The main focus of previous research on the electoral bases of extreme right parties has been to construct a prototype of an extreme right voter; however, in many cases this task has proved almost impossible. It is extremely difficult to obtain meaningful samples from the various large mass surveys (e.g. Eurobarometer and European Social Survey) conducted across EU member states. The number of self-declared extreme right voters is often very small, and the parties of interest to scholars of extreme right politics are often excluded from these surveys as too small or peripheral to the party system. Unlike researchers of other party families, we cannot therefore rely on an arsenal of survey data. The few comparative studies conducted often highlight interesting but inconclusive findings about this elusive electorate. They have often point to contrasting characteristics of the extreme right voter not just across countries, but also within given party systems. In this sense, some social groups may be larger and more prominent in some countries than others; therefore, if this social category is susceptible to the discourse and ideology of the extreme right, parties competing within those particular party systems will be in a better position to exploit the potential extreme right vote.

Using the case study of France by Mayer (1998) as an example of the rapid changes in extreme right electorates, we can see that the steady rise of the extreme right in France from the mid-1970s to the early 2000s was to a large extent caused by the defection of blue-collar workers from the array of left-wing parties. In the 1988 presidential election, support for Le Pen was higher than average among voters belonging to the working class. These voters were the largest bloc to move *en masse* to the FN. Alongside working class voters, small business owners and farmers, drawn to the stridently pro-capitalist and anti-interventionist aspects of the FN strategic-discursive platform have also regularly supported candidates of the Front National

(Kitschelt, 1995:112). In a study of the Swiss SVP and Austrian FPÖ, McGann and Kitschelt (2002) find that these two sub-groups of the population are most likely to be attracted to the discourse of the extreme right. A similar pattern is reported in an analysis of the Italian Lega Nord voters in Northern Italy. Betz and Immerfall (1998) maintains that these small commercial and artisanal entrepreneurs and blue-collar workers in the Northern periphery accounted for much of the Lega's resurgence in 1996. Indeed, studies focused on the profiles of extreme right voters often draw contrasting conclusions. The existing literature sometimes points to specific groups such as blue-collar workers and self-employed small business owners (Mayer, 1998) that are susceptible to the appeal of extreme right parties.

Comparing voter characteristics across countries, little evidence exists, however, of any putative homogeneity of potential or actual extreme right voters. Studies such as those of Svåsand (1998) and Andersen and Bjørklund (2000) of extreme right voters illustrate that such voters represent a cross-section of the electorate; in some countries such as Denmark and Sweden, few social groups are exempt from the appeal of extreme right parties. Extreme right parties can draw upon a reservoir of support from a variety of stable social groups. Blue-collar workers, small and independent business people, and professionals all seem susceptible to extreme right discourse, and this interesting mix of social groups dissects boundaries usually associated with the traditional left-right socio-political cleavages.

Demand for extreme right discourse

Extreme right parties can often retain a certain amount of flexibility with regard to discursive appeal. They can often manipulate salient issues and change direction because they are not tied to exclusive bases of electoral support. In contrast to many other mainstream parties, whose electoral bases are often supported by traditional socio-economic cleavages, extreme right parties are sometimes able to combine a discursive appeal (within the confines of their natural ideological habitat) with various heteroclit proposals that may attract a diverse cross-section of social categories. Issues such as immigration, law and order, national identity, and European integration have been heatedly debated in the public sphere and can contravene the traditional political left-right scale. The increased salience and visibility of these issues have recently created opportunities for the extreme right. These issues are natural topics of discussion for the extreme right, and many such parties throughout Europe have latched onto this new dynamic and fought successful election campaigns as a result.

In this sense, Petrocik (1996) states that certain issues can become synonymous with or owned by one party, and that the electorate often regards the party as more credible or legitimate if it competes on this specific dimension. Parties such as those of the extreme right may therefore be able to score an advantage with voters by emphasising distinct issues such as immigration and the enforcement of law and order whilst other mainstream parties prefer not to discuss these issues openly. Budge and Laver (1986) argue that political parties may decide to compete by accentuating issues on which they have an undoubted advantage, rather than by putting forward contrasting policies on the same issues. Parties may therefore try to differentiate themselves (even if caused by their extremist nature) from other competitors by emphasising unique ideological positions, as voters can then clearly identify their discourse and policies. This also relates back to the question of definition. Authors such as van der Brug and Fennema (2003) describe the prominence of the issue of immigration in the discourse of extreme right parties, referring to them as anti-immigrant parties. Similarly, discourse analysts such as Scarrow (1996) and Pelinka (1998) note that parties of the extreme right can be typified by one particular discourse that symbolises their raison d'être; for example, Scarrow emphasises the theme of anti-party discourse amongst extreme right parties, whilst Pelinka focuses on the populist premise of the Austrian FPÖ. Once again, we are reminded that we need to reconceptualise our definition of extreme right parties. Although this section helps us to understand why some parties might be more successful in tapping into their potential extreme right reservoir, it opens up new questions about how extreme right parties can seduce their core electorate and appeal to their potential voters.

In summary, the current literature contains no overwhelming agreement as to why some parties are more successful than others. Existing studies often exclude party-centric explanations derived from the analysis of discursive strategies, organisational factors, or leadership capacity. On the other hand, although demand-side explanations contribute to our understanding of the variation in electoral success, no social group is regularly classified as the main reservoir of extreme right electoral support. Certain social groups (students and highly educated professions) seem consistently immune to the appeal of the extreme right, yet the electoral support of extreme right parties in Europe appears to stem from heterogeneous social categories across countries.

1.5 The puzzle

Although these approaches have tried to capture what is happening at the aggregate level, these models exclude an extremely important piece of the puzzle: the extreme right parties themselves. Indeed, van der Brug et al. (2005) argue that a properly specified model of electoral support for radical right parties should contain demand-side and supply-side factors. Few studies try, however, to explain the success of individual extreme right parties by examining the characteristics of the parties themselves. How do these parties use their discourse to differentiate themselves from their competitors? Are some types of parties more successful than others? This series of questions requires a shift from considering the traditional supply and demand approaches. We are reminded by van der Brug and Fennema (2007) that 'this amazing variation [in electoral scores] calls for an explanation that goes beyond the socio-structural model of voting behaviour, since the social conditions that supposedly caused the surge of radical right parties do not vary much between the different European countries and hence cannot account for their different fortunes'. We therefore need to implement a framework of analysis that tries to identify the ideological unity of the extreme right party family and that attempts to understand the variation in electoral success. We believe that by bringing 'parties back into the picture' we can try to understand the phenomenon of variation better by studying what renders these parties different and/or similar to one another.

Throughout the preceding discussion, we highlight the difficulties we face as scholars studying the extreme right party family. Traditionally, studies have not regarded the specificities of the party itself as an important component of the electoral success equation, which is what we propose to change with our model. We believe we can construct a typology of extreme right parties based on an empirical and comparative analysis of their ideological discourse. Extreme right parties are not puppets of the party system. Ultimately they are similar to any other political party: capable of determining their own destiny with the strategic help and the right blend of discourse. A niche or political space may provide an extreme right party with a foothold on the ladder to the mainstream political stage, but how can these parties maximise this potential? The parties themselves need to acknowledge the existence of a potential extreme right electorate and adapt their strategies and discourse appropriately in order to obtain the best electoral results. We draw upon the findings of Carter (2005) and Golder (2003), who suggest that some ideological discourses may be more successful than others in securing votes for extreme right parties. Carter (2005) finds that, with other variables held constant, parties with a xenophobic programme or image have a greater chance of winning votes than do the more neo-Nazi or neo-fascist parties. Particular combinations of discursive strategies can therefore be expected to help the extreme right score greater electoral success, as some types of ideological discourse are more attractive to the potential electorate than are others.

Throughout this book, we highlight two intriguing and entwined puzzles in the study of extreme right parties: the puzzle of ideological unity and the question of differing successes and constituencies. In order to understand the underlying ideology of extreme right parties we must conduct empirical research that aims to dissect their ideological discourse. Existing studies have failed to propose an empirically tested definition of the extreme right party family that not only captures commonalities within the ideological discourse of all extreme right parties but at the same time understands their differences. No study so far has provided a conclusive model or widely accepted evidence to explain cross-national inconsistencies with regard to both overall success and the type of voters each party tends to attract. In order to address these problems, this book uses a framework of analysis tailored to the specificities of this particular party family. A one-size-fits-all definition must be avoided if we are to analyse variations in the behaviour of extreme right parties. We need to develop a new framework of analysis that tries to understand the essence of extreme right ideology and that can be empirically tested in comparative research. In summary, this book addresses the following research question:

How does the ideological location of each extreme right party vary and how does it affect the individual voters and overall electoral success they will attract?

This research question entails two sets of operational questions that will guide the research design and empirical framework of this study.

1. *Similarities and Differences in Ideological Discourse:* What distinguishing ideological dimensions structure the discourse of the extreme right party family? How can we define and locate extreme right parties within their specific ideological space, and how can we conceptualise extreme right ideology in a way that will help us understand the logic of their variations over time, stratae, and parties?
2. *Extreme Right Ideology and Voter Preferences:* What are the ideological preferences and perceptions of potential and actual extreme right voters? Can we map their ideological distribution and match this with the locations of the extreme right parties that compete within the individual party systems? Do the strategic-discursive choices of extreme right parties and their match with individual voter preferences affect their success at transforming potential supporters into actual voters?

This book therefore explores the question of whether and how the extreme right can be defined as a multidimensional party family based on two strategic-discursive dimensions, and the extent to which the conceptual map of extreme right ideology will help us assess the impact of these various ideological identities on extreme right party electoral success via the types and numbers of voters they attract.

1.6   Two birds, one stone ...

We propose a conceptual map of extreme right ideology to help us reconceptualise our definition of extreme right parties and a research design to allow us to confront why some parties are more successful than others based upon their ideological discourse. We aim to answer our research question within a unified framework by creating a new typology of parties specifically tailored to the extreme right family.

Before we detail how we approach the research question, we must decide which term to use for the parties we are concerned with throughout this book. For various reasons, we prefer the term 'extreme right' over the plethora of recent terms and labels assigned to this particular party family. The term extreme right predates most other labels attached to this party family in the literature and is widely considered the most traditional term of reference for this political ideology. 'Extreme right' is one of the most easily identifiable ways of referring to this particular party family as it is meaningful to the electorate when they think of the types of parties they need to choose from. other more specific labels such as 'new populist right' or 'radical right wing populism'. As this study uses comparative analyses of extreme right parties, it was important to choose a term of reference that is transportable across countries. In all three countries studied here, the term extreme right is readily and easily understood by all, not just those familiar with the academic literature in this field. Finally, as we have seen in the review of the literature, although many new labels and terms have been proposed, scholars in the field have not agreed unanimously that any of these should replace the existing term extreme right; most such terms and labels fail to stand the empirical test in a way that would validate their conceptual and analytical framework.

As mentioned earlier, there has been controversy in the literature regarding which parties belong to the extreme right family. In order to test our model, we include in the empirical analysis parties deemed in some of the existing literature to belong to the extreme right which have scored at least 1 per cent of the vote or equivalent in a recent national election in the political systems included in our analysis (see Chapter 3). Conceptually, however, based on the model we expose in Chapter 2, we propose to define an extreme right party as a political organisation running in elections (whether at the European, national, or local level) and whose main ideological identity (as conceived by the conceptual model) is based on a negative expression of identity via cultural or civic references, and a discursive support for a form of social or political form of authoritarianism. In the next paragraph, we outline how we approach the research design and the conceptual model.

Using a party-centric approach, we conducted interviews with party elite and text analysis of party manifestos to locate parties within a defined ideological space that is unique to the extreme right party family. We contribute to comparative analyses by examining how the different sub-types of parties prioritise two structuring ideological dimensions: authoritarianism and negative identity. Each dimension has two possible ideological conceptions. The authoritarianism dimension has a social (reactionary) mode and an institutional (repressive) conception. The negative identity dimension has cultural (xenophobic) and civic (populist) conceptions. These two dimensions create four sub-types of parties within the extreme right party family. We locate each party based on its ideological discourse, which we establish empirically through the analysis of party manifestos and interviews of party elite. This conceptual map of extreme right ideology helps us to define the ideological identities of 25 extreme right parties in 17 party systems.[4]

Using case studies from the United Kingdom, France, and Germany for examples of multi-extreme-right-party systems, we also investigate internal party competition. Analysing party manifestos, we map the position of each individual extreme right party within its given party system. Then we focus on three party systems in order to understand better the ideological identities of these parties. Adopting an analytic narrative style, we recreate the strategic-discursive choices each individual extreme right party may face within its given party system. We study a 'within party family' model of party competition in order to describe the ideological space at stake when extreme right parties compete alongside each other.

The conceptual map of extreme right ideology contributes to our understanding of the fundamental ideological dimensions that structure the extreme right party family, and allows us to address why some parties are more successful than others in their quest to capture their potential electorate. In this respect, we expect the four sub-types of parties to have varying levels of electoral success, as their ideological message will appeal to different sub-sections of the electorate and influence their strategies for party competition. Our framework of analysis therefore helps us understand the subtle differences and core similarities existing within individual party systems and across the party family.

We also incorporate into our study an empirical investigation of the ideological preferences of actual and potential voters of extreme right parties.[5] By studying the location of each party and the corresponding ideological distribution of the electorate in a given system, we can assess whether some parties are relatively more successful than others at capitalising on their potential. Analysing the discourse of extreme right parties and mapping the ideological distribution of the electorate within the extreme right ideological space enable us to evaluate the match between the parties' and voters' positions within their given party systems. Whether such a match may be conceived as natural congruence or a strategic effort by extreme right parties to 'follow' their potential voters, we expect that more successful parties can imitate the ideological preferences of their potential electorate and transform potential votes into actual votes.

In other words, the overall objective of this study is to map precisely the boundaries of the extreme right ideological universe and understand how extreme right parties and their voters vary within this conceptual model. In order to understand the intense rivalries between competing extreme right parties within the same party system, we evaluate the extent to which the critical choice of location made by each party within this universe corresponds to the preferences of the potential extreme right electorate within each system.

1.7 Chapter structure

This book contains nine chapters, which:

1. Summarise the state of the existing literature;
2. Outline our methodology;
3. Define our theoretical and analytical model; and
4. Provide our empirical analysis using:
   a. Interviews of extreme right leaders in multiple European countries,
   b. Twenty-five European extreme right parties' latest manifestos and five series of press releases over several years, and
   c. An ad hoc mass survey in eight countries.

A breakdown of the subsequent chapters follows:

Chapter 2. Introduction of the theoretical framework, research design, and model.

Chapter 3. Discussion of the triple methodology used to test the conceptual model and justify the case selection.

Chapter 4. Substantiation of the model of extreme right ideology by analysing interview extracts obtained from the extreme right party elite.

Chapter 5. Analysis of party manifestos in order to examine the strategic-discursive choices made by each party.. This allows us to ascribe an ideological identity to each party within the defined extreme right ideological space.

Chapter 6. Study of the dynamics of internal party competition within the extreme right party family in Great Britain, France, and Germany.

Chapter 7. Overview of the variations of strategic-discursive preferences of five parties over time using a systematic time-series analysis of their press releases.

Chapter 8. Evaluation of the ideological distribution of the extreme right electorate and an individual-level model of extreme right potential and actual voting; view of the aggregate-level success of extreme right parties over time.

Chapter 9. Conclusions and issues for future investigation.

2
Theoretical Framework and Conceptual Map

2.1 Beyond the problem of definition

This chapter describes the specifics of the conceptual map of extreme right ideology that forms the theoretical framework of this book. We propose a new approach to help us understand the ideological specificities of the extreme right party family. This approach must be systematic and empirical in order to identify both the similarities and differences within the ideological core of this particular party family. Four main theoretical arguments structure our research design, to explain the fundamental importance of our conceptual map in defining the sub-types of parties within the extreme right party family.

As discussed in Chapter 1, scholars of the extreme right are consistently confronted by the problem of how to define the term extreme right, and the theoretical misunderstandings and empirical inconsistencies surrounding their choice of definition. Our definition must incorporate the subtle differences as well as the fundamental similarities between parties of the extreme right family. No consensus appears to exist as to the common features and distinctive criteria uniting the various members of the extreme right party family. As a result, we are often presented with complex theoretical frameworks that fail to withstand empirical investigation or that make sense empirically but do not withstand theoretical scrutiny. Our proposed model keeps these considerations in mind.

In this chapter, we present the framework of analysis and the structure of our conceptual map.

2.2 Models and approaches of defining the extreme right party family

Several attempts have been made to unite the plethora of competing models within the existing literature that describe the multiple characteristics of the extreme right party family. Mudde (2004) adopts an approach used by Wittgenstein' (1953) whilst detailing five types of approaches used to define and characterise members of a political party family. He typifies these approaches as

1. Prototype;
2. Lowest common denominator;
3. Highest common denominator;
4. Family resemblance; and
5. Ideal type.

The prototype model proposed by Wittgenstein identifies one 'perfect' reference to which all other categories are compared, a model that also makes sense in the Weberian ideal type approach. In terms of the extreme right party family, one party would serve as a prototypical example to which all other potential members of the family would be compared. This method emerged because political scientists wanted to test a hypothesised link between the contemporary extreme right parties in Europe and pre-war fascist and Nazi parties (Eatwell, 1996; Harris, 1997). More recently, several authors have used the French Front National (Mayer & Sineau, 2002) or the Italian Movimento Soziale Italiano (MS-FT) (Ignazi, 1997) as their prototype model. The problem with the prototype model approach is that it is highly inductive. It unilaterally crowns one given party as a 'perfect' specimen of its family, in a way that can be endlessly discussed and cannot be falsified.

The second approach, using the *lowest* common denominator of extreme right parties across time and systems, describes only the minimal features common to all the members of the party family. This approach would be extremely difficult to operationalise with respect to extreme right ideological discourse. Discourse varies across time and countries, according to the local legal norms, specific social and historical contexts, and social acceptance of certain discourse and rhetoric. For example, although some parties occasionally adopt openly racist stances Britain, others refer to migrants or asylum seekers (the French FN or the Austrian FPÖ), or to large ethnic groups residing within the country (such as the French-speaking community, for the Vlaams Belang). Finding a common denominator in such discourse relies largely upon the social scientist's interpretation and opens the way for criticism that such a common denominator is in fact of little importance (Pedahzur & Avarham, 2001).

The third approach finds the *highest* common denominator between extreme right parties. This approach implies an arbitrary case selection, as the parties must bear any set of similar characteristics such as size, history, and electoral success; however, if the chosen extreme right parties are of equal size, campaign in similar party systems, retain the same organisational structure, and are offered opportunities to participate in coalition governments, one may indeed find greater commonalities between their discourse, programmes, and proposals, simply because the case selection is partially biased (Anderson, 1996).

The fourth approach is based upon a theory of family resemblance: within the context of political party families, this theory assumes individual members have some common features but no single feature will ever be shared by all of the family members. In this sense, we have to evaluate and compare the fundamental features associated with each party and the party family to identify how many and which features need to be shared by a member to be deemed part of the extreme right party family. This approach is also inductive, and it is hard to establish which family features concern broader groups of parties than the extreme right family. In this sense, a theory of extreme right family features is hard to falsify, all the more so that no overarching feature is needed for a party to be considered of the extreme right.

Pedersen (1982), on the other hand, emphasises the potential worth of typologising parties according to their lifespans. The principal implication of the lifespan theory is a process of evolution: surpassing 'thresholds of legitimisation', resolving crisis events in ideological and strategic terms, and changing roles from inception to participation in government. The evolution and progression of a political party are often determined by the individual politico-institutional setting and the level of electoral demand, so it is difficult to find commonalities across several party systems or time frames. These lifespan developments are indeed common to all political parties, but to date European extreme right parties present a diverse array of completed and ongoing lifespans within a relatively short time as many fragment, internally combust, or are even, in the case of several German or Dutch extreme right parties, prohibited.

Gallagher et al. (1995: 181) argue that a genetic component can be used to define members of a party family, implying that parties of the same family should have mobilised during similar historical circumstances or set out with the intention of representing similar interests. Although this theory is relevant to parties representing the dominant cleavage-based interests (social-democratic, conservative, Christian democratic, or agrarian parties), it is difficult to apply to the extreme right, a party family that regularly transcends the traditional left-right dimension. Some older extreme right parties have roots from the inter-war period, but many post-war parties suffered a schism, disbanded, or were prohibited. Some parties were founded and socialised in the immediate post-war period (German Sozialistische Reichspartei Deutschlands, SRP),[1] whereas others made their debut in the past decade (Danish Progress party). A condition that they be mobilised in similar historical contexts is therefore clearly not relevant when defining the membership of the extreme right party family.

Some authors use membership of transnational groups in the European Parliament to determine the eligibility of party families (Bardi, 2003). This point of reference is hard to apply to the extreme right party family; even though there have been several parliamentary groups, on the whole they have been inconsistent, short-lived expedients, and susceptible to fissure. The most notable group to be established by an extreme right coalition was the 'Identity, Tradition and Sovereignty' (ITS) group, created in January 2007 and chaired by French MEP Bruno Gollnisch (from the Front National). The ITS group collapsed after ten months, when members of the Greater Romania Party withdrew from the group; however, a few weeks before the European Parliament elections in June 2009, Gollnisch claimed he could resurrect the group, saying he was in regular contact with the British National Party, the Bulgarian Ataka, and the Austrian FPÖ.[2] At the same time, many parties belonging to the extreme right party family prefer to remain outside trans-European parliamentary groups and thus remain unaffiliated MEPs within the Parliament. For example, the Hungarian extreme right party, Jobbik, won 14.7 per cent of the vote in the 2009 elections and three seats, but has so far remained unaffiliated within the Parliament. Similarly, some parties belonging to the extreme right party family simply do not gain enough votes in the elections to return any representatives to the European Parliament. This renders the party family difficult to define, as some of the obvious members will undoubtedly be excluded or some odd ones might be included such as the British conservatives. Authors such as Müller (1989) have directed their attention to the political origins of party leaders and officials in order to trace the roots of the political ideology of the party; yet, how would one select a representative sample of leaders from whom a party's ideology can be defined? How can some leaders and officials be more representative of the entire party than others are? Indeed, some leaders and officials have openly declared links to inter-war or post-war fascist groups (Schönhuber, former leader of die Republikaner); others have not or are simply too young to have experienced the fascist era firsthand (Nick Griffin, leader of the BNP). Such leaders would indeed have been socialised in completely different contexts and presumably equally different ideological mindsets.

The preceding approaches are wholly plausible in defining membership of a party family, but for many reasons these particular avenues are unsuitable in the context of the specific ideological space of the extreme right party family. As a result, our framework of analysis must be tailored to the specificities of the extreme right party family, and empirical testing is fundamental to the success of defining the individual parties within it. In the next section, we highlight some main definitions of the extreme right party family in the existing literature and discuss their advantages and shortcomings with regard to empirical reality.

2.3   How can we define the extreme right party family?

Alongside the debate of how to define the extreme right, we are also confronted by the uncertainty of whether we should even be speaking of a unified extreme right party family. As we briefly see in Chapter 1, little consensus exists about who should or should not be defined as extreme right. The same disagreements surround the debate on the existence of a party family on the extreme right. When confronted by the task of defining parties, most scholars use the concept of party families, in which political parties are grouped across countries predominantly on the basis of their ideology (Michels, 1911; Duverger, 1951; Lipset & Rokkan, 1967).

More recently, Von Beyme (1984) constructs several typologies based on important ideological criteria forming different '*familles spirituelles*' using two criteria to classify each individual party: (1) the party's name, and (2) voter perceptions of party programmes and ideological positions. The first criterion based on the party name is extremely difficult to operationalise in the context of the extreme right party family. Party leaders and officials retain the full decision to name their parties as they want, and party names can be extremely ambiguous. For example, the Russian Liberal Democrats can be classified as members of the extreme right party family, and the National Socialist Party in Germany was certainly anything but social democratic. In addition, parties such as the German Peoples' Union (Deutsche Volksunion or DVU) or the Austrian FPÖ certainly do little to acclaim their allegiance to extreme right ideology.

Party families can usually be distinguished by comparing policy output across a number of parties. This method is highly appropriate for the analysis of parties that operate within government and have a direct impact on policy-making. Remember, however, that with at least four exceptions (FPÖ, AN, DF, SVP) most extreme right parties have never participated in their national government; even where they have participated, they were only junior partners in governing coalitions. This renders it nigh impossible to distinguish the specific policies they have directly influenced versus the initiatives of other parties. Indeed, often when they reach government they form a coalition with other parties who on the face of it would seem hostile to extreme right values, which may well prevent their true ideological discourse from being expressed through policy.

Problems also arise when trying to use voter perceptions of party positions along the ideological spectrum, as they tend to be inaccurate and unreliable estimates of the given party's real location. Indeed, the issue dimensions used to measure voter perceptions of parties are often one-dimensional, when the interaction of political issues is actually dynamic and multidimensional. In addition, we fail to understand the essence of political parties or the basics of party competition if we assume parties are static and can only be judged on a particular set of policies or stances at one given point in time. Parties often change direction or adopt new stances during the course of a year or even within an election campaign. They also react and adapt to the campaigns and policy proposals of their competitors, external influences, or internal pressures from the party members themselves (Laver et al., 2003). Moreover, voter perceptions of party ideologies are difficult to measure, as the categories used by political scientists for such measurements might not be natural for voters. For example, it would be unfair to assume that voters always think of extreme right parties as primarily right wing. Some elements of extreme right discourse overlap with those of neighbouring party families. In this context, it would be hard to imagine that voters who affiliate with the right wing ideology of conservative or Christian democrat parties and would never contemplate voting for an extreme right party would have a different perception of extreme right party ideology than would other voters.

Some authors prefer to typologise parties based upon some specified ideological characteristics or dimensions. Ignazi (1992, 2003) distinguishes between 'new' and 'old' extreme right parties, a typology that focuses on three dimensions: spatial, ideological, and attitudinal-systemic. As a result, parties are characterised first with regard to a presence or an absence of a fascist legacy and, second, in relation to an acceptance or a refusal of the political system. He argues therefore that extreme right parties in Europe can be divided into two main categories:

1. 'New' extreme right parties, such as the FN, the VB, and the FPÖ, which build upon an anti-systemic, populist legacy; and
2. 'Old' parties, such as the BNP and the Italian MS/FT, which focus on the more traditional neo-fascist ideology.

Serious questions remain about the exact basis for classification in Ignazi's analysis. There is little doubt that the arbitrary distinction between new and old extreme right parties artificially masks the underlying but obvious complexities surrounding the definition of the extreme right party family. Mudde (2004:328) states that 'sometimes parties are classified exclusively on the basis of the party ideology, yet at other times they are judged by the attitudes of their members or even their voters'. He adds that 'similar parties seem to be classified differently, because of the presence or absence of other parties'. To illustrate his critique, Mudde uses the example of the classification of the Lega Nord, which Ignazi describes as an anti-system but not an extremist party on the basis that the MS-FT already occupies the most extreme position on the right-hand side of the political spectrum. This assumes there is only enough space for one extreme right party in each party system. We question, however, how Ignazi would apply this assumption if more than one party belonging to the extreme right party family competes within the same party system. This approach exposes many empirical inconsistencies. In many European party systems, multiple parties compete for their share of the potential extreme right vote (see Chapter 6 on party competition). There are as many as three main German extreme right parties (the NPD, the DVU, and Die Republikaner), three main parties of the extreme right in France (the FN, MNR, and the MPF) and this pattern can be seen in other party systems such as in Italy, Poland, and even in systems in which the extreme right has not been particularly successful (the Britain, for example).

Eatwell (1989), on the other hand, insists that in order to identify a new radical right party we must distinguish:

1. Whether it is a party that its competitors perceive to be located on the right and not a viable coalition partner; and
2. When the party appeared on the political scene.

This categorisation seems vague and extremely difficult to operationalise. For example, how far right should a party be located for it to be a member of the extreme right party family? Surely, this question should not be answered purely theoretically but should also incur some empirical testing, as the specificity of the party system, socio-economic context, or the political climate of each individual country is undoubtedly extremely important in determining this outcome.

The criterion that the party should not be a viable coalition partner does not work, as several parties belonging to the extreme right party family have participated in coalition governments (for example, the MSI-AN and the Lega Nord joined Berlusconi's party, Forza Italia, in a coalition government after the 1994 elections). With regard to the final criterion, when the party appeared on the political scene, it is also difficult to define extreme right parties according to this, as many parties have emerged, disappeared, and then re-emerged under a different name or new personnel.

Many authors base their definition on particular case studies in order to appreciate the full value of country-specific detail; however, an overload of these details can add a further problematic facet to the puzzle. Scheuch & Klingemann (1967) base their definition of right wing extremism on what the *Verfassungsshutz* (Office for the Protection of the German Constitution) defines as political radicalism and extremism. It states that *radikalismus* (radicalism) constitutes a radical critique of the constitutional order without any anti-democratic meaning or intention; whereas *extremismus* (extremism) defines an anti-democratic, anti-liberal, and anti-constitutional approach (Backes & Jesse, 1993). This distinction between the two forms of right wing extremism is interesting, but its usage outside the German political system is limited as each country has its own peculiarities and benchmarks to which the terms radicalism and extremism can be compared, which is undoubtedly salient in the context of the German political system.

In summary, as seen in the preceding discussions, it is extremely difficult to characterise or define the membership of the extreme right party family. The various attempts so far to define systematically and coherently what it means to be a member of the extreme right party family have failed both a robust theoretical and confirmed empirical test. As a result, the existing literature lacks a unified theoretical framework that can explain exactly who belongs to this party family, why, and on what basis. Defining theoretically and empirically what actually constitutes an extreme right party is perhaps one of the most difficult hurdles this book faces. We argue that in order to understand further the extreme right party family, we need to refocus our attention on the parties themselves and provide a conceptual definition of these particular parties based on their ideological discourse. In the next section, we look at how we can study party ideology to identify the various sub-types of parties within this specific party family.

2.4   The study of party ideology

Research on political parties and party families based on ideology has been limited in both range and quantity (Mudde, 2000: 183). In the field of comparative politics, it is surprising to find that few studies actually adopt an ideological approach to studying party families or groups (Lawson, 1976:15). This is particularly true in the context of extreme right parties. The few comparative studies that have adopted the ideological approach are fairly restricted to comparisons of either one party through time (Sainsbury, 1980) or country-specific case studies (Hoogerwerf, 1971; Borg, 1966), or try to infer a transnational group that loosely represents the core of the party family (Gardberg, 1993; Mudde, 1995). As widely applied in the study of coalition governments (Budge & Keman, 1990; Laver & Schofield, 1990) to the analysis of policy output (Esping-Andersen, 1985; van Kersbergen, 1995), political parties have been grouped into broader party families, which has often resulted in vague and tenuous linkages between parties and their supposed siblings.

Party discourse and ideology can be extremely difficult to analyse. Such analysis can be time-consuming and can often require knowledge of multiple languages if primary literature such as manifestos and press releases are to be studied. One of the most remarkable achievements in this area stems from the Comparative Manifestos Project.[3] This approach has been most widely used, and forms the basis of the European Manifestos Project that analyses the policy stances of most of the large party families in Europe (Budge et al., 2001). The Comparative Manifestos dataset is the most extensively validated set of policy estimates available within the discipline of political science, but is of limited use to this research as it includes few extreme right party cases. In addition, the project focuses on policy rather than structuring ideological dimensions. Clearly we need to construct our own conceptual map to test the specificities of extreme right discourse.

Some authors suggest extreme right parties could be defined based upon their ideological characteristics. Betz (1994: 413), for example, underlines a 'rejection of socio-cultural and socio-political systems...and of individual and social equality' within the discourse of the extreme right parties. Similarly, Kitschelt & McGann (1995) identifies new radical right parties on the basis of their location on three dimensions: citizenship (cosmopolitan versus particularistic), collective decision modes (libertarian versus authoritarian), and the state allocation of resources (re-distributive versus market-liberal). Eatwell (1989) defines the new radical right (preferring not to use the term extreme right party) as retaining the following features: moral conservatism, political authoritarianism, and economic liberalism. Again, authors disagree on the fundamental elements constituting the core ideology of the extreme right party family. Fennema (1997), for example, has analysed the ideology of extreme right parties and movements using a historical perspective, and concluded that there are four key features of extreme right ideology: ethnic nationalism (or ethnoculturalism), anti-materialism, anti-parliamentarianism, and he formulation of conspiracy theories.

Although most of these models of definition outline particular characteristics of extreme right ideology, many of them refer to specific case studies or a small selection of countries and are thus limited in their comparative explanatory power. Moreover, these definitions of sub-types of parties or character lists are often vague and ambiguous, non-exclusive to the extreme right party family, and are usually based upon the expert judgement of parties or loose interpretations of extreme right ideology rather than on the actual discourse of these parties.

Some authors suggest there are too many differences between parties of the extreme right, rendering it impossible to conceive a unified party family. We argue, however, that by dissecting the extreme right party family into different sub-types of parties we can truly appreciate the subtleties of this group of parties within and across party systems. We can only truly define extreme right parties by conducting in-depth analysis of their discourse in order to reveal the most important aspects of their ideological identity.

In order to study the logic of the variations in discourse we encounter within the extreme right party family, we need to analyse the strategic-discursive choices each party must face when deciding upon its unique discourse and ideological identity. We can gain insight into the logic of these choices by analysing official discourse such as party programmes and manifestos. Indeed, Mudde (2000) claims studies of extreme right parties have not benefited so far from the interesting insights that can be gleaned from the study of party programmes. The analysis of extreme right party discourse allows us to reveal some of the core dimensions at the heart of extreme right party family ideology. The vast majority of party specialists agree that a party manifesto is the closest thing to an official view of a party's ideological discourse. A party manifesto remains arguably the one fundamental document in which a party defines its identity. Because party programmes are officially endorsed by their leaders and members and are subject to conference scrutiny and debate, they are 'considered to represent and express the policy collectively adopted by the party' (Borg, 1966: 97). Manifestos are designed with a clear and simple objective: set a coherent ideological standpoint, attract potential voters, and increase visibility of the party during electoral periods and campaigns. Everything from their emphasis to their proposals via their stylistic and rhetoric choices corresponds to a certain exercise of self-definition expected of every party in a given party system. It therefore seems logical to assume that party manifestos serve as a good proxy to estimate the official discourse of each individual extreme right party.

By defining each party according to its discourse, we gain a valuable insight into the ideology underpinning the party family. Party manifestos cannot, however be taken at face value. Because manifestos are drafted for a mass audience in order to attract potential voters, their rhetoric may be considerably more moderate or even completely different than the discourse and ideology of members and activists. Indeed, Rose and Mackie (1988) distinguish between extrovert and introvert party activity, and between front-stage discourse, belonging to the extrovert activity, and back-stage discourse, belonging to the introvert party activity. We nevertheless gain valuable insight into the manner in which extreme right parties communicate and frame their discourse and ideology. In addition, simultaneous analyses of party manifestos enable us to incorporate a truly comparative and empirical framework and allow us to explore the conceptual map we have proposed. We move on to discuss the ideological criterion that also must be taken into account when we attempt to define and conceptualise the extreme right party family.

2.5   The conceptual map of extreme right ideology

Within the scope of this study, we focus specifically on extreme right party ideology. Ideology can be conceptualised in many ways, one of the most common of which is an inclusive concept: 'a body of normative or normative-related ideas about the nature of man and society as well as the organisation and the purpose of society' (Sainsbury, 1980:8). This infers that ideology is a set of normative ideas on how society or man are versus how they ought to be (Mudde, 2000), and would include a basic rationale of how society should be ordered and by whom. Infinite configurations are undoubtedly possible.

Although a party family ideology seems impossible to simplify, let alone that of a single party, we should provide an ideological conceptualisation that can be 'sufficiently abstract to travel across national boundaries' (Rose, 1991: 447) to allow comparative analysis across the countries included in the study. The theoretical elements of extreme right ideology should be captured, as should the empirical reality of what is being communicated by party discourse. We propose to study two facets of party discourse: the external and internal perspective. By combining analysis of external party communication (e.g. analysis of party manifestos, programmes, pamphlets) with interviews of extreme right party elite and leading officials, we should achieve valuable insight into the true discourse of the extreme right. Analysis of party communication directed toward the general electorate and potential voters should provide a fairly broad and detailed insight into the institutionalised party ideology (Sainsbury, 1980:17; Holzer, 1981).In-depth interviews with party elite present another facet of the discourse of the extreme right. The following section outlines the logic and rationale underpinning the conceptual map and highlights the core ideological dimensions of extreme right ideology that we outline as the defining structure of the extreme right party family.

Many parties in an extreme right party family retain their discursive specificities and are grounded within their own unique historical context, although two fundamental ideological dimensions are common throughout the entire party family. Indeed, some of the variation in discourse we witness across parties of the extreme right can be attributed to several factors such as the personality of the leader, the strategic-discursive choices each party has to make when drafting its manifesto in the face of competition and pressure from activists, different legal and electoral frameworks, and varying socio-political contexts.

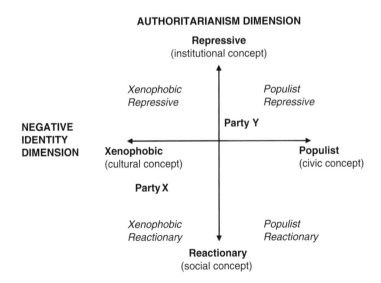

Figure 2.1 A conceptual map of the extreme right ideological space

We posit that extreme right ideology is structured along two ideological dimensions (see Figure 2.1):

1. Authoritarianism, featuring social (reactionary) and institutional (repressive) conceptualisations; and
2. Negative identity, including a civic (populist) and cultural (xenophobic) mode.

These two dimensions are stable and consistent, and occur within and across party systems. Extreme right parties must make a series of strategic-discursive choices when deciding where to locate within the extreme right ideological universe and which unique aspects of their discourse to showcase in order to provide simple and clear-cut ideological cues to voters and potential voters.

Extreme right parties have to make a series of ideological choices within this defined and bounded ideological space, strategic-discursive choices that define their ideological identity. This conceptual map of extreme right ideology (see Figure 2.1) enables us to locate the parties in our analysis relative to each other within their domestic party systems and across external party systems. An original contribution of this book is to define empirically the ideological specificity of the extreme right party family within a unified conceptual framework that allows us to determine which parties belong to this fast-growing party family. We posit that each extreme right party uniquely combines a dominant emphasis on two conceptions of the four main ideological pillars and is thus given an ideological location on the conceptual map. The extreme right party family can, therefore, be sub-divided according to the location of each party based on the strategic-discursive choices the parties make within their ideological discourse.

Each individual extreme right party's style and blend of discourse varies along two dimensions (hence the impossibility to simply divide the extreme right into two sub-party families), and is tailored to the party's internal pressures and constraints, its target electoral market, and the institutional and contextual specificities of the political, electoral, and party systems it operates within. The unique location of each extreme right party within the conceptual map has an impact upon its ability to seduce voters, its electoral potential, and the shape of internal (within the extreme right) and external (vis-à-vis other parties) party competition.

The two dimensions of authoritarianism and negative identity create four possible ideological conceptions. First, a social authoritarian conception embodied in a reactionary formation and an institutional authoritarian conception embedded in a repressive format. Second, the negative identity dimension can assume two different forms: a cultural conception resulting in a xenophobic discourse and a civic conception that encapsulates a populist discursive theme.

2.6 The four ideological pillars

In the next section, we introduce the two ideological dimensions, discussing each conception. We first examine the two conceptions of the authoritarian dimension: the reactionary and repressive modes. Subsequently, we develop the two conceptions of the negative identity dimension: the xenophobic and populist forms.

The authoritarianism dimension: reactionary conception

In essence, the social conception of the authoritarian dimension is a utopian ideology and entails devotion to a posited ideal civilisation. This civilisation may take the form of a city, town, locality, or, in the most extreme case, the entire world. In this ideal community, all perceived evils of society (e.g. poverty, crime, misery) are replaced by a harmonised and homogeneous society. It characterises a society striving to perfect itself and its people. Utopian ideology is often strongly opposed to, and even sometimes rejects, the existing status quo (Mannheim, 1960). The nature of utopian thinking has changed historically, depending on whether or not utopia was regarded as realisable. As such, it often constitutes a critique of social institutions (Goodwin & Taylor, 2009). With the French Revolution came suggestions that the course of history could be diverted, and utopia (of a sort) could be implemented: abstract ideals could be incarnated in society by deliberate human action. As utopia depicts an ideal form of social life which by definition does not currently exist, we expect parties espousing reactionary discourse would refer to a glorious past or golden age and encapsulate euphoric visions of the future.

The implication for current political life is that retrenchment and conservation to prevent worse decline are the only proper forms of political action. A major assertion of the extreme right utopian claim is that the inefficiency of political structures cannot be resolved *within* the traditional democratic system. Extreme right parties propose solutions *outside* the liberal democratic framework of Western societies. Overall, an ultra-conservative ideological component leads parties of the extreme right party family to postulate a glorified social order. With regard to the alleged imperfections of contemporary society, they threaten to impose a utopia by force (Merkl & Weinberg, 1997). Traditional society had its balance, its natural order, something new generations fail to understand and have lost. Standards of authority and order were respected before some disruptive influences diluted them by promoting some deviant alternatives in the names of modernity and egalitarianism. The solution proposed is authoritarian but does not involve state interference in private affairs. Quite the contrary, as it requires the state to withdraw to its rightful place to allow the common sense of good citizens to reign with a return to old values and solutions, which may no longer be legal in democracies which have lost their way to political correctness.

Within the reactionary discourse of extreme right parties, there is a certain devotion to community, whether it is the national community, regional/local networks, or simply the family. Parties of the extreme right point to the 'erosion of family, clan, neighbourhood, and social class' (Heitmeyer, 1993: 22), and often reinforce the need for a revival of the group mentality. This group mentality is embedded and reinforced in the extreme right ideological frame of 'man is a *Gemeinshaftswesen* and can only develop fully within a community'. The community's needs almost become superior to the existence of the individual. There is 'a belief in the authority of the state over the individual; an emphasis on natural community [...] limitations on personal and collective freedoms; collective identification in a great national destiny [...] and the acceptance of the hierarchical principle for social organisation' (Ignazi, 1997: 49). We now turn our attention to the second conception of the authoritarianism dimension, the institutional repressive mode.

The authoritarianism dimension: repressive conception

The repressive conception of the authoritarianism dimension firmly rests upon a form of social control characterised by strict obedience to the authority of a state or organisation. This often entails the maintenance and enforcement of control through the use of oppressive measures. Even though most contemporary extreme right parties couch their platforms and appeals in terms of democratic respect and institutional fair play, the underlying tone of some of their propositions has often been subtly anti-democratic. Remember one of Goebbels infamous quotes about the NSDAP: 'we want to make use of democratic means in order to gain power and after seizure of that power we would ruthlessly deny to our opponents all those means which they had granted to us during the time of our opposition'.[4] In order to combat impending chaos and threatened anarchy, extreme right parties often claim that they will entrust a strengthened state with the task of (re)enforcing law and order. The state must use repression to eradicate errant fragments of society. The affirmation of stability, authority, and submission of the individual to the ideological goal are paramount in much of their discourse. There are obvious differences between the levels of radicalism and the extent to which the party endorses anti-democratic behaviour. Because of the very nature of anti-systemic rhetoric, most parties proposing radical departures from the existing status quo are relegated to the peripheries of their respective party systems. Extreme right parties that want to compromise on this particular element and emphasise other aspects of their discourse are perceived more palatable to the wider public tend to be more populist in tone; such parties generally represent opposition against the incumbent government and other mainstream parties rather than against the system per se (see 'The negative identity dimension: populist conception' later in this section).

For the purposes of this study, we distinguish between authoritarian ideology and the authoritarian personality.[5] In order to reinforce anti-systemic and anti-party claims, extreme right parties propose an extremely centralised and autocratic leadership of their movement, a characteristic that threatens the party's existence when the current leader steps down from office. The majority of extreme right parties are dominated by a strong and autocratic leader. The French National Front has its Le Pen, the Austrian FPÖ its Haider, the Italian Alleanza Nazionale its Fini. Extreme right parties are often 'possessed' in a patriarchal manner (in the Weberian sense). Fortuyn gave his name to the party and Le Pen contradicted the internal hierarchy of the National Front to name his daughter Marine his designed successor. We use the lens of the authoritarian personality to capture the effect of the leader on the party and to establish whether there is a leadership cult. Obviously, the authoritarian ideology of an extreme right party is extremely difficult to assess, as the party has had no chance to implement any of its policies or influence government; however, we look for hints of authoritarian ideology throughout the text analysis of party manifestos., An emphasis on the authoritarian personality is more easily captured via the interviews of the elite and of high-ranking officials.

We now turn our attention to the negative identity dimension, first discussing the essence of the xenophobic conception, then examining its populist counterpart.

The negative identity dimension: xenophobic conception

In Bruter's (2005, 2009) model, cultural political identity is broadly conceived as a sense of belonging to a human community with which one shares some values, history, cultural references, or heritage. It is a measure of relative perceived proximity, whereby one feels closer to those within the community than to those outside it. Similarly, the cultural pole of the negative identity scale excludes those seen as essentially different from the community: in the broadest meaning of the word, 'foreigners'; hence, the reference to a xenophobic pole of the negative identity dimension. By contrast, positive references will be made to the Nation, the People/Volk, historical national figures, and so on. The concept of *Volk* (the people) is often fundamental to the discourse of the extreme right party family. Klandermans and Mayer (2006: 271) claim that this is 'the first, most important in-group'. The same authors state that the nation takes on almost biological image 'as a natural consanguine community, with its territory, its language, its culture, that surpasses all others – family, work, religious ties' (ibid.: 271). This type of discourse adds another dimension to the in-group structure, that is, the sense of belonging that requires a 'total devotion to nation and cultural assimilation' (Klein & Simon, 2006a:168), which leads to a 'collective identification in a great national destiny, against class, ethnic, or religious divisions' (Ignazi, 2002: 24).

Broadly defined xenophobic, racist, or anti-Semitic elements are perhaps the oldest aspect of extreme right politics to be identified by political scientists. Arendt's (1958) study of anti-Semitism highlighted its role as a key element in the very definition of Nazism. Similarly, Adorno et al. (1950) considered racism and xenophobia to be two core elements of extreme right ideology. Some authors think of these attitudes as so central to the extreme right ideology that they focus broadly on the anti-immigration stance of extreme right parties or think of 'anti-immigrant parties' as a more suitable label than 'extreme right' (van der Brug et al.,, 2000, 2005). Xenophobia and racism[6] are terms that often used to describe the rhetoric of the extreme right. Banton (1983) has documented how the concepts of race and racial inequality dominated much of the public discourse during the nineteenth and the early twentieth centuries. The general belief was that one should 'preserve racial hygiene', races had to be 'maintained' and their purity 'attained'; fighting for 'one's race' or to 'awaken racial consciousness' was seen as legitimate. Kitschelt and McGann (1995) argues extreme right demagogues use these themes in response to the increasing multiculturalisation of Western European societies. Extreme right parties almost unanimously agree that restrictions should be placed upon immigration; as a policy theme, immigration has indeed been a salient issue for the majority of extreme right parties since their inception.

Extreme right parties also draw upon a notion of identity that is intrinsically linked with the physical notion of the nation but is largely expressed and mobilised through the more politically charged term nationalism. The nation, by contrast, is a psychological characteristic, a concept individuals are able to identify with and claim to be a part of. Delanty (1996) argues that nationalism appeals to identity now rather than ideology, and that ideology is being increasingly refracted through identity discourse.[7] Under the guise of a need to belong, identity often becomes a mystical phrase, a call for a return to traditional roots. The accentuation of national peculiarities creates an artificial in-group that is simultaneously reinforced by reference to a supposedly obvious out-group. Many parties akin to the extreme right assume that full-fledged membership in the national community requires that individuals share a common identity, language, religion, ideology, culture, and/or history. The dominant community is taken as the reference group to which all other identities should be compared. This refers both to the distinguishing features of the group and to the individual's sense of belonging to it. Any group that does not fit the nationalist mould would, therefore, not be considered as a legitimate member of the national community and would be consequently brandished an out-group.

With regard to our specific interest in the construct of the extreme right discourse, the dichotomy between identity frames and oppositional frames is important. The 'us'-versus-'them' category is used as a frame to present the discrimination of relevant out-groups and the inherent preference for the rights and privileges of the in-group; thus, a distinction is regularly made between them and us within the identity politics of the extreme right that allows parties to construct scapegoats and conspiracy theories that frequently blame such groups as foreigners, ethnic minorities, homosexuals, Jews as the perpetrators of society's ills. Extreme right parties present outsiders as a threat to the very fabric of their society in an era of social and moral malaise and cultural decadence. This leads us to the centrality of principles of inclusion and exclusion: right wing extremists combine an external exclusiveness (Mudde, 2000: 43) with an internal homogenisation (Mudde, 2000: 68). The in-group is presented as a homogeneous set of actors (represented by the party), which defines itself as the opposite of the out-group.

Renan (1882) and, more recently, Brubaker (2004) argue that membership in the national community should be viewed as voluntary (a nation is any group of people aspiring to a common political state-like organisation); however, most extreme right parties believe ethno-cultural traits should determine one's admission into the national community. Indeed, countries differ as to how states manage the question of how to define the nation and who can be seen as a member of its community. In the French method of inclusion, essentially anyone who accepts loyalty to the civil state is a French citizen; however, in practice a considerable degree of uniformity must be enforced. In contrast, the German method, required by political circumstances, was to define the nation in ethnic terms. Ethnicity in practice came down to speaking German and (perhaps) having a German name. The state as a political unit is seen by nationalists as the protector of the national community, charged with promulgating the traditions and heritage of the majority ethno-cultural group. In the next section, we present the populist conception of the negative identity dimension.

The negative identity dimension: populist conception

In contemporary political discourse, populism[8] is often perceived as a rhetorical instrument based on demagogy that provides a generalised label for a number of politicians from Bossi to Le Pen via Berlusconi, each accused of using simplistic slogans to threaten traditional representative democracy and the legitimacy of political institutions. Similarly, parties of the extreme right, including the French Front National, the Belgian Vlaams Blok/Vlams Belang, the Austrian FPÖ, and the Italian Northern League, have often used a populist dynamic to complement their authoritarian values and anti-system sentiment (Scarrow, 1996). Extreme right parties often express contempt for their fellow politicians and their parties. Parties of the extreme right party family sometimes claim not to be political parties at all, a claim that often extends to civil society as they refuse to acknowledge the legitimacy of the mass media, trade unions, or any organisation that openly express refusal of extremist and racist ideology. At the heart of the extreme right's electoral appeal to ordinary people is a desire for a radical transformation of the socio-political system by attacking the social-democratic consensus (Swyngedouw, 1998). Extreme right parties often suggest that colluding mainstream parties defend the same conception of politics and that they (the extreme right parties) are the only real alternative to the existing political governance.

Populist discourse regularly consists of simply constructed arguments based upon several common propositions. The sovereignty of the people is often championed alongside a complete denunciation of the political elite and institutions. Once the demagogues have deconstructed the establishment, they suggest that the only viable solution is to restore popular sovereignty and that they can be the only ones trusted to do it. By portraying themselves as the true defenders of democracy, they construct a barrier to differentiate themselves from traditional elected representatives to legitimate their claims vis-à-vis their competitors. Le Pen's campaign slogan, 'mains propres, tête haute' [clean hands, straight head], was meant to illustrate the moral and legal 'virginity' of his forces as opposed to the common levels of corruption and misuse of public goods by the four main parties labelled the 'bande des quatre' [gang of four].

Many contemporary leaders of extreme right parties decry mainstream politicians as being out of touch with ordinary citizens, claiming that these public servants have alienated the people they are supposed to represent. Leaders of extreme right parties exclaim that the will of the people should rule and that they would, given a chance to govern, root out the alleged corruption of the existing elite who try to usurp the power from the people. Recognising the electoral potential of populist themes, some parties have focused on such themes in election campaigns. This phenomenon has been noted extensively by the existing literature. For example, Scarrow (1996) focuses on the unifying theme of anti-party discourse amongst a number of extreme right parties; Betz (1994) and Betz and Immerfall (1998) believe that populism plays such a key role within the ideology of extreme right parties that they prefer to talk of 'right wing populist' parties or 'new populist' parties as opposed to extreme right or far right parties.

An empirical and analytical difficulty remains in that there is no definitive specification of the populist discourse. Although this type of discourse can be occasion-specific within the context of a given electoral campaign, it can also be more durable and define the very ideological identity of a party. Chirac in 1995 and Berlusconi in 2001 probably illustrate the first scenario; a number of reactionary nationalist parties such as the Austrian FPÖ or the French FN are characterised by the second. Hassenteufel (1991) used the case study of Austria to illustrate that the anti-system function was performed simultaneously by both the FPÖ and the BRD (Greens). Both parties have had to face the difficulties posed to their legitimacy as anti-system parties after agreeing to participate in the coalition government. Consistent arguments that the mainstream parties and their politicians are corrupt and do little to represent the concerns of real people soon become irrelevant when the said extreme right party is then invited to share power in a coalition government.

In summary, the strategic-discursive location chosen by each party defines its ideological identity within a defined extreme right ideological territory.

These two dimensions create four possible quadrants of extreme right ideology: xenophobic-reactionary, xenophobic-repressive, populist-reactionary, and populist-repressive. Parties are not expected to use only one of the two possible types of references on either of the two dimensions. Instead, ideological references to xenophobic and populist discourse on the one hand, and reactionary and repressive discourse on the other hand, are not only conceivable but also expected. Nevertheless, we believe that within both dimensions a certain tension exists between the two conceptions, as they refer to different solutions to societal problems (reactionary versus repressive conceptions) and highlight different scapegoats or culprits as the cause of these problems (xenophobic versus populist conceptions). As we illustrate empirically in Chapters 4 and 5, these tensions are confirmed empirically as pillar scores are negatively correlated within dimensions.

If we look first at the authoritarian dimension, the state-based solution in the form of institutional authoritarianism is often considered the culprit when it comes to the social authoritarian argument. Indeed, rigid bureaucratic or legalistic rules, and excessive taxation may prevent the priest from being heard, the father from smacking his child, or the teacher from instilling respect for the morals associated with traditional values. On the other hand, when the focus is on institutional authoritarianism, the state must be stronger, tougher, and harsher even if it means curbing individuals' power of decision and the authority of competing social or moral forces, historically including religion. Recent studies focusing on profiles of the electorates that vote for extreme right parties have tended to separate moral authoritarianism and traditionalism from the discourse that focuses on ethnocentrism (Billiet & De Witte, 1995; Swyngedouw & Ivaldi, 2001). When it comes to the negative identity dimension, the tension is as deep in essence although less obvious. Philosophically, accusing foreigners of not respecting their host society, abusing social benefit/welfare systems, and causing crime is fundamentally different from blaming past and present governments for attracting immigrant workers under false pretences and creating inner city ghettoes that cause misery and conditions propitious to high unemployment and crime.

In this context, we also refer to political communication theory that suggests parties must communicate a core and non-conflicting message to their electorate (Simon & Iyengar, 1996). The party must decide who it is going to blame for societal chaos: is it the fault of the politicians who have engineered the multicultural experiment or the immigrants that have settled here and taken jobs and burdened the social security structure? If the party argues that the blame should be equally shared between foreigners and politicians, the ideological message communicated to their electorate will be incoherent and ultimately inefficient at mobilising them on a key ideological theme. Authors such as Betz (1994), Kitschelt and McGann (1995), and Lubbers et al. (2000) have stated that extreme right parties have steadily moved toward emphasising social and moral issues, with a particular focus on issues of immigration, law and order, and moral rectitude; however, we expect extreme right parties to emphasise a particular conception of the two dimensions in order to make their discourse succinct and clearly identifiable by potential voters. The relative positioning of every extreme right party on each dimension and its consequential location in a given quadrant gives a unique pedigree to its fight, discourse, and strategy. This specific ideological identity will affect the dynamics of party competition within the extreme right party family, the types of voters it will potentially seduce, and ultimately the electoral success it obtains.

2.7   Theoretical expectations from the conceptual model of extreme right ideology

In this section, we outline the theoretical expectations that have shaped our research design (see Section 2.8) and discuss how our conceptual map of extreme right ideology contributes to our understanding of the ideological specificity of the members of the extreme right party family. In other words, without necessarily testing formal hypotheses, this section discusses what the extreme right world would resemble if the model exposed in Section 2.5 is correct. If these theoretical predictions are upheld throughout this book, then one could argue that a network of concordant indications supports our model. Based upon our conceptual map of extreme right ideology, this section first illustrates how different combinations of discursive strategies would lead to the formation of different sub-types of parties within the extreme right party family. We then underline the expected consequences of the model upon patterns of extreme right internal party competition when more than one extremist party addresses a national electorate. Next, we outline the predicted theoretical impact of the model on the variation in electoral success that the extreme right experiences within given party systems across countries and electorates.

Discovering sub-types of parties within the extreme right party family

Extreme right parties can be defined by their unique discursive positions on two fundamental ideological dimensions: negative identity and authoritarianism. The negative identity dimension ranges from a cultural conception (xenophobic) to a civic one (populist), and the authoritarian dimension ranges from a social conception (reactionary) to a institutional one (repressive). We try to discover whether these ideological dimensions are salient within the discourse of extreme right parties by counting discursive references (frequency of words) to these ideological pillars in the manifestos of the 25 extreme right parties we study here. We expect each party to have a dominant mode on each of the two structuring ideological dimensions;

that is, they will predominantly emphasise one of the two conceptions of each dimension. This will provide each party with a dominant discourse within the four quadrants of the conceptual extreme right ideological universe: xenophobic-reactionary, xenophobic-repressive, populist-reactionary, populist-repressive. In other words, if our model is correct, then we would expect all four types of dominant strategic-discursive combinations to be represented by some extreme right parties in the three countries studied. This would be an important finding. As discussed in Chapter 1, the extreme right party family is traditionally believed to be either monolithically xenophobic or singularly populist in its very definition.

Exploring the dynamics of multiple extreme right party internal competition

Multiple parties within the extreme right party family can successfully coexist in a given party system if they choose different ideological locations within the four quadrants of extreme right ideology. In a sense, this departs from most conceptions of single-ideological-line spatial models that simply order parties on a left-right scale, which implies that the co-existence of multiple parties towards the same extreme right segment of the scale is somewhat illogical or unlikely. In our model, each extreme right party is expected to capture a target electorate in order to coexist alongside competitors within the same party family. For example, an extreme right party might distinguish itself from its rivals by emphasising different conceptions of the core ideological dimensions that are unique to their particular party family. By carving out an ideological identity that is different to its competitors, this party should be able to coexist alongside other larger or pre-existing parties within the party family.

If, however, a new extreme right party chooses to imitate the discourse and ideological identity of a pre-existing party, it will fail to capture a unique electorate of its own, as it will be encroaching on the ideological territory of a larger or pre-established rival. Such a new party will find survival a challenge. This being said, if a new challenger chooses to emphasise a divergent discourse to that of the historic party, then it will have a better chance of survival. By combining different conceptions of both ideological dimensions to the one occupied by the existing historic extreme right party within its discursive strategic choices, the new party is not encroaching on the electoral territory of the former party and will instead carve out an electorate of its own.

Finally, in order to be successful within a competitive party system, a party must communicate a clear and coherent ideological message to its potential electorate. In other words, a party must choose a dominant emphasis or mode on each of the two ideological dimensions if the electorate is to understand the ideological cues it is receiving from multiple parties within the same party family. If a party's ideological identity is unclear, for example if it straddles both conceptions of the same ideological dimension, it will be threatened by parties in neighbouring quadrants, rendering its chances of survival weaker.

Investigating the match between extreme right party ideological identities and the ideological distribution of the electorate

We try to discover the ideological dimensions at the heart of the extreme right party family, using the conceptual map to investigate their ideological identities by examining the salience of discursive strategic references. More importantly, we also use a mass survey to assess how the actual and potential electorate perceive the four pillars of extreme right ideology. With these two aspects of the research design in mind, we try to match the two components in order to evaluate whether there is a match between the discourse of parties and the ideological preferences of the actual and potential extreme right electorate.

Here we expect that some combinations of discourse such as populist-reactionary that highlight the power of the people over corrupt elite and emphasise nostalgia for the good old days will appeal to a broader segment of electorate than that associated with the xenophobic-repressive discourse that focuses on isolating immigrants as the root of all societal problems and empowering the state with authoritarian control. Parties espousing the softer elements of the core extreme right ideology are expected to appeal to a greater audience than those preferring to stick to their harder traditional reservoir of extreme right discourse; however, this expected outcome is also influenced by the distribution of the electorate across the four quadrants of extreme right ideology. In some countries, the electorate will be more susceptible to a particular type of discourse than in others. If the actual target electorate is seduced by a harder type of discourse, then this type of party could also be electorally successful (see 'Investigating the match between extreme right party ideological identities and the ideological distribution of the electorate' in this section).

The underlying argument throughout this book is that an extreme right party that manages to secure a 'match' between its ideological location and that of its potential electorate is more likely to be successful electorally than other parties in the same party family would be. A party that fails to capture the ideological preferences of its target electorate within its discourse will fail to attract viable or sustainable support.

In the following section, we discuss the overarching research design of the book and how this framework structures the methodology and the empirical and analytical approach of the book.

2.8   Defining ideological identities via interviews and text analysis of party manifestos

The conceptual framework at the heart of this book revolves around the necessity empirically and analytically to define and locate the positions of the parties within the extreme right ideological universe. To accomplish this goal, we propose using a conceptual map to define each extreme right party and locate its position within the extreme right ideological universe in relation to its counterparts not only within the same party system but across European party systems. By analysing the discourse of extreme right parties, we should be able to demonstrate whether they belong to the extreme right family, and, if yes, the sub-category of extreme right party to which they belong. Each party is defined by its ideological identity relative to its unique focus on the two structuring dimensions of extreme right ideological discourse. These strategic-discursive choices affect internal party competition and, ultimately, electoral success.

In order to substantiate our conceptual map of extreme right ideology, we use extracts and from the interviews of extreme right party elite and leading officials. In Chapter 4, we highlight the subtleties of each of the four ideological pillars that structure the conceptual map of extreme right ideology by detailing the discourse of the extreme right party leaders we interviewed in France and in the Great Britain. We then test the conceptual map of extreme right ideology in Chapter 5 by analysing extreme right party discourse in the manifestos of 25 parties. Chapter 6 focuses on the effect of mapping extreme right party ideology on the dynamics of internal party competition. We argue that the series of strategic-discursive choices parties have to make in terms of their ideological identity and their unique location within the extreme right ideological space can have serious implications on intra-extreme right party competition when several parties compete for a share of the potential extreme right electorate. In several countries, the emergence of multiple extreme right parties competing for the same vote reservoir has aroused little attention. It is not surprising that more parties wish to fight long-established extreme right competitors to capitalise on a newly discovered electoral reservoir.

What renders the emergence of a new party (within a multi-extreme right party context) within a given party system successful? The success or failure of multiple extreme right parties must not depend solely on their location within the universal left-right continuum, let alone on external context; their location within a potential ideological territory that is relevant to the extreme right and its potential voters also matters. The relative success of a party depends upon the distribution of the potential electorate within the extreme right ideological territory. Each quadrant of extreme right ideology retains different potential electoral payoffs depending upon the ideological distribution of the electorate across the four pillars created by the two ideological dimensions. In other words, the more or less dispersed a given electorate is on one conception of an ideological dimension, the more or less scope there will be for a happy coexistence between the various extreme right parties in competition.

2.9   Match or mismatch? Survey analysis of extreme right electorates

We now turn to the part of the study that involves an analysis of the extreme right electorate. We wish to re-examine the discrepancies in the existing literature to understand better the profile of an extreme right voter. In order to reflect the demands of the electorate, extreme right parties will use different strategies to seduce different types of voters. Not unlike other political parties, extreme right parties try to reach as broad as possible a range of voters within their specific ideological catchment area. People who vote for extreme right parties may have varying reasons for doing so (e.g. ideological affiliation, strategic voting, protest vote) and thus will undoubtedly retain strikingly different characteristics. The final component of this study is to test whether the type of extreme right party has an impact on the level of success a party can hope to achieve.

Across Europe, parties in the extreme right party family register significantly different electoral records. Some parties manage to harness the potential extreme right vote; others fail to get their message across to the voters. In party systems with several parties competing for the potential extreme right vote, some parties are more successful than others. In Chapter 7, we overview briefly the electoral success of the eight parties in the United Kingdom, Germany, and France in order to highlight the relatively successful parties and the parties failing to communicate effectively their ideological message to their target electorate. In the second part of Chapter 7, we analyse the characteristics of potential extreme right voters, which in turn helps us evaluate the match between these potential electorates and the positions of the extreme right parties competing in each system. We use the results of the party manifesto analysis to map the locations of the parties themselves, then compare these findings to the results of a mass survey which illustrates the ideological distribution of the actual and potential electorate.

In summary, this book examines the dynamic interaction between:

1. The ideological preferences articulated by party leaders and representatives in order to develop the conceptual map;
2. The ideological identity of each party as a unitary actor via the official discourse embodied by the manifesto;
3. The implications of each party's ideological identity on patterns of party competition; and
4. The match between a party's ideological position and the ideological distribution of the electorate within the individual party systems.

In the following chapter, we discuss each aspect of the methodology in greater detail, highlighting the specificity of each approach within the research design and model.

3
Case Selection and Methodology

3.1 Introduction

This chapter describes how we intend empirically to develop and test our conceptual map and its impact on patterns of party competition, dynamics of ideological discourse, and individual and aggregate dimensions of the vote by detailing the main methodologies to be combined. Our research question raises the issue of the pivotal role of the discourse of extreme right parties in shaping parties' and voters' ideological identity. Our analytical and empirical objectives are ambitious. We wish to investigate the logic of the emergence and internal evolution of the discourse of individual extreme right parties, but also the dynamics of the match between extreme right party discourse and voter ideological preferences. While conceptualising the map of extreme right ideology, we considered a various approaches that would address the research question in order to evaluate which particular methods would be most suitable to test our model. In order to capture the specificity of extreme right ideological discourse, we use a combination of qualitative and quantitative methods. In this chapter, we describe how our main methodologies are operationalised and fit together to create a coherent whole, and explain the logic that underpins our case selection for each part of the research design.

This complex multi-layered research design includes analysis of party manifestos and press releases, in-depth interviews of extreme right leaders and elected representatives, a mass survey of citizens and potential extreme right voters, and analysis of aggregate-level time-series electoral data over 30 years.

3.2 Overarching empirical structure and methodology

The first part of our empirical investigation uses in-depth elite interviews to address the spontaneous references of extreme right party leaders. This is done in Chapter 4, where we explore the subtleties of the ideological discourse associated with the two dimensions and its four conceptions by presenting a series of selected quotes from the in-depth interviews of extreme right party elite in the Britain and France.

The next key part of our research design captures the ideological identity of extreme right parties in a comparative and empirical manner by empirically testing the conceptual map of extreme right ideology developed in Chapter 2. We assess each party's ideological identity by examining strategic-discursive choices presented in party manifestos. This gives us a typology of extreme right parties based on the two dimensions that structure the ideological discourse of the extreme right party family. The results are presented in Chapter 5, where we use text analysis of party manifestos to test the conceptual map, investigating each party's main ideological identity and unique location on the two dimensions, and illustrating how each party emphasises certain elements of extreme right ideological discourse. We are thus presented with a conceptual map that defines the ideological location of each party relative to its competitors in their respective party systems.

Mapping the ideological location of each party relative to its competitors has obvious implications as to the dynamics and strategies of party competition. In Chapter 6, we thus explore the complex world of extreme right party family party competition and discuss the empirical repercussions of each party's ideological location with respect to it competitor's location and the likely chance of electoral success.

In Chapter 7, we look at the time-serial dynamics of extreme right party discourse. In contrast to the party manifesto analysis, which deals with extreme right parties' strategic-discursive identity at one point in time, we analyse how each party's discourse evolves over time by aggregating quarterly over several years the discourse contained in each party's complete press releases and contrasting it to the discourse found in the manifestos of five parties. This allows us to inform our understanding of extreme right party discourse by focusing on five European extreme right parties.

In the final empirical chapter, we look at the match between extreme right party and potential voter preferences and its electoral impact at the individual and aggregate level. Indeed, we first investigate the ideological preferences and characteristics of potential and actual extreme right voters. We move on to some fully specified models of extreme right voting whereby we evaluate, among other things, the respective effects of adhesion to the four basic pillars of extreme right ideology identified by our model, the strategic-discursive location of extreme right parties, and the match between the said ideological location of each party and that of individual voters on the propensity to vote for the extreme right, as well as actual electoral decisions of individual voters. In the second part of the chapter, we examine the long-term electoral success of each sub-type of extreme right party over countries and over three decades.

This combination of approaches and methodologies allows us to capture these three interactions in a way that is comparative and connectible.

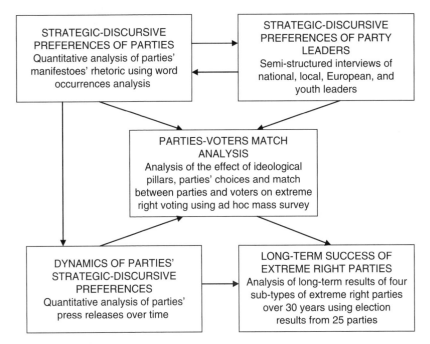

Figure 3.1 Methodological integration of the project

Moreover, the superimposition of this combination of quantitative and qualitative methods enables us to triangulate our findings in order to achieve more robust, generalisable, and meaningful results. Figure 3.1 illustrates the overarching framework of analysis.

In the following section, we discuss the rationale underpinning of our choice of cases used to test each component of the research design. We include a variety of parties that differ in terms of electoral success, organisational structure, and, of course, ideological discourse.

3.3 Case selection

We use a multi-dimensional matrix of methods to address our complex research question, including in-depth interviews and analysis of party manifestos, press releases, an ad hoc survey, and aggregate-level election results over time. This multiplicity of methods also implies a careful balance between broadly comparative elements when we analyse the quasi-totality of Europe's main extreme right parties, and more focused work based on a few selected case studies in other parts of our research design.

Two key elements of the empirical analysis, analysis of manifestos and of the longitudinal analysis of party electoral results from 1979 to 2010, are developed using a broad comparative perspective on European extreme right politics, whereby we included every significant party deemed to be on the extreme right by some part of the existing literature in 17 European countries with significant extreme right parties.[1] This broad perspective on European extreme right politics gives us a general perspective on the European extreme right landscape for these two crucial elements of our empirical analysis, and highly generalisable findings on extreme right ideological variations, and the conditions and reality of the electoral success of the party family over time.

We also wanted to analyse in-depth a smaller number of case studies. This was the case for the interviews, the longitudinal analysis of press releases, the study of internal party competition, and the individual-level analysis of the ideology of individual potential and actual extreme right actual voters. The choice of case studies in these more specific cases is not, by any standard, easy if we want to keep the element of comparability and generalisability of the whole design. Indeed, many elements must be considered when deciding which of the 25 parties in the general sections of our analysis to select as specific case studies in other sections. Such elements include the main political system's characteristics (e.g. federal or unitary, proportional or majoritarian, one or two elected chambers of Parliament), extreme right characteristics (number of extreme right parties in competition, average level of success, representation in local and national politics, in the European Parliament, in government, age of extreme right parties in the country), and regional characteristics (Northern, Southern, Western, or Central and Eastern Europe). Model-specific characteristics were also considered (e.g. to some extent, we aimed for a representation of all four subtypes of extreme right parties identified in our model), as were the needs of specific design components (Chapter 6 on internal competition between extreme right parties obviously required countries in which several extreme right parties compete with each other; Chapter 7 on the dynamics of party press releases over time required the use of parties competing for at least five years). These criteria led us with three sub-groups of parties for case-study purposes.

For a second series of empirical tests that required the inclusion of whole political systems with multiple extreme right parties, we focused our empirical analysis on three countries: the Britain, France, and Germany. We chose these three countries for a variety of reasons. We wanted to focus our analysis on countries with several parties belonging to the extreme right party family competing within the same party system. These three countries also have an extreme right made up of different types of parties, with different longevity, different patterns of national dominance, and different levels of overall success. We selected the following parties to study:

1. Britain: the British National Party and the UK Independence Party.[2]

2. France :the Front National, the Mouvement pour la France (MPF), and the Mouvement National Républicain (MNR);
3. Germany: the Deutsche Volksunion, the Republikaner, and the Nationaldemokratische Partei Deutschlands.

The variety of parties within three very different party systems allows us to discover the ideological discourse of each party and how it varies within and across party systems. This diversity of cases helps us not only to understand the ideological specificity of each of the parties in the three different party systems but also to gain a deeper insight into the dynamics of multiple extreme right party competition within the defined ideological space of the party family. We balanced the need for variation within and across party systems with the desire to gain in-depth country-specific detail. In choosing parties that vary widely on the dependent variable (level of electoral success) we minimise the effects of selection bias on causal inferences. The parties analysed vary significantly in terms of their size, style, history, roles within party systems, and structures. This broad diversity of cases in this study allows us to improve our overall understanding of the extreme right party family. We focus our analysis on parties representative of the entire spectrum of success within the party family in Europe: Germany (weak overall but strong in specific regions), United Kingdom (weak overall but strong in specific elections), France (strong) for a long time but no access to government).

Each party system also varies as to historical references and extreme right political traditions. For example, the United Kingdom has no strong governmental tradition; in France, the Vichy experience is largely dismissed as a parenthesis by mainstream parties and politicians; Germany has the omnipresent legacy of the Nazi regime. Each party no doubt reacts differently to its particular ideological heritage, which also frames the ideological message interpreted by the electorate. A historical legacy may also impede the electoral advancement of an extreme right party if electoral thresholds or prohibitions are imposed by their respective democratic and constitutional frameworks. We include cases that retain a variety of electoral and political systems. For example, in terms of electoral systems, we have plurality (UK), majority (France), mixed (Germany). In terms of political systems, we have semi-presidential (France) and parliamentarian (UK, Germany); federal (Germany), devolution (UK), and unitary (France), with significant power attributed to the regions.

For a section on the dynamics of extreme right party discourse, a focus on France, Germany, and the Great Britain is not satisfactory. This time, there is no need to focus on entire political systems with multiple extreme right parties. Cases in which a single extreme right party is represented should be included, as such parties have more freedom to change their strategic-discursive focus over time, as should cases of parties belonging to multi-extreme right systems that are thus more constrained. It is also of paramount importance to include case studies from all four main sub-types of extreme right political parties: xenophobic-reactionary, xenophobic-repressive, populist-reactionary, and populist-repressive. Also included are parties occupying much of the literature on the extreme right where they are often perceived as important prototypes of extreme right parties. We focus on the French FN, British BNP, Austrian FPÖ, Swiss SVP, and Danish DF. We would have liked to have included one of the major extreme right parties from Central European countries, such as the PRM or Ataka, but none has enough press releases available (five years of press releases was our minimum for systematic analysis of meaningful variations, but no central European party in our universe could provide more than two years worth of continuous press releases).

Finally, for the individual-level analysis of the match between the ideological preferences of extreme right parties and those of their potential and actual voters, the case selection needs are mostly based on the characteristics of countries rather than parties or party systems. For that section, whereby we use part of an ad hoc, made-to-measure survey financed by the Economic and Social Research Council (see footnote 24), we thus use a cross section of all major types of political and party systems in Europe, selecting nine of them for the analysis: France, Germany, the Great Britain, Italy, French-speaking Belgium, Dutch-speaking Belgium, Austria, Denmark, and Romania. We thus have small and large, relatively wealthy and relatively poor countries, republics, and monarchies, centralised, decentralised, and federal political systems. Northern, Western, Southern, and Eastern Europe are represented, and systems include the use plurality, majority, mixed, and proportional electoral systems, countries in which extreme right parties are strong and weak, represented in government, represented in Parliament, or neither, single or multiple.

We therefore have four different series of case selections for the six empirical components of our study: a 70-country, 25-party pan-European sample, a multi-extreme right parties three-country sample, and a five-country classic extreme right parties sample. Let us now look in greater detail at the actual contents of each of the methodologies.

3.4 Capturing the ideological preferences of extreme right party leaders

One of this book's main objectives is to understand the specificity of extreme right ideology. We aim to capture the essence of extreme right ideology by investigating the various strategic-discursive choices each party makes within its discourse. To do this, we need to draw a distinction between the official unitary ideological position of parties, usually expressed by their manifesto or party programme on the one hand, and the ideological preferences of party leaders, who may diverge more or less significantly from the party's official platform on the other. In many ways, models of ideological heterogeneity of party representatives are implicitly and intuitively conceived by Miller and Stokes (1963). Both because of their own individual ideological specificities and how they perceive their electorate's preferences (conceived quite literally in Miller and Stokes's work, possibly more broadly here), party leaders will develop their own sets of ideological and policy preferences. These preferences may be somewhat similar to the core ideological corpus of the party but will also probably retain some divergence or specific emphasis.

Although much analysis – starting with Miller and Stokes' 1958 data, which deals with members of the same institution in a context of low partisan discipline – focuses on the individual preferences of party leaders and representatives, there are also reasons to believe that institutional learning will lead to systematic differences in preferences according to the intra-partisan and extra-partisan reference structures of party leaders (e.g. Rohrschneider, 1996). For instance, the European Parliament representatives of an extreme right party may well share certain ideological preferences because of their own electoral situation, the types of debates taking place in the European legislature, and the types of colleagues against whom they want to argue (Déloye & Bruter, 2007). By contrast, national-level leaders with hopes of national parliamentary positions or even cabinet portfolios may have other marked influences; something similar could be said of local and regional leaders as a whole and vis-à-vis each other. Finally, Bruter and Harrison (2009) show that young party members in general are quite different from older party members in their preferences and positioning; here again, we may expect the same to be true of young extreme right leaders responsible for the parties' young party organisations, student unions, or simply representing the age-18-to-25 or age-18-to-30 generations.

For all these reasons, we try to gauge as accurately as possible the ideological preferences of European, national, regional and local representatives in order to substantiate our proposed conceptual map of extreme right ideology. Unlike parties (as unitary actors) that communicate officially through their manifestos and other documents, individual party leaders or representatives have no unified corpus of published material representing their preferences. If one were interested only in the most prominent national-level leaders, such as party chairs, one might rely on speeches and addresses; the same could not be said of less visible leaders, for instance at the local or regional level, let alone of young party leaders. Instead, to establish leaders' true strategic-discursive true preferences in order to compare them, one essentially has a choice between ad hoc surveys and interviews. A survey would be tempting insofar as it provides a completely equivalent pattern to measure the preferences of all the leaders and representatives targeted; however, it would raise significant problems both methodologically and practically. Methodologically, authors such as Wodak and Kryzanowski (2008) suggest that rhetoric and discursive preferences are far better captured by interviews or text than they are by surveys, which, in comparison, are relatively dry pieces of textual evidence.

Considering the problems associated with the use of multiple open-ended questions in surveys (Sudman & Bradburn, 1982), it would also be extremely difficult to capture the spontaneous strategic-discursive emphasis of party leaders. Instead, one would have to use predominantly leading questions which would be hard to compare with the totally different exercise of manifesto design, in which no social scientist plays the role of questioner. In practical terms, because many extreme right politicians are well known to dislike any exercise which could be used against them', they would likely consider a survey an extremely suspicious data gathering tool. By contrast, interviews leave respondents the space they need to express their preferences freely. In the context of semi-structured interviews, such as the ones chosen here, spontaneous unprompted preferences and more targeted ones could both be solicited by the interviewer. This allows respondents to express their priorities entirely in their own words, before we capture their preferences systematically with regard to the two components of each of the two strategic-discursive dimensions on which our conceptual framework is based.

We chose to focus our case selection for the face-to-face interviews on two countries: the Britain and France. By focusing on two cases we could concentrate on four parties, each representing one quadrant of our ideological map. We were therefore able to conduct a relatively large number of interviews across different regions and levels of representation. In terms of sampling, the elite are by definition a limited number, so it can be difficult to obtain a sufficient number of respondents. As we wanted to recruit leaders and activists of extreme right family parties as respondents, we were also aware they may be reluctant to volunteer or co-operate with our requests for interviews for fear of being trapped or tricked into saying something that can be used against them or their party. In terms of case selection, we tried to include representatives in local, regional, and national office, representatives at the European level and across all levels of responsibility, whether they are leaders of youth organisations or elected Members of the European Parliament. We wanted a mix of female and male respondents, different age groups (young, middle-aged, and older members), and geographical areas (villages, towns, cities, urban, rural). We systematically targeted leaders and representatives, including national-level leaders, party heads, deputy-heads, ministers, MPs, members of national party executives, members of the European Parliament, regional and local representatives such as members of regional or local assemblies, heads of branches or national/regional organisations, and leaders of young party organisations at the national, regional, or local level. We tried to ensure a well-balanced case selection, interviewing respondents from small and large branches, highly active and barely active, living in rural and urban settings, women and men, and a wide range of age groups and socio-economic backgrounds.

Initial contact was made with senior party leaders or officials within each of the parties (e.g. MEPs, local, regional, national representatives, branch leaders) in order to 'officialise' our research credentials and gain clearance from party personnel to conduct interviews with party leaders and officials. Although we encountered problems accessing some individuals, most of the respondents we interviewed were extremely helpful and informative. Most respondents were wary initially but after we assured them of the anonymity of the research and the purely academic nature of the findings, the majority of the interviewees were happy to expand upon their beliefs and opinions. Numerical references were assigned to each party in order to render the interview transcripts anonymous. Biased or selective reporting can be a risk in analysing interview transcripts, but we endeavoured to avoid both in our discussion of the interviews in Chapter 4.

We interviewed 92 extreme right party leaders and officials across the four parties.[3] Only a few people refused to participate in the interviews. The interviews were conducted in places convenient to the respondents, ranging from cafes to bars, homes, and local/branch offices. The length of the interviews varied depending on the time made available by the interviewees and the elaborateness of their answers, but was typically one and one-half to two hours. Fewer than 10 per cent of interviews lasted under an hour, and fewer than 10 per cent lasted over two and one-half hours.

We used semi-structured interviews for three main reasons:

1. A mixture of closed but mainly open-ended questions gave the respondents latitude to articulate their responses fully, as this type of question allows respondents to organise their answers within their own frameworks rather than that of the interviewer.[4]
2. An interview protocol with set themes of questions maximizes response validity across countries and parties.
3. Respondents tend to be more open and honest if they are not constrained by closed-ended questions. They prefer to articulate their views, explaining why they think what they think. This consideration was important to us, as we expected that most of our respondents would want to justify their views and opinions to us. Moreover, we were aware that some respondents assumed we were going to trap them into saying things or would misinterpret their responses during the interviews.

This semi-structured design, specifically the second part of the interview that focused on the four conceptions of the two ideological dimensions, allowed us to capture the ideological preferences of extreme right party elite.

We followed an interview template outlining the general themes in the first part, with the second part guided by the four ideological components of the conceptual map in order to ensure as much comparative analysis as possible. The two sections were not obvious to the interviewees but served as a mere transition point from the spontaneous introduction of the interview to the more structured second part that focused on the ideological components of the conceptual map. The first part of the interview was largely spontaneous. The respondents were asked about their political involvement and their own objectives as party leaders/officials. In order to find out more about how they frame their decision to join the party, we also asked respondents direct questions about their joining the party: when, how, why, and so on. We inquired about the impact of friends and family: Were they recruited? Did a friend or family member persuade them to join? Have they convinced others to join their party? We were also interested in finding out how others perceived the respondent's decision to join the party in question: for example, were they supportive or critical of them? This first section eased respondents into the interview to make them feel comfortable talking about their political activism and their individual story of membership. The first part of the interview is not presented in this book, as we focus our analysis on the ideological component directly related to the research question. The interview template is reproduced in Appendix B.

Following these relatively unstructured sections, we prompted respondents to detail their preferences as to or ideological stances on dimensions corresponding to the strategic-discursive elements detailed in the conceptual map of extreme right ideology. For instance, with regard to the reactionary end of the authoritarianism dimension, they would be asked if they think that society used to be better 40 years ago. Respondents would also be asked if they thought crime control should be a higher priority and whether they believe the state should be willing to intervene more directly in people's lives when they seem to act against the interest of the nation and the broader public interest. This section always remained semi-structured, so that we could use different types of formulations depending on what the respondent had mentioned earlier and the way the discussion was going. In practical terms, we felt that it would be extremely difficult to obtain in-depth and robust answers from respondents using a recorder during the interviews, especially considering the suspicion with which our requests for interviews with the extreme right party elite were met. We therefore took extensive handwritten notes throughout all of the interviews. This practice of note taking is preferred in large segments of the literature, as it often provides a better quality of answers without significant loss of reliability (Bruter, 2005; Page & Wright, 1995). This creates lower levels of self-censorship and decreases the risk of deception as widely evidenced by the existing literature.[5] As stated earlier, our research design allows us to superimpose our methods and approaches in order to triangulate our findings; therefore, we use extracts from the interviews to substantiate our proposed conceptual map and corroborate our findings from the text analysis of party manifestos in Chapter 5 in order to map the ideological identity of each party.

3.5 Capturing the official ideological preferences of extreme right parties

Uncovering the ideological identities of extreme right parties lies at the heart of our model. We propose to do this by analysing their ideological discourse via their party manifestos. As seen in Chapter 2 and in line with the existing literature, we believe manifestos are a suitable proxy in determining the official ideological positioning of extreme right parties.[6] Most of the traditional party literature views parties as unitary actors. Although it is simplistic and unrealistic to assume that political parties would accurately aggregate the multiple preferences of their members, the most intuitive way of legitimising the unitary assumption is to consider that in many political systems, particularly in Europe where parliamentary government remains the norm, voters can associate to some extent a unified set of preferences with each party that competes for their vote.

This unified set of preferences can be conceptualised in many ways. From the voter's point of view, many rational and subjective perceptions alike may come into play when assessing a party's positions. The vast majority of party specialists agree, however, that the closest thing to an official account of a given party's set of ideological preferences is its manifesto. Party programmes are officially endorsed by the leaders and members of the party through party conference and represent the external image of the party to its potential electorate. Manifestos, have a predominantly external orientation (Flohr, 1968), but 'represent and express the policy collectively adopted by the party' (Borg, 1966:97).[7] Although manifestos have an undoubtedly moderate façade to attract potential voters, these official documents offer important insight into the strategic-discursive choices made by extreme right parties. Fleck and Müeller (1998) suggest that a more radical backstage exists behind the seemingly moderate external showcase of the party programmes; however, we argue that these documents allow us to uncover the ideological identity of each party via the extreme right conceptions they emphasise, as well as their style and rhetoric. This corresponds to a certain exercise of self-definition every party is expected to embrace when making strategic-discursive choices. We therefore consider party manifestos the best possible proxy for the official unitary positioning of an extreme right party. Moreover, as stated earlier in this chapter, we triangulate our findings throughout this book in order to validate our analysis and combination of methods. In this sense, we can use interviews of the party elite to reaffirm the ideological identity of each party and for insight into the preferences of the internal organisation.

In each of the 25 cases, we used the most recent manifesto available, most of which were published between 2005 and 2009 (with exceptions such as the Republikaner's 2002 manifesto). As is well discussed in the manifesto analysis world, party manifestos can have different meanings and purposes. For some parties, the manifesto is similar to a party's Constitution and is stable over time. In other cases, a manifesto is considered a short-term election-specific document highlighting the party's programme should it be in a position to enter government after the election. For example, the German Republikaner clearly has a stable constitution-like manifesto whereas the British UKIP has a special pamphlet on Europe and several policy papers on issues ranging from immigration to crime to identity cards. Similarly, the Swedish Democrats had something akin to a short programme of basic principles in addition to some idea documents; the FN has a lengthy document detailing many of the party's ideological beliefs. Most of the parties also author material especially for the European Parliament elections but we focus on national election material to avoid skewing toward a European bias. The nature of the various manifestos also affects their length and level of discourse. For instance, the DVU's manifesto was only 2019 words long, whereas the FN's had 29,820 words.

All of the manifestos were accessible online and available for public download. Party websites are an important point of contact with the general public, activists, and potential voters.[8]

In order to study the variations in discursive patterns across parties and party systems, we tailored our study design to the specificities of the extreme right party family. Little data existed for us to utilise in studying the discursive strategies of extreme right parties across countries. In terms of existing data, the Comparative Manifesto Project was not suitable for our research design because it only included some of the parties classified as extreme right. In addition, the framework used in the Comparative Manifestos Project is structured along traditional left-right scales and focuses on policy not ideological dimensions, which was inappropriate for our study as our foci of interest would almost universally be placed at the most extreme position on the scale. We decided, therefore, to construct our own database on the ideological preferences of extreme right parties.

We used text analysis to digest the content of party manifestos. This method is regarded to be 'a systematic, replicable technique for compressing many words of text into fewer content categories based on explicit rules of coding' (Stemler, 2001) and coincides with the specifications of our research design. Computer-assisted content analysis offers a way to surmount the difficulties of traditional content analysis while producing results that are entirely consistent with it (Allum, 1998). Software such as Nvivo enables the researcher to analyse vast amounts of text quickly and cheaply (Laver et al., 2002). This method has recently captured the attention and imagination of political scientists such as Gabel and Huber (2000), Laver and Garry

(2000), and Laver et al. (2002), and has received well-deserved praise. This type of text analysis involves applying a coding framework to the text or discourse that is to be analysed, and words/word families are highlighted and counted.

For this aspect, we chose a quantitative analysis of word counts rather than a qualitative discourse analysis, as we wanted to capture the salience of each word category within the four pillars of extreme right ideology. This allows us to evaluate the individual word scores of each conception of the two ideological dimensions. In terms of procedure, we are primarily interested in the substance of the text. We wanted to gauge the salience of the four strategic discursive pillars outlined in our conceptual map of extreme right ideology. Content analysis of discourse enables us to examine how particular arguments are constructed, highlight issue salience, or remark upon the absence of certain themes. It also gives us an opportunity to scrutinise emerging patterns and trends within the discourse, whilst recording the rhetoric in a comparative, systematic and comparable way.

One essential aspect of our text analysis methodology (whether for manifestos, press releases, or leaders interviews) is that our model of analysis is one of association, not connotation. In other words, when coding manifestos (and other data) we search for words that evoke themes that could resonate in the minds of potential voters, rather than references that are explicitly xenophobic, populist, reactionary, or repressive. This means that a reference coded as part of the xenophobic pillar may talk of Black people, Muslims, Jews, or foreigners with no negative connotation whatsoever in the discourse of the party. The model suggests that mentioning foreigners a number of times, even without a negative connotation or animosity, would prime readers (and thus potential voters) to consider foreigners an important focus of interest of the party. Similarly, numerous references to the nation, without any positive connotation, would be enough to evoke to the potential reader that the party cares about the nation and resonate in the minds of potential voters who also care about it. The names of the corresponding pillars are directly derived from the existing literature and the values, priorities, and concerns much of the literature identifies as central to potential extreme right voters and supporters over time.

The conceptual map of extreme right ideology is a critical means of explaining some variation in electoral success by defining the sub-types of parties within the extreme right party family. Insights into extreme right party ideology and discourse derived from the existing literature combined with the findings of the interviews with extreme right party leaders enabled us to construct a tailor-designed coding frame in order to scrutinise the official partisan discourse of each party. In the pilot study, we extended the analysis of party manifestos to include all of the mainstream parties in each system.[9] This expansion of the analysis allowed us to highlight the specificities of the extreme right discourse in each party system, minimising risk of misinterpreting the results.

Using the four conceptions of the two ideological dimensions as core themes, we allocated words, word families, and word categories to the four types of extreme right discourse:

1. Civic conception of negative identity (populist);
2. Cultural conception of negative identity (xenophobic);
3. Social conception of authoritarianism (reactionary); and
4. Institutional conception of authoritarianism (repressive).

Our framework of analysis is designed to capture the substance of the text, that is, the salience given to the four strategic-discursive pillars and how this discourse interacts and compares. The coders read manifestos and suggested lists of words considered representative of the two dimensions (negative identity – populist and xenophobic forms and authoritarianism – reactionary and repressive forms) at the heart of extreme right ideology. The multilingual lists were then compared. Several manifestos were blindly multi-coded for test purposes, and, in all cases, both lists of words were attached to a relevant pillar, and their coding (i.e. the pillar they fit) was over 95 per cent reliable. The other five per cent were discussed, and final coding decisions were made regarding the remaining few words to retain and how, and those to exclude for ambiguity.

In total, we obtained a list of 827 words that were then collapsed into 509 word categories representing the two dimensions and four pillars of extreme right ideology. References to these words and word categories[10] were coded manually and critically. For example, if a word appeared that was on the list of word categories but was used in a completely different context, we excluded it from the total count. Following is an extract from the BNP 2005 General Election manifesto to highlight how we coded the words and assigned them to one of the four ideological pillars:

> It is the *'average' man and woman* who *suffers* from the *failings of our politicians* to grasp the issue and *restore genuine democracy.*

The italicised words were coded and assigned to the populist pillar, as they refer to discourse embodied by the civic conception of the negative identity dimension.

In the next extract, we coded the bold text as discourse related to the xenophobic pillar of the negative identity dimension. Again, the italicised words refer to the coding of the populist pillar:

> The **British peoples** are embroiled in a long term **cultural war** being waged by a *ruling regime* which has abandoned the concept of '**Britain**' in

pursuit of **globalisation**. We are determined to win that **cultural war**, and to that end, we must **take control of our national borders**.

The word occurrences were systematically registered. We then counted the total word occurrences for each pillar and each party and expressed them as comparable proportions of word occurrences. Our first measure expressed the coded words as proportions of the total words in each programme; however, this is a linguistically unrealistic tool of comparison to the extent that the different languages used in the 25 manifestos have different proportions of wasted purely grammatical words. For instance, French and German use far more prepositions and articles than do English, Bulgarian, and Russian.

We thus created a second count to express each word occurrence as a proportion of the total valid words in each programme, that is, the total words excluding neutral grammatical items. We used this count when we required comparisons of gross word occurrences in the parties' discourse.

A third count expressed word occurrences as a proportion of the total coded words: the proportion of the ideological words used by a given party that fit the xenophobic component of the negative identity dimension and its populist counterpart, and the reactionary component of the authoritarianism dimension and its repressive counterpart. This third, relative count is used in the analysis when comparing the different types of parties within the extreme right party family.

In the next section, we introduce the third component of the research design, which involves analysis of the ideological positioning of each party and the relative match between this and the ideological distribution of the actual and potential extreme right electorate in each of the three party systems.

3.6 Analysing the dynamics of extreme right ideology through party press releases

The next section of the work corresponds to an investigation into the dynamics of extreme right party discourse over time. Fundamentally, the methodology used in this section is the same methodology used in the manifesto analysis component: same pillar operationalisation, word lists, counting methods, and distinction between total, valid, and coded words.

Unlike the manifestos, which constitute unified documents, the press releases had to be aggregated. All press releases published by each party were aggregated by full calendar quarter: 1 January to 31 March (Q1), 1 April to 30 June (Q2), 1 July to 30 September (Q3), and 1 October to 31 December (Q4) over a period of five to ten years depending on historical press release availability for each party.

As mentioned earlier, this particular section is limited to five case studies: the French FN, British BNP, Austrian FPÖ, Swiss SVP, and Danish DF.

3.7   Matching the ideological identity of extreme right parties and voters

As seen in the previous chapters, the extreme right party family offers a full spectrum of examples of electoral successes and failures. In the fourth empirical component of the research design, we investigate the match between the ideological identities of the parties and the ideological distribution of the electorate within nine party systems. The series of strategic-discursive choices each party has to make in order to determine its ideological identity can affect its chance of survival against competitors (as seen in Chapter 6) and determine its electoral fortune. We expect that the strategic-discursive choices that parties make matter affect their ability to attract larger or smaller numbers of potential and actual voters. We also hypothesise that parties will be more successful at gaining the support of individual voters when their ideological identity matches that of potential extreme right voters, and less likely to convince them when there is a mismatch between the ideological preferences of party and voter. Ultimately, it would be logical to assume that the party that has chosen an ideological identity that mimics the ideological distribution of the electorate will be likeliest to obtain higher levels of electoral success.

The first part of Chapter 8, which deals with voters' ideological preferences across the four pillars of extreme right ideology, is based on the results of a mass survey conducted in June 2009 during the week that followed the European Parliament elections. The survey was conducted as part of a project on European identity and citizenship funded by the Economic and Social Research Council.[11] The survey was conducted by public opinion company Opinium and its partners using a total sample of 31,269 cases across the 27 member states of the European Union, and mixed methodologies (Internet, face-to-face, and telephone/CATI). Quota samples were used for the Internet-based samples, and randomisation for the face-to-face and telephone samples. The questions on extreme right voting were asked in eight countries: Austria, Belgium (French- and Dutch-speaking sub-samples), Denmark, France, Germany, Italy, Romania, and United Kingdom (Great Britain and Northern Ireland sub-samples; no major extreme right party competes in Northern Ireland, so that part was not included in the analysis). The samples used for each of these countries were as follows:

Austria: 1006
Belgium (French-speaking): 813
Belgium (Dutch-speaking): 1201
Denmark: 1001
France: 2000
Germany: 2010

Italy: 2000
Romania: 1013
United Kingdom (Britain): 2054
United Kingdom (Northern Ireland): 100.

We selected a few specific questions related to the ideological distribution of the extreme right electorate (see Appendix C; the results are analysed in Chapter 8). The survey questions on which we focus our analysis follow:
Three formulations of the dependent variable:

1. Vote choice: two questions asked respondents which party they voted for in the recent European Parliament elections, and which party they would vote for if a general election (or first order election equivalent, depending on the country) took place next week. Respondents were first asked if they had voted (would vote) (alternatives included not being able to vote and abstaining), and then for which party. The results of the two questions were indexed in order to create a single extreme right variable coded 0–2, for which 0 means that the respondent did not or would not vote for any of the extreme right parties competing in his/her party systems in either European or general elections, 1 means that the respondent either voted for an extreme right party in the recent European elections but would not in forthcoming general elections or the other way around, and 2 means that the respondent both voted for an extreme right party in the recent European elections and would do so again in forthcoming general elections.

2. Propensity to vote: the survey used the propensity to vote questions used by van der Eijk, Franklin, and their colleagues in recent European Elections Studies.[12] Respondents are asked how likely they would be to vote for party X in the future, and the question is repeated for each of the main parties competing in the respondent's party system. In this specific case, respondents were also asked about their propensity to vote for each of the extreme right parties included in the analysis. The question used a 0 to 10 scale. Operationalisation is that propensity to vote for an extreme right party is the maximum of the propensity to vote for all extreme right parties competing in a given party system.

3. Potential extreme right voter: the propensity to vote question was recoded into a dichotomous variable whereby people who exclude voting for an extreme right party ('0' to propensity to vote question for all extreme right parties competing in the system) are considered self-excluded voters (0), whereas people who answer that they would consider voting for at least one of them (1 or more) are considered 'potential extreme right voters'. This formulation is used as a control variable in some of the multivariate models.

In addition, a series of questions was used to capture respondents' placement on each of the four pillars of extreme right ideology. The measures used agreement scales asking respondents the extent to which they agreed with eight different statements, two statements per each conception of the four pillars of extreme right ideology: the reactionary, repressive, xenophobic, and populist conceptions.

The two reactionary questions measured agreement with one statement suggesting that their country was a better place to live 20 years ago than today, and another claiming that their national values and cultural heritage are not sufficiently respected by the younger generations.

The two repressive statements asserted that criminals are not punished with sufficient severity in our society, and that the state should be stronger to guarantee order.

The two xenophobic statements claimed that there are too many foreigners and immigrants living in our society, and that some ethnic minorities do not respect the national traditions sufficiently.

Finally, the two populist statements declared that politicians do not care much about the interests of ordinary citizens in their country, and that there is still quite a lot of corruption and dishonesty amongst the national elite.

In the analysis, we used both actual average placement on each scale and how these scores fit relative to the mean of the eight countries. We used the means and standard deviations to compare how citizens are ideologically distributed on each of the four pillars of extreme right ideology, on average, across and within each country, how these pillar placements vary according to the propensity to vote for extreme right parties as well as the actual decision to vote for them in European or national elections.

3.8 Types of parties and their electoral success

Following on from the analysis of individual-level data, the second part of Chapter 8 looks at the aggregate-level success of all the extreme right parties included in the general analysis (25 parties, 17 party systems) over time from 1979 to 2010.

In that section, in order to maximise comparability we focus solely on general elections (also called legislative or parliamentary elections in some countries) in every political system. We focus on vote as a percentage of expressed vote, as is most standard in aggregate-level electoral analysis (thus discounting abstention), and use official publicly available results from electoral commissions or their equivalent.

In the case of the PVV (Partij voor de Vrijheid), we also use the results of the List Pim Fortuyn in 2002–03 before the PVV emerged as the Netherlands' leading extreme right party. In the case of the SVP, we exclude the 1979 elections, as the vast majority of the literature considers the SVP simply a liberal party until the 1980s. In the case of Belgium, we express the scores of the VB and the FNB (Front National Belge) as part of the vote in the electoral constituencies where they mostly run (Flemish-speaking and French-speaking, respectively), as opposed to proportion of the vote in the entire kingdom of Belgium.

Finally, for the part of the analysis in which we aggregate the results of extreme right parties by sub-type of party, we use the results of the manifesto coding in Chapter 5 to create our typology of the extreme right party. This is the simplest and most straightforward way of grouping parties into the four sub-types: xenophobic-reactionary, xenophobic-repressive, populist-reactionary, and populist-repressive. The obvious limit of this methodological choice is that some of the extreme right parties included in the analysis may have changed quadrants once or even several times over the 31 years of our analysis; however, absent longitudinal data about manifestos over time, this remains the best possible estimate of the long-term success of each of the four sub-types of parties over time.

3.9   Summary of methodologies

Our study is based on the related evaluations of party programmes, discourse dynamics, leaders' ideologies, and (potential and actual) voter preferences. Only this complex equilibrium can allow us to map extreme right ideology in Europe and to assess its impact on extreme right parties' long-term electoral success.

The study of political programmes is a central component of our research design but by itself cannot determine the true ideological core of extreme right parties or tell us which parties differ in their discourse. In the analysis of party programmes, we should at least expect to find some evidence of the underlying themes of extreme right ideology but the terminology and discourse may be sufficiently cautious or ambiguous to attract a wider audience rather than overtly racist or decidedly xenophobic in style. For a deeper insight into the ideology of the extreme right, we look at the variations in party press releases over time and speak to party representatives. Face-to-face interviews help us pick up on themes usually left out of party manifestos, such as authoritarian-style leadership and attacks upon parliamentary democracy. By gathering information from various official party documentation and from interviews, we should better be able to make inferences about the ideology and discourse of the extreme right parties we are including in our study. Moreover, the third empirical component investigates the match between the ideological identity of each party and the ideological distribution of the electorate within each particular party system. This final aspect of the analysis allows us to triangulate the findings gathered from party ideology, leaders' discourse, and voter preferences and behaviour in order to elaborate a coherent model of extreme right aggregate-level success across time and political systems.

4
The Conceptual Map and Extreme Right Elites

4.1 Introduction

In this chapter, we refine the conceptual map at the heart of this study by incorporating the ideological discourse of extreme right party leaders. As explained in Chapter 3, we interviewed a significant number of party leaders from UKIP and the BNP in the United Kingdom, and the FN and the MPF in France (the full interview protocol is also detailed in Chapter 3). Consequently, this chapter is based on the data thus gathered, analysed in terms of general trends and using specific excerpts and quotations.

This qualitative exercise serves several important goals. First, it helps verify via semi-structured discussions whether the pillars detailed in our conceptual map make sense, fleshes them out, and ties them to the reality of an everyday political discourse by those who, in many ways, represent the voice of their parties. This discursive illustration of the ideology at the heart of extreme right parties thus helps us substantiate the four main quadrants embodied in our conceptual map. Not only does this chapter look into the details of the two ideological dimensions and draw upon examples extracted from the interviews, it is also an extremely important prerequisite to understanding the full meaning of the findings of the following chapter. In Chapter 5 we test the conceptual map by analysing the official discourse encapsulated within the party manifestos of extreme right parties in the United Kingdom, France, and Germany.[1]

In this chapter, we use case studies of France and Britain to illustrate some of the main ideological references that represent the conceptual map of extreme right ideology.[2] We conducted a series of elite interviews with four parties: the British National Party, the United Kingdom Independence Party, the French Front National, and the Mouvement Pour la France. These parties represent some of the most interesting cases of intra-country rivalry within the extreme right party family, with all parties competing in major elections. In addition, as confirmed in the next chapter, these parties represent different aspects of the extreme right ideological spectrum, with a different story to tell in terms of electoral success. In total, we conducted 92 interviews across the four parties.

In the next section, we describe our interviewees. A few details are provided here regarding the interview protocol; the full briefing of the methodology is found in Chapter 3.

4.2 Interviewing the extreme right party elite

As detailed in Chapter 3, we interviewed party leaders from each of the four parties in order to add a qualitative dimension to the testing of our conceptual map. Reliance only on a quantitative analysis of the official party discourse contained within their manifestos might mean overlooking important facets of extreme right discourse and ideology. Face-to-face interviews with extreme right leaders (from small local party executives to national party leaders, via elected representatives in regional assemblies or the European Parliament)add a fundamentally important aspect to the study of extreme right discourse, which will help us locate and identify the different tenets of the conceptual map.

Who are the party leaders and activists? Core party leaders, the party elite who direct and steer the party organisation, are fairly easy to identify. This group is limited in number and will have a certain level of adroitness in handling questions from researchers, interviewers, and the like. For this reason, we included some lower-level party executives and officials in our interviews in order to avoid receiving just the official party line repeated by national headquarters staff. Interviews were conducted across different regions within the United Kingdom and France.

As mentioned earlier, Chapter 3 describes our methodology more fully, but we recap a few details here in order to set the scene for the empirical analysis in Chapter 5. The semi-structured interviews were designed to capture the essence of extreme right ideology within the individual discursive formulations of extreme right party leaders. Although the interviews allowed some flexibility, we kept them as comparable as possible by retaining specific themes related to the four pillars of extreme right ideology. Most of the interviews lasted between one and one-half and two hours; some interviews took up to three hours when the respondent was particularly excited and talkative about his or her involvement. The interviews were conducted in a location convenient to the respondent.

In Chapter 2, we describe the conceptual map that posits that the extreme right ideological space is structured by two dimensions: authoritarianism and negative identity. Each party will have a unique position (ideological identity) according to the discourse it espouses in the official party manifestos as well as the rhetoric of its party elite. In this chapter, we look at the ideological discourse of the extreme right party elite through the medium of face-to-face interviews. We expect party leaders and officials to refer to components of extreme right ideology also found in the conceptual map. To recap, the negative identity dimension consists of a cultural conception which forms the xenophobic pillar, and a civic conception that assumes the guise of populist discourse. Similarly, the authoritarian dimension consists of a social conception that forms a reactionary pillar, and an institutional conception known as a repressive discourse. The interviews were designed to tap into these specific ideological dimensions in order to gauge the relevance of these pillars in the discourse of the extreme right party elite.

In the following section, we present the analysis of the elite interviews. We use excerpts from the interviews in order to understand the ideological discourse within the hearts and minds of extreme right leaders as well as to substantiate and expand the conceptual map of extreme right ideology.

4.3   The authoritarianism dimension

As explained in Chapter 2, extreme right parties occupy an ideological space with two fundamental dimensions: authoritarianism and a negative identity scale. We look first at the authoritarian dimension. Numerous authors have insisted on the willingness of extreme right parties to present themselves as the champions of order, or even as the only ones capable of restoring order in societies, which they claim have become chaotic or anarchic. Many commentators have argued that in the 2002 French presidential election campaign the Front National benefited from a focus on the theme of insecurity. At the same time, Polish parties such as the League of Polish Families or Self-Defence (SD) largely build their electoral campaigns on the idea that contemporary Poland had lost the yardsticks upon which its order and cohesion relied. We argue that the authoritarian stance of extreme right parties can take two distinct forms depending on the solution that they advocate to restore order:

1. A return to a previously existing utopian order, whereby traditional society and values are deemed the answer to today's anarchy (reactionary pillar); or
2. A stronger state, expected to be capable of atomising the elements that make society hell for good citizens (repressive pillar).

The reactionary conception

We see in Chapter 2 that the first possible expression of the authoritarian dimension is a social conception we identify as reactionary. Proponents refer to a utopian past, a lost Eldorado betrayed by modern times and modern leaders. What can we expect these reactionary references to be in the discourse of corresponding extreme right party leaders? Certainly open references to past times, use of the rhetorical field of deterioration, worsening of social, economic, and political conditions, but also, as defined in Chapter 2, a suggestion that the state and public authorities have interfered with a natural order in which the authority of institutions such as the church, parents, or teachers has either subsided or been relegated to the same level as unreliable alternatives in the name of political correctness (typically, a complaint that the dominant church would be put on par with a loony sect or that legitimate parental discipline be brandished as violence).

Let us now see how this is effectively reflected in the discourse of the extreme right party elite that we interviewed. We expect to find numerous references to an idealised civilisation or community during interviews of the extreme right party elite. In order to illustrate their utopian vision of a structured society, leaders may refer to the perceived chaos of modern day society and all its woes, including increasing levels of poverty, crime, and social and cultural malaise. We also expect leaders to advocate a return to traditional morals and values and uphold the precious link between religious and family loyalties. A glorious past or golden age is referenced alongside a vehement criticism of contemporary institutions perceived to reinforce the imperfections of society. At the same time, extreme right party leaders may reinforce their connection with the key nucleus of the community by claiming to represent the interests of the traditional family. They advocate that standards of authority and order be upheld and thoroughly respected in the face of modernity and egalitarianism. The reactionary solution to these problems is authoritarian, but does not involve state interference in private affairs. In contrast to the repressive conception of authoritarianism, the reactionary discourse requires that the state withdraw to its rightful place to allow the common sense of good citizens to reign with a return to old values and solutions, which may not even be legal anymore in democracies which have lost their way to political correctness.

When it comes to traditionalism, no institution is more emblematic of a utopian past than the traditional nuclear family, the ultimate cell of society. The traditional family is seen as a microcosm of what society as a whole should be, where the individual learns the basics of respect and authority while benefiting from love and protection; in short, the first school of life where all the values of a good citizen will be instilled and experienced. The following British interviewees express the significance of traditional values and morals within the ideology of the extreme right. Both respondents stress the importance of family as the nucleus of the community and believe that society should be a coherent and cohesive unit that protects community interests:

> Instead, I think we need to protect the values of our country. Protect families first because family is the basic cell of the nation. For example, why not offer mothers – if they want it – some money not to work? That

way, they could take care of their children and they would be less likely to wander the streets and sometimes be up to no good. (UKIP011)

There are an increasing number of broken homes in this country. The family should be at the heart of the community. I believe core values are about a stable education system, family values, the family as a unit, and restoration of discipline. In recent years, there has been a break-down of the family as a core unit. Many homes now don't even have a dinner table. People eat dinner off their knees and at separate times. (UKBN007)

In both examples, the ruin of the very notion of family as an untouchable yardstick, a system of values, and a cell of reference is seen as a 'cancer' within society in the sense that it is likely to spread to neighbouring cells and institutions to the point that the whole society would consequently be endangered.

Similarly, within the context of this particular ideological component, almost all of the respondents wanted to re-emphasise the importance of preserving local traditions, history, and culture, to protect the homogeneity of the national community. Such fond references to history and tradition, a fatherly conception of patriotism, and a national heritage deposited in the hands of the new generations also serve to strengthen the in-group's culture and homogeneity. The following examples typify the importance ascribed to the traditional values of family, the national community and its heritage:

To me, the founding values we want to defend are the defence of the country, of its traditional values, of family, of nation, of traditions. (FRMF005)

As I am becoming more mature, I have come to realise how proud I am to be French. This is an amazing country and it has one of the richest heritages in the world. I don't think that a country which doesn't respect its ancestors or pretends that other people's ancestors matter as much as ours is a country which respects itself. You need to respect our past too. Like all our great (wo)men, for example Jeanne d'Arc, of course. But even, also, all the unknown soldiers, all the family mothers and so on. (FRMF010)

We should be investing in local traditions, history and culture. Leicester council invested thousands of pounds into the celebrations for Diwali so why couldn't they do anything for St. George's day. (UKBN021)

The idiots here banned a true representation of a Christian scene. There was no Christmas tree or nativity scene. There was no sense of excite-ment or celebration. We decided to take it upon ourselves to broadcast over a PA system some Christmas carols to instil some festive spirit. We plan to also make our own special arrangements for the other festivities such as Easter, St. David's Day, and St. George's day. We need to preserve our traditions for the sake of future generations. (UKBN013)

The EU smacks in the face of British history. We shouldn't replace the British flag with the European one. It is wrong. (UKIP012)

To me, to be French is to accept French history as a whole. 1500 years of history with its good and bad moments. As Le Pen says, we are not the owners but the tenants of our country, and as a result we do not have the right to let France disappear. (FRFN014)

Note the multiple references to national historical figures: Jeanne d'Arc or 1500 years of history for the French extreme right elite, old Christian celebrations of St George's day and St David's day for the British ones. It is interesting to see here, in the context of the reactionary pillar, that the emphasis is predominantly on symbols and heritage rather than practical risks or dangers. Reactionary extreme right party leaders appear to be portraying themselves as the depositaries of a conception of a nation that no one else is defending.

Public education is often seen as an integral part of the national infrastructure. In France, 'l'école républicaine' is regularly described as the mould which helps shape the national coherence of values and citizens. Extreme right parties thus often emphasise their impression that education systems have deteriorated and lost their way. They claim to regret the old ways and want to reform the school system, to instil discipline into unruly children who have no respect or manners. They want to reinstate education as the backbone of society and re-educate people so that they understand the traditions, values, and heritage of the country they live in. The following excerpts are from French and British interviewees and highlight the importance attached to education within the ideology of the extreme right"

Education needs to be reformed to. The education of the 'éducation nationale' is a scandal, it is really politicised education and it is bankrupt, now young people don't even know how to speak or right properly. I don't even understand it, now it's phone text language, now people say 'lol' if they want to tell you they find something funny, it's taken me days and days to understand it!! Knowledge has been degraded. (FRMF003)

Everything revolves around education. I was taught everything but British history or Christianity or for that matter anything about paganism. They should be taught about the important customs that were and still are important in Britain. We have a responsibility to future generations and our children. (UKBN004)

Schools are rubbish. Yobs dominate. We need to instil discipline and create a stable situation for children. They have to the role models of mother and father. The world is going crazy. For example, what is the thing with super-nannies? No incentive for good behaviour. If you are bad you are sent to the naughty step. What good does that do? If I was bad, I was smacked. I think spanking is ok as long as it teaches the child right from wrong. It should be positive and negative reinforcement. (UKIP010)

Within the extreme right party discourse, one is frequently exposed to numerous references to an apparent 'Americanisation of culture' (or standardisation thereof). This discourse was also present within many of the interviews we conducted with the leaders and high-ranking officials of the extreme right parties. The following examples are taken from the two British parties and the French MPF:

> The values and moral codes of our parents and grandparents are polluted by SKY TV and American TV channels. (UKIP002)
>
> We are less British than we used to be. We have become more Americanised. Everything is changing and not for the better. (UKBN001)
>
> The word 'chav' has Americanised gang culture here in Britain. (UKIP004).
>
> We would never let TF1 [largest French TV channel] show more American films than French one! This is a betrayal of our whole culture! (FRMF008)
>
> Don't expect me to take the grandkids to 'McDo' as grandparents do in their TV ads! We didn't have that when I grew up and they love the 'fetes de villages' as much as I did when I was growing up. (FRMF010)

Interestingly enough, although the United States is often used as reference model by many right wing parties, notably in Britain but even sometimes in France, the discourse of extreme right parties usually equates it with standardisation, generalisation of a lowest common denominator, and a 'reign of mediocrity'. Once again, we should emphasise how the elite discourse is concerned with symbols, not just with substance, which reinforces the very utopian nature of the reactionary pillar. By relying on symbols, politicians avoid engaging with a level of specification which could make the past sound less glamorous or vivid, or the present less scary and dramatic.

A common aspect of the reactionary conception of extreme right ideology is nostalgia for the golden age, a harkening back to the good old days. Extreme right parties tend to compare the contemporary disastrous state of affairs to that of a time when all things were harmonious and joyful, everything and everybody knew its place and role within society. Here again, we see that traditional values and morals of a bygone age are heralded as superior to those of today's society. The following interview extracts illustrate this perception of the past and today's society quite succinctly:

Values such as fair play, common sense, patriotism, loyalty, duty, and self-reliance to name a few are passed on from one generation to the next. There would be no morals without this kind of fabric of society to hold it together. Take these things away and you debase society. (UKIP024)

When I was growing up, I grew up on a council estate. Everyone had a job and the gardens were tidy, houses were clean. Now if I were to go back today the people would be on welfare, there would be drugs everywhere and the gardens would be overrun and dirty. (UKBN008)

We used to have a stiff upper lip. We need to toughen up a bit I think. We need to bring back the values I knew as a kid. (UKIP022)

People always make fun of elderly people saying 'in my time we used to ...' Well, my time was better 1. (FRMF002)

Yep, that was the 'good old time'! (FRFN019)

Most of the interviewees, across all age groups and parties, referred nostalgically to an idealised glorious past. This finding was also confirmed by the Klandermans and Mayer (2006) study of extreme right activists in five European democracies. In the next section, we discuss the second conception of the authoritarian dimension. The repressive conception of authoritarianism proposes an institutional solution to the problems that society faces, preferring to summon the strength of the state to deal with delinquents and a repressive order of society.

The repressive conception

The repressive conception of the authoritarianism dimension is built upon a form of social control characterised by strict obedience to the authority of a state or organisation. Thus, we expect extreme right leaders to espouse the enforcement and maintenance of political control via oppressive measures. Despite most of the contemporary extreme right party elite vows to uphold and compete within the regulations and rules of their respective constitutional democratic frameworks, their discourse often has a subtle anti-democratic tone. As a result, we expect the affirmation of stability, authority, and the submission of the individual to the ideological goals of the party to be paramount in the discourse of many extreme right party leaders.

In line with the repressive ideology, party leaders may advocate fighting chaos and threatening anarchy by trusting a strengthened state to eradicate errant fragments of society; therefore, we expect numerous references to a strong state and the enforcement of law and order within the discourse of leaders and officials, as well as to the strong, charismatic leader of the party (be it the current leader or previous figureheads). The majority of contemporary parties are personified by an autocratic leader and retain an extremely centralised and hierarchical organisation. As a result, we expect leaders and officials to refer to the extraordinary capabilities of their leaders in comparison to other politicians and look upon them as saviours of their respective nations.

The following examples from interviews of extreme right party leaders emphasise the restoration of law and order. As witnessed across the two countries of France and the United Kingdom, most interviewees spoke of the importance of law and order within a coherent society and were convinced that their parties had the means to sort out today's societal problems:

> I think that discipline and order need to be reinforced in our country. Le Pen is the only one who proposes to change that. (FRFN011)

> People want more order, more police, more authority – they tell us that all the time. (FRFN021)

> I feel strongly about the absence of law and order in this country. Something has to be done. (UKIP015)

> We need to strengthen law and order. We have to confront several problems associated with gangs; lack of job opportunities, working class estates, no money to go to cinema, etc. they haven't got anything else better to do than cause trouble. (UKBN020)

Beyond the general glorification of order enforcement and authority, extreme right leaders venture into specific proposals for a stronger, more authoritarian and punitive state. No area is as 'natural' a field for the expression of repressive preferences as the fight against crime; thus, many of the interviewed extreme right party leaders also spoke about tougher penalties for criminals and agreed that prison sentences should be tougher in order to deter people from committing crimes in the first place. The majority of the respondents derided the influence of political correctness and the hypocrisy surrounding crime and punishment. The following extracts from several interviews shed light upon these beliefs and detail some possible solutions to society's problems:

> How can things work well without criminals realising that crime is punished? We need to have tougher policies on crime. (FRMF006)

> The police arrest them, then one hour later they release them – that's what our justice system has become, and it's the good citizens who live in fear. (FRFN005)

> We have always been clear – zero tolerance policy and we will make crime go down. Judges are not here to be social workers they are here to punish criminals. (FRFN012)

I joined UKIP because they take a firm line on crime and they propose proper punishment of criminals. (UKIP015)

There is an insidious influx of human rights and political correctness entering this country so that punishment is not fairly distributed. (UKBN009)

We need an extreme political party to get this country back onto an even keel. Society has become far too liberal, whether it is with drugs, litter etc. They need to be punished. (UKBN022)

In contrast to the reactionary pillar of the authoritarianism dimension, which we see emphasise education, values, and morals, the repressive conception of the same dimension is much more coercive and direct. Some interviewees focused on the reintroduction of the death penalty as a means of instilling law and order into society. The following examples highlight this trend within the extreme right parties in Britain and France:

He proposed big popular referenda on the important decisions: A good one to start with would be death penalty; it should be the people's choice. (FRFN001)

I don't see how anyone can be against death penalty for monsters that have raped and killed some innocent children. (FRFN021)

The public have the right to know whether repeat sex offenders live in their local area. We should introduce the death penalty with the advance of DNA evidence and proof of evidence. Don't need anything else. The majority is what's important. The Conservatives introduced a bill to bring back the death penalty in 1954 but it was scrapped by Labour. (UKBN023)

There is a minority of UKIP members that want us to do more on the social authoritarian dimension like the reintroduction of the death penalty. (UKIP019).

We should shoot drug dealers and this would control the horrible drug problem this country is facing. (UKBN012)

We should have the death penalty for some crimes. It is crazy that with the ethics of human rights the perpetrator of the crime is often more protected than the actual victim of the crime. (UKBN008)

Although the repressive pillar of authoritarianism naturally emphasises the popular theme of toughness on crime (and on criminals), it would be wrong to believe that it is limited to the topic of police and justice. Political authoritarianism is not just a policy principle, it is a whole conception of governance. In addition to their tougher stances on crime and punishment, the respondents we interviewed emphasised having a strong party leader with charisma, excellent communication skills, the ability to relate to the common man', and trustworthiness to make the right decisions for the party and society at large. We encountered a certain sense of awe when respondents spoke about their leader. All of interviewees were committed to their leader's cause and believed that he was the right man for the job, as briefly illustrated here:

> Le Pen is simply someone exceptional. The first time I met him, I was shivering for hours afterwards. (FRFN013)

> In meetings, it's extraordinary, he steps on the scene and everybody understands that they are going to witness something exceptional. (FRFN004)

> De Villiers is a true leader, without him, France wouldn't be the same country at all. (FRMF013)

> Nick Griffin is a true leader. He is strong willed and knows what he is talking about not like the rest of the politicians. (BNP001)

In summary, we found several common traits among the fundamental tenets of extreme right ideology within the hearts and minds of the leaders we interviewed. The party was often described as a close-knit family, a circle of trust and acceptance, where individuals can voice their opinions without prejudice. This sense of belonging to a group or community was prevalent amongst the leaders of the British BNP and the French FN. The group-oriented identity of extreme right militants has been explained as a reaction to the erosion of family, clan, neighbourhood, and social class (Heitmeyer, 1993). This group mentality is embedded and reinforced in the extreme right ideological frame of 'man is a *Gemeinshaftswesen* and can only develop fully within a community'. The community becomes almost superior to the individual. There is also 'a belief in the authority of the state over the individual; an emphasis on natural community; distrust for individual representation and parliamentary arrangements; limitations on personal and collective freedoms; collective identification in a great national destiny [...] and the acceptance of the hierarchical principle for social organisation' (Ignazi, 1997:49).

To a certain extent, there was a cult of leadership. Each party's leader was highly regarded, and many expressed admiration, awe, or even love for him (her). The leader was considered as the only person who could restore faith and common sense, and put the country back on an even keel after the many years of abandonment. Local issues were strongly emphasised within all four parties, but some respondents spoke of links with other European and international groups with whom they occasionally met and organised joint rallies and events with strong neo-nationalist themes. For example, the young BNP organisation met regularly with the FNJ, the youth organisation, and reportedly held meetings with the Swedish Democrats. Most of the interviewees, particularly the highest-ranking leaders of the group, wanted to portray an image of unity and consensus within the party organisation; however, some respondents suggested that this was not indeed the true picture. In some of the interviews it emerged that there was little internal coherence and leaders often found it hard to coordinate the varied interests of members who were far from ideologically homogeneous.

4.4 The negative identity dimension

We discuss the conceptual nature of the negative dimension in Chapter 2. Large segments of the literature have underlined the propensity of extreme right parties to exclude or oppose, but the various targets of this exclusion or opposition (e.g. foreigners, immigrants, asylum seekers, minorities, other parties, systems, corrupt politicians, bureaucrats) have usually been considered independent or discrete. Instead, our conceptual map suggests that these possible targets of opposition and exclusion fit together on a negative identity dimension, which runs from a civic negative identity to a cultural one, mirroring the two main pillars of political identities identified by Bruter (2005). The identification of an out-group is fundamental to this dimension of negative identity as featured in both the populist and xenophobic conceptualisations, albeit in different ways.

The stigmatism of out-groups is used to simplify references to a presumed unified and obvious identity of the core in-group of the nation (Meinhof, 2002; Wodak, 1996). Here, we identify two different out-groups: politicians are the main point of reference for the populist discourse, whereas foreigners (however broadly conceived) are the out-group victims of xenophobic discourse. This particular theme of discourse is discussed in detail throughout the following description of the two conceptions of the negative identity dimension.

On the whole, the cultural conception of negative identity broadly corresponds to xenophobia; its civic conception is referred to as populism. These two conceptions of negative identity serve the same purpose, and the discourse of extreme right parties alternates emphasis from one to the other.

The xenophobic conception

In our conceptual map, the first strategic-discursive pillar of the negative identity dimension is xenophobia, which relies on cultural identity exclusiveness, contrasting the true national community with its 'parasitic' foreign elements, be they influences, norms, values, institutions, or people. References to this foreign out-group may specify a foreigner within the national community (e.g. ethnic minorities, religious groups) or outside (e.g. other countries). We anticipate that leaders will express this cultural negative identity in many forms and guises, but they may focus on the foreign elements of modern day society in contrast to the assumed homogeneity of the nation. Leaders may also highlight a xenophobic discourse that contrasts us versus them and expresses foreign elements as a threat to the cherished national identity and interest. We also expect the elite to embellish their xenophobic discourse by attributing the problems of today's society to the presence of the increased number of immigrants, asylum seekers, or members of some minorities.

In the following interview excerpts, immigration policy is on the top of the agenda for many of the extreme right party leaders. A recurrent theme within the immigration discourse of extreme right parties contrasts the needs of the national community to that of the immigrant population. As a result, many parties use slogans such as 'British jobs for British workers' or 'Les Français d'abord'; similar slogans can be found within the discourse of a variety of European extreme right parties from the German NPD to the Danish DF.

The only problem we have is over-population. If we grasp it and articulate it in the right way, we will be on a winning straight. We are not in the same class as the BNP. Enoch and Howard have both made mistakes when it came to articulating immigration policies. There is no other political quest that it is harder than to try and articulate immigration policy without sounding racist. (UKIP002)

I am against uncontrolled mass immigration. We have to impose a defined limit to the numbers of people coming into the country. It is a well-known fact that the UK is over-populated. There is huge pressure on markets, housing, jobs etc. The high population density however you look at it is a massive strain on the country. Our main concern is the large population growth, which is directly linked to immigration. Death and birth rates cannot be controlled but immigration can be. It is the only variable of population growth that can be controlled. An aim of zero population growth is the only sensible policy to pursue. (UKIP020)

To me, it is all summarised in the motto 'Les Français d'abord!'. It is the beginning and the end of it all. To me, it is really down to the old saying 'charité bien ordonnée commence par soi-même'. I'm not at all against helping others, but I think that one needs to start by helping his own. (FRFN008)

We don't hate foreigners, but the French must come first, it's just normal. (FRMF012)

If you have only one steak, won't you give it to the people from your family before donating it to others? The nation is our family. (FRMF010)

The motto is France, France, France. (FRMF006)

The connection between xenophobia, race, and identity is extremely intertwined within the discourse of the extreme right. Although many contemporary parties disavow their allegiance to racist rhetoric and questions of how they actually define the national community they propose to defend, we see from the following examples that it is not that straightforward. Some leaders of extreme right parties still view racial ancestry, differences between cultures and races, and even social Darwinism as obvious references to the national community or identity should be defined:

British identity is of course intertwined with racial ancestry. If you go down this route, you are not doing anything wrong. It is not racist it's a fact. Negroes born in this country could never be British in the way I am. It is a question of human nature. British values are a function of British racial ancestry too and its people. The British are a product of a white European race. We built the churches and the roads. They are not like us. They are different because they evolved differently. They are not the same. Look at the figures of Richard Lynn (shows me the book again) the making and meaning of Britishness. He shows that they have different IQ scores etc. Prof. Sykes at Oxford has shown that every British woman is one of the 7 daughters of Eve. You are the descendent of one of 7 women. British white Europeans evolved differently. We had to cope with an ice age, scarce food, draughts, the survival was key. We are from the same genetic stock of Northern Europe. (UKBN022)

Different cultures and races do not naturally mix. We have seen this in the conglomerate of Eastern Europe, Africa, India, Indonesia, and the UK. It's a cultural clash. The increasing numbers of Muslims and blacks create a divide from the whites. Take Bradford, for example, the Hindus are being driven out by the Muslims there. It's not racist; it's just a simple fact. (UKBN004).

People cluster around common identities and work together through cooperation. The idea of destroying this process, this 'organic' growth is ridiculous. It screws up the natural progression of the survival of the fittest. It's the basics of social Darwinism. These are my people. I have homogenised with these people. Now we are threatened by this outside force. We at the BNP aim so preserve our identity and protect our culture at all expense. (UKBN007).

France is not a country that was born yesterday, and the French were not a people who were born yesterday. You can't just bring anyone in out of the blue and claim 'ok, let's redefine France so that it adapts to you'. (FRMF017)

Yes, of course it was a bit easier to integrate people like the Poles or Italians who were white and Catholic in the 1930s than people who are Muslim and come from a completely different background today. (FRMF003)

The American notion of a 'melting pot' is a myth! (FRFN003)

Other interviewees voice their xenophobic discourse by targeting mass immigration as a threat to national identity, the coherence and homogeneity of the national community, and, in some cases, the root of society's decline and cultural malaise. The following examples illustrate the connection that extreme right party leaders establish between the impact of immigration and the fight to preserve their national identity:

> I want to protect my own country like the Aboriginals in Australia and the Native American Indians in North America were fighting for the same thing. They wanted the whites out but look where that got them. (UKIP009)

> If we don't preserve our British identity, then it will be lost forever and we might never be able to regain it. We are also fighting to live freely on our own land. (UKBN004)

> If you don't understand your past, then you can never fully understand your present or future. Who are British people and where did we come from? Opponents of our say that Britain is a country of immigration but most of the people who came to live here hundreds of years ago assimilated to the British culture and identity. (UKIP013)

> We don't want concentration camps or to deport everyone. We are what we are. We want to maintain and preserve our identity and democracy. (UKBN005)

> We created this country. Our people fought in wars, laid the roads, railways and waterways. It's our bloody country. Everyone has to have their own patch that they can call their own. We must reclaim our identity. What would we do without a name? It is getting to that point now in this country. People don't know who they are any more. (UKIP014)

> Yes, I do think that French identity is under threat. (FRMF011)

> It is not just us saying it, with the current policy, there is a real risk that in 20 years, there might be more minarets than church towers. (FRMF012)

> We need to protect our borders – that's rule number 1. (FRFN021)

> What we always say is that we don't 'own' France – it has really been entrusted to us, and this is why it is our duty to protect her, watch for her, and ensure that what makes her identity is not betrayed and sacrificed in the name of the political ambitions of a few politically correct politicians. (FRFN016)

> The tchador [Islamic veil] is simply not part of the French identity. These are not the women described by Victor Hugo and Lamartine! (FRMF009)

Similarly, mass immigration and the subsequent growth of multiculturalism are often accused of being a threat to national traditions and cultures.

The following examples are drawn from our French sample of interviews. It is interesting to note the underlying change in tone of the French extreme right parties from a virulent anti-immigrant stance to one of criticising the government for letting the immigrants into the country in the first place:

> De Gaulle said himself that France is 'a white country of Judeo-Christian tradition'. Politicians have let it become a 'café au lait' country of Islamo-Judeo-Christian tradition instead. They have let scores of recent non-European immigrants come and settle in, millions of them, whilst earlier, the French habit was to let a few dozens of thousands of European immigrants who could assimilate far more easily. (FRFN011)

> Contemporary immigration is completely different. You take a North African immigrant, tell him to come with his customs, and plant him with his family in a district full of other immigrants. The customs are very different; the Poitiers battle still represents a major fracture in the history of Islamic people. So it simply cannot work like that, it is really the politicians' fault. (FRMF002)

Many of the extreme right parties that have flourished throughout Europe over the past few decades share this rejection of all 'others', immigrants, foreigners, refugees (Ivaldi, 2001); however, their predominant tendency in the interviews was to highlight the rights and privileges of the nation over all else. This national preference was often used in conjunction with framing the xenophobic discourse; for example, stressing the homogeneity of the nation and what it means to be British/French also ultimately says a lot about what and whom they do not consider to be a part of this in-group or national community (however vaguely defined by the parties or the individuals). In other cases, respondents took the opportunity to emphasise the out-group distinction with regard to the language issue. The following interview excerpts exemplify this discourse. They discuss the problems that arise from the use of multiple languages and its effect on local communities. One of the French extreme right party leaders also questions whether anyone could indeed feel French who does not speak the language.

> In some schools in Bradford and Leeds, English is not the first language. In some it's French because of the high numbers of black Africans. No wonder standards are slipping if children can't even communicate with each other. (UKIP023)

> The number of Eastern Europeans, especially Poles, here in Grantham has dramatically increased over the last few years. There are whole sections of town that are dominated by the Poles and if you walk down the street all you can here is Polish and not one word of English. They have no car tax but they live and work here. If we did that, we would be in a lot of trouble.

These little things grate on me and I get hacked off. That's why I listen to what the BNP says as most of it makes sense to me. (UKBN010)

How can you feel French if you don't speak the language? (FRFN009)

Of course, the French language has always been a big part of French identity, so yes, when I see some groups of youngsters who speak together in Arabic, it shocks me to an extent. (FRMF018)

Extreme right parties that compete in regular elections and try to increase their share of the vote have in recent years tried to tone down the more radical xenophobic discourse focused on immigrants and foreigners. Instead, some extreme right leaders prefer to speak of the damage that has been inflicted on the national community by the treacherous politicians that have instigated mass immigration into the country. The following interview extracts of extreme right party leaders highlight this change of strategy that is increasingly evident in their discourse:

They have engineered mass immigration. The interbreeding with Negroes and half-castes is very convenient for the globalisation plan. (UKBN014)

I can't blame the immigrants themselves for their take, take, take attitude and I don't hate the asylum seekers either. They are being offered everything on a plate and who would say no. The people I do hate are those white politicians that have sold this country down the line. (UKBN002)

The government is sweeping the problems under the carpet, which ultimately results in problems and violence as there was in Bradford during the riots. The UK is the most overcrowded place in Europe, with over twice the population of France and four times that of the US. The unchecked immigration has had a huge strain on the welfare bill and created terrorism. (UKIP007)

I don't agree with their multi-cultural experiment. The government has purposely concentrated different ethnic groups and races into small areas so they fight against each other and not against the government. It is a case of 'divide and rule' as the saying goes. (UKBN011)

We say attack the government that is letting all these people in not the individuals. The immigrants before were of a different type. They didn't want to change the country. My parents didn't want to come here and impose their views on other people living here. Now, they want halal, ban the use of alcohol hand wash in hospitals so they are not clean. The labour party is letting them do this. (UKBN016)

It is a question of space not race. It is not a race issue but we don't want to give criminals open access. (UKBN013)

People are not naturally racists but as I see it they are merely reacting to the swamps of immigrants coming into the country putting increased pressure on the economy, jobs, housing, NHS etc. (UKIP012)

It's not even the fault of immigrants either, they are also the consequence, it is the fault of those who let them in without counting. (FRMF002)

Yes, I always say that the politicians who opened all the doors are more to blame than the poor people who chose to pass them. (FRFN007)

They invited them all in when they had no business to do so. (FRFN017)

A shift toward criticising Islam within the rhetoric of the extreme right has been manifested via an increasing number of references to the impact and influence Islam has on the national community and its way of life. The following examples echo some of the references we encountered in the text analysis of party manifestos:

I don't want to see minarets in every French city, but I don't think this is the right focus. It's always the same here, in France, we always tend to tackle what you can see instead of the root of the problem, it's the same with the veil, and the rest. (FRMF009)

The threat of Islam is not recognised by the other parties. They don't want to talk about it. They are importing a huge problem. It is a time-bomb. It is the fastest growing religion not just here but in the world. To underestimate the threat is the biggest act of treason this government has made. (UKBN003)

It is a fact that Islam is a polar opposite to everything that represents the values of the western world. (UKIP008)

I do not want to live in 6th Century Saudi Arabia. If they do, then they can go home. (UKBN012)

The extreme right often presents its exclusive identity concept by contrasting an opposed external 'other' with the in group of the nation. In the following cases, we encounter the European Union as the perceived 'other' with its alleged foreignness contaminating national systems, corrupt bureaucracy running amok, and suspected undemocratic institutions and representatives making a mockery of national political and legal systems:

The EU is an alien system run by countries (mainly Germany) that have an alien tradition of politics and very different legal systems. It is just outrageous to subordinate our system to theirs. (UKIP006)

We were the only ones who voted against the 10 new members of the EU. All of UKIP MEPs voted against Romania and Bulgaria. We didn't want them in. (UKIP021)

It's bureaucrats trying to replace democracy by their technocratic system. (FRMF001)

The EU is becoming more powerful by the day and laughs when citizens express their disagreement. This is scandalous. (FRMF008)

It was ridiculous to open the door to countries like Romania, and now, of course, Baoso, Sarkozy and Merkel are intent on bringing in Turkey. They know 99 percent of the people are opposed to this but they don't give a toss. (FRMF015)

Turkey is intent on joining, and they are happy to try the back door against European public opinions. (FRMF007)

Most of the xenophobic discourse of the extreme right focuses on the identification of an 'other', be it immigrants, minority groups, or even a foreign country or a political system or institution. In some of the interviews, we experienced some virulent anti-American rhetoric usually in the form of an attack on globalisation and the effect it has on UK or French culture. The following examples show that a country, the United States of America and Germany in this context, can also be singled out as the enemy of extreme right ideology:

I used to like America but now I hate them. Invading countries is not good or clever. What right does he have? They wanted the oil but it is not that important anymore. I don't believe the story of the September 11th attacks now. I think America did it to themselves to justify the war. (UKBN004)

There is something about the US that is aggressively imperialist, and as they always side with the same, like Israel, England, or some dodgy South American regimes, it is clear that in a way they are trying to rule the world. (FRFN002)

American culture is trying to annihilate national cultures on its way. (FRMF009)

We have to be very suspicious of Germany, especially as they seem so intent on taking over the EU. If history has taught us anything, we should be very careful. They are still our number one enemy. (UKIP027)

Well, Germany was France's public enemy number 1 for 150 years, so it is a bit odd to suddenly ask the French people to pretend they are our biggest friends. (FRMF019)

One of the main keystones of extreme right discourse is the elevation of the national interest over the interests of the foreign outside world or defined out-groups within the community. Glorification of the national patrimony alongside a desire to preserve national traditions and culture serves to diminish and minimise the impact of globalisation, multiculturalism, and the influence of US culture on the national heritage and culture.

We now move on to discuss the second aspect of the negative identity dimension, encapsulated by the populist civic conception.

The populist conception

At the other extreme of the negative identity scale lies the contrast between the people and the parasitic and devious influence of the elite, who are accused of betraying the national interest and its heritage and traditions. In Bruter's model of identity (2005, 2009), the civic pillar of political identities represents the way citizens define themselves as part of the political system, focusing on their civic rights, their political duties, and their relationship to and experience of the relevant institutions. A negative civic identity can therefore be expressed by voicing criticism against the existing system and accusing political institutions and their representatives of betraying the interests of the national community.

Similar to that of the xenophobic conception, the civic populist reference may target a variety of victims: political parties (the extreme right is often implicitly assumed to be outside the corrupt circle of the mainstream parties and are presented as a non-party or a movement), the media (considered to be unified, hostile, and often under the control of other powers), economic and bureaucratic elite, alongside pressure groups (from trade unions to human rights groups to civil society organisations). Extreme right leaders may claim that one of their prime objectives is to retrieve the power of the people from the corrupted elite of the mainstream parties. We expect them to draw upon the contrast between the man on the street and the parasitic and devious politicians, who are accused of betraying the national interest and the people's will. We anticipate that party leaders will emphasise their allegiance with the people, stating that their party listens to their concerns and is the true representative of their interests.

During all of the interviews we conducted, respondents were keen to mention populist themes with jibes at politicians, incumbent governments, the media, and even their enemies at large. One of the most common themes within the populist discourse of the extreme right is the accusation that the existing parties and their politicians are out of touch with the mass public. The party of choice is often portrayed as outside the existing system and status quo and untainted by the corruption and scandals allegedly haunting the other parties. Extreme right leaders explained that their party would solve societal problems by listening to what the man on the street wants and applying a common sense approach to politics. The interview extracts highlight the sentiment of a BNP leader who outlines how the BNP is differs from the other mainstream parties and a young French FN leader who believes politicians are out of touch with real people:

The ruling liberals are out of touch with public opinion. They just don't understand what normal people think especially the middle and lower classes. We are different because we listen. We are different from all the rest of the other parties. We don't believe people should be told what to do or think. We don't believe that politicians are the masters of people. That's not democracy. The politicians think that people must be told about this and that, but they are out of touch. (UKBN003)

All the elites come from the same mould. All the leaders come from the ENA, it is a very elitist clique with very few people who are represented. The elites, as a result, are completely disconnected from the people. (FRFN011)

Similarly, a UKIP representative for the European Parliament voices his thoughts about the mainstream parties and how the existing parties are seemingly unequipped to deal with the problems of the general public:

In terms of British politics, there is nothing left to vote for. The mainstream parties all propose more of the same. I hate the sight of the puffy face of Cameron. It tells you all you need to know about him – he has never had a tough day in his life. He has had everything given to him on a silver spoon. (UKIP013)

The following respondent laments how the existing parties and their politicians seem to have little regard for the average man on the street and feels that the BNP, on the other hand, appears to have the concerns of real people at the heart of its campaign.

The existing parties in the British party system are completely and utterly useless. They don't have anything in common with real people. They have never lived like an average person so why they should pretend to understand our concerns and views. They have no idea about us or how the man on the street lives. They are not average people, they are professional politicians and we all know how they lie. The BNP is different. It is made up of average people like me and you. They seem to understand the man on the street and our concerns. They want to bring the country back. They want to look after the country, not give it away. They would restore morale. (UKBN005)

A common theme within the extreme right populist diatribe is a search for truth within a corrupt and misrepresentative world of politics. The extreme right party, in contrast, is portrayed as the champion of truth. In the following examples, respondents echo these populist sentiments. A young BNP party leader believes that truth should be paramount in politics. A young party activist of the FNJ (the FN's youth organisation) and a member of the MPF repeat similar themes within their interviews.

> If you are not telling the people the truth then there is no point. What is the point of voting otherwise or doing anything really if you are not telling the truth to the people who have elected you? They are the real people who matter. (UKBN010)

> One of the reasons why I am a true FN supporter and activist is that we are the only ones trying to put an end to conditions of unfairness in this country. (FRFN002)

> Honestly, I think that current politicians should be tried for High Treason in front of the High Court of Justice because this is really what they are doing: betraying the country: Mitterrand, Chirac, Sarkozy et al. (FRMF008)

Interviews with extreme right leaders also evoke criticism of the media, with references to a pact between the media and the established parties and to alleged collusion between the media and the mainstream parties against the extreme right party in question. A local leader of the UK independence party expresses his suspicion of the media. Similarly, two leaders of the MPF and the FN explain their mistrust of the media and their cooperation with the elite.

> To me, this misportrayal, this manipulation is predominantly the fault of the media; they are really quite close to the main parties. (UKIP012)

> There is really no difference between the parties. They are all the same, and the media support them. In fact, 'democracy' is only a name in this country. (FRMF011)

> So many French female journalists are married to politicians that it is pretty obvious how intertwined the big parties and the media have become! (FRFN006)

Many respondents affiliated with the BNP referred to an overload of political correctness in the United Kingdom; for example, the following respondents tell us about their paranoia and conspiracy theory stories surrounding the infiltration of the BNP and suggest that the current trend of political correctness is orchestrated by the liberal internationalist elite in a bid to control the people. A UKIP member also shares her frustration with the incumbent government and the detrimental influence of political correctness on society. In addition, a BNP activist suggests that the feminist movement is responsible for the increased number of women in the workforce and that this has forced them to abandon their procreative role in favour of employment.

> The media are like prostitutes: they have enormous power but no associated responsibility. The fight will be won or lost in the media. Why do they want to dismiss the BNP? I understand now that it is all associated with political correctness. There is a blatant agenda by the liberal internationalist elites to control the people. (UKBN018)

> There is an institutionalised political correctness scheme against the BNP. (UKBN013)

> The Government is so politically correct now. You can't say anything but they let people off for beating up the elderly. It has got to the stage where it is over the top. (UKIP001).

> The feminist movement has convinced women in their 30s not to have children. They have beguiled them from their natural role of reproducing. (UKBN016)

> Nowadays, political correctness is everywhere. (FRFN001)

> I really think that political correctness is used to vilify ['diaboliser'] those who have things to say that disturb the governing majority. It is nothing less than a dictatorship of the unique, prescribed thought that most politicians and media believe in and that the people don't. (FRFN021)

As we expected, the populist discourse of the leaders and officials of UKIP predominately directed harsh criticism toward the European Union. In line with the theory of issue ownership, we see in the next section that UKIP has made the question of Europe its own. Petrocik (1996) emphasised that certain issues can become synonymous or owned by one party. Party supporters develop a certain degree of brand loyalty based either on past party performance (Fiorina, 1981) or on previously staked-out party positions (Shepsle, 1991). The majority of respondents from UKIP criticised the overwhelming bureaucracy and the allegedly undemocratic character of the European Union.

> The duly elected politicians have illegally sold us to Europe. We now find ourselves in a dictatorship. The EU system of government is totally undemocratic. (UKIP001)

> The EU is an absolute tyranny. The losses of freedoms have exposed oppression by tyranny. The EU is the risk. The growing embryo of the EU is dangerous to the peace of the world. (UKIP010)

> We have lost things such as a true system of parliamentary democracy, control of crime and punishment and we will eventually lose the unwritten constitution as we will have to convert to the 'European' way. When

you lose it, you will know what we have lost and that will be the British identity. People just don't realise the danger yet though. The British people didn't fully realise the threat Hitler posed then and they still don't realise the threat the EU is now. (UKIP008)

The EU is the polite way to impose undemocratic decisions on the people without them being able to rebel. (FRMF019)

No system so undemocratic has been used in France for hundreds of years. (FRFN027)

Both of the following interviewees highlight their criticisms against the European Union and refer to the behind-closed-doors decision-making in the EU bureaucracy:

People are now beginning to see and realise for themselves the real consequences of the EU on our country. The Parliament is not the supreme authority it is meant to be. It has been super-seeded by the European Commission, who are a bunch of unelected bureaucrats and their staff are above the law now. We are not allowed to find out what they are up to, what they do or what they are even supposed to do. The European Parliament is a front to their activities. It is not a parliament at all. It forms no policies, laws, government or taxation. It is all part of a big fraud scheme. We should withdraw immediately and UKIP is the only viable to commit to that mission. (UKIP025)

The EU's main aim is to proceed by stealth. Have you heard of the term useful idiots? Well, the EU is full of them. They are useful to the cause but they delude themselves over the real nature of the EU. Look at the SEA and all the rest of the treaties. Why do we need them? (UKIP023)

When asked to describe how to locate the ideological position of his/her party, one young French FN party member explains that the FN is a true populist party and emphasises the importance of common-sense values. In addition, an older member of the UKIP states that the political ideological spectrum does not force people to view parties as left or right; for him, right or wrong. This again highlights a populist discourse that accuses the elite of corruption and stresses the virginity of the extreme right as a party of opposition to all that is bad within the system.

If anything, I would say we are a true populist party. We are a popular party and we have the common sense values. We are a nationalist populist party I suppose. (FRFN006)

I don't see UKIP as left or right politically, but more simply right or wrong morally. (UKIP002)

Throughout the interviews, respondents across all parties described the deficiencies of the current political system and contrasted the forces of the extreme right against the corrupt political elite and other institutional representatives. Leaders believed that their party would be the saviour of true democracy and the guardian of the national interest. They also claim to be the real voice of the people, who are misrepresented and alienated by the professional politicians.

In addition to the more obvious distinction between the in-group and out-group in terms of the national community versus foreign elements, throughout the interviews many respondents recalled a tangible feeling of exclusion from society as a result of their membership. The stigmatism attached to membership in an extreme right party can lead to a perception of injustice and frustration. This sentiment appeared self-reinforced within the party, as did the bond between the inner circle of party activists. Some activists recalled accounts of blackmail and persecution because of their partisan affiliation. Others reported that they were frightened of losing their jobs and friends if their activism became public knowledge. Klandermans and Mayer (2006) indeed reported this observation in their study of extreme right party activists in the Netherlands. They point out that this element of stigmatism in connection with extreme right partisan affiliation reinforces a second dimension of in-group/out-group tension, this time between members and non-members of extreme right parties.

An important element of our proposed conceptual model of extreme right ideology is to suggest that parties and politicians have some choice as to where they should be located on the negative identity and authoritarianism dimensions. We expect a certain tension between xenophobic and populist references on the one hand, and between reactionary and repressive preferences on the other hand. Using manifesto analysis (see Chapter 5), we could compare pillar occurrences systematically. In the context of the interviews, it things are not as straightforward. First, the interviews were qualitative and not based on random samples of party politicians, which would make any generalisation problematic. Second, after an initial spontaneous phase of the interview, politicians' views were systematically probed as to all four pillars, somewhat evening out' references across politicians and parties. Based, however, on the spontaneous part of the interviews, the differences between leaders of various parties were quite striking. For instance, in the French context, MPF politicians made frequent reactionary references but FN politicians did not. Similarly, UKIP politicians made more populist references, but the references that pertain to the field of the xenophobic pillar were far more sustained in the speech of BNP politicians. Although this impression has not been quantified, the insistence on the two competing pillars was clearly imbalanced and almost symmetric between MPF/FN on the one hand, and UKIP/BNP on the other hand.

4.5 Summary

In this chapter, we use the interviews conducted with leaders of extreme right parties in the United Kingdom and France to illustrate qualitatively the essence of the four pillars within our conceptual map. We find elements of each of the four pillars in the discourse of extreme right party leaders and officials in both France and the United Kingdom. In the context of the authoritarian dimension, we see references to a reactionary component based on the return to a traditional way of life with the instillation of established values and morals. We also experience a repressive element within the authoritarian dimension that emphasises the rule of law and order within a structured society led by a strong state and an authoritative leader. Similarly, with respect to the negative identity dimension, extreme right leaders and officials highlight the xenophobic conception by contrasting the interest of the national community with that of the foreign 'other'. Scapegoats for modern day society's problems are found in references to immigrants, migrants, asylum seekers, or, more generally, foreign elements. In addition, numerous references to a populist discourse identifies politicians and the institutional elite as the common enemy, stating that the way forward is to place power in the hands of a party that could restore the people's will and follow policies inspired by common sense.

Based on the interviews, we can already see that some parties clearly emphasise certain strategic-discursive conceptions. In the United Kingdom, the BNP discourse leans toward a xenophobic-repressive ideological identity, and UKIP is more aligned to the populist-reactionary discourse. In contrast, leaders and officials of the FN in France largely emphasise the populist-repressive dynamic of extreme right ideological discourse, whereas the MPF's elite identify mostly with the xenophobic-reactionary pillars of the conceptual map. These preliminary findings are empirically tested in Chapter 5 when we analyse the manifestos of the French, German, and British extreme right parties.

5
Capturing the Ideological Identities of Extreme Right Parties

5.1 Introduction

Having defined our bi-dimensional, quadri-polar model of extreme right politics and grounded it qualitatively on the actual discourse of various extreme right leaders interviewed in several European countries, it is now time to map systematically the official discourse of extreme right parties across the European continent.

The extreme right party family in Europe consists of many parties that seem to have an ideology in common but one that is marked by substantial discursive variations. We argue that each individual party has to make a series of strategic-discursive choices that will determine an ideological identity that defines each party within the family group. In this chapter, we test our conceptual map of extreme right ideology by mapping the discourse of 25 extreme right parties across 17 party systems. These countries span the broader European continent, from the United Kingdom to Russia and from France and Austria to Bulgaria, Greece, and Turkey. They include political systems in which some parties usually considered on the extreme right have been in government (e.g. Austria, Italy), others where they are strong and meaningful (e.g. France, Belgium), and others where they are traditionally fairly weak (e.g. Sweden, Greece). A number of political systems have only one meaningful political party; others have two or three apparently competing against each other, seemingly defying traditional models of partisan politics (see Chapter 2). The parties whose discourse we have coded include old and new, large and small, national and regional political parties, but all have had an impact on the political scene of their country; all were selected along the lines defined in our methodological section.

We use comparative text analysis of party manifestos to show how these parties retain different ideological identities. Although the quantitative analysis of ideological references is extremely interesting as it provides an overview of the global ideological discourse, we must not overlook the value of a brief but crucial qualitative analysis of the manifestos. Some excerpts of discourse from the manifestos of the British extreme right parties (the BNP and UKIP) are therefore presented to illustrate the various types of strategic-discursive rhetoric. We discuss the ideological location of each party within the defined, bounded territory of the extreme right party family and ascribe each party to a sub-type that identifies their ideological and discursive emphasis. As explained earlier, the 17 party systems vary greatly in terms of institutional background, electoral systems, territorial organisation, democratic history, and so on. They respectively include one, two, or three extreme right parties. The 25 parties themselves vary greatly in terms of their discursive strategies and retain quite different electoral records. This provides us with a unique testing ground in which to learn and understand the core ideological discourse of multiple extreme right parties within a given country and across several party systems.

In Chapters 1 and 2, we discuss some of the conceptual and definitional problems faced by scholars studying the extreme right party family. Although the existing literature is plagued by competing models and lingering doubts whether these parties are so different that they do not constitute a real party family, we propose to test an empirically defined map of extreme right ideology that is tailored to the discursive specificities of this particular party family. In order to capture the subtle differences between these parties, we require a robust empirical framework that can be transposed to various party systems while retaining conceptual validity. A central tenet of our argument throughout this study is that the variation within the discourse of extreme right parties, which seems to be so troubling when looking for common postures, is symptomatic of constrained ideological choices that every single party has to make. Far from being disruptive and exceptional, these subtle differences should be discussed and taken into account when defining the ideological heart of the extreme right party family.

Indeed, as we describe in Chapter 2, each party retains a unique blend of discourse that varies along two fundamental ideological dimensions (authoritarianism and negative identity). Furthermore, we argue that there is a natural tension between the two competing conceptions of each dimension. The emphasis placed on the different conceptions of each dimension allows us to define each party based on its location on the conceptual map. Each party's ideological identity varies according to internal ideological pressures and constraints, its target electoral market, and the institutional and contextual specificities of the political, electoral, and party system.

At this stage, it is important to re-emphasise that our model of manifesto analysis is not one of *connotation* but one of *association*. We are not interested in explicitly populist, xenophobic, reactionary, or repressive references; rather, we look for evocations of the *themes* that support them and can trigger an association in the minds of potential voters who would be attracted to the four pillars of extreme right ideology highlighted by our model. Thus, we are looking for words or references which evoke notions of cultural identity (e.g. nation, minority, foreignness), civic identity (e.g. parties, elite, partisan cartels), the past (e.g. history, heritage, transmission), and state-controlled order (e.g. crime, justice, punishment), regardless of their connotation. We expect such references to resonate within the minds of potential extreme right voters and echo their ideological preferences (Roskos-Ewoldsen, Roskos-Ewoldsen et al., 2002). In exactly the same way, a social democrat's talking of inequality, even without any explicit connotation, will ring a bell in the minds of potential voters, or liberals when the word freedom is repeated in their manifesto.

As seen in Chapter 6, the specific ideological locations of extreme right parties within each system will shape internal (within the extreme right) and external (vis-à-vis mainstream parties) party competition. Moreover, as we test in Chapter 7, each specific sub-type of party is expected to have different levels of likely electoral success according to the ideological distribution of the electorate across the four quadrants of extreme right ideology.

The four pillars of extreme right discourse make intuitive sense; however, throughout the next section we provide examples of the discourse coded in our textual analysis of British party manifestos to help the reader better understand the subtleties involved with the discourse of the extreme right and conceptualise the locations of the parties on the ideological map.

5.2 The negative identity dimension: xenophobic and populist pillars

As seen in Chapters 2 and 4, the first defining feature of the negative identity dimension contrasts the identity of the national community with that of the defined out-group. The ideological discourse associated with this dimension tends to emphasise the exclusion of specific groups or minorities, whether they be foreigners, immigrants, asylum-seekers, countries, minorities, other parties, systems, politicians, or bureaucrats. Our conceptual map of extreme right ideology suggests that references to the negative identity dimension can embody a *civic* negative identity or a *cultural* negative identity. This distinction of civic and cultural identities draws upon the inspiration of Bruter's model of political identities (2005, 2009). The cultural conception of negative identity broadly corresponds to xenophobia; its civic conception corresponds to populism. To recapitulate, the cultural conception opposes the assumed homogeneity of the national community (as it is defined by the extreme right party in question) to an assumed out-group. Similarly, the civic conception of the negative identity dimension contrasts the will of the people to that of the self-interested corrupt ruling elite. Each party will have a dominant mode on one of the two conceptions according to their relative emphasis within the discourse of their party manifesto (see Chapters 2 and 4 on the tension between the two conceptions).

The cultural conception of the negative identity dimension: xenophobic pillar

As stated, the cultural conception constitutes the *xenophobic* conception of the negative identity scale. We expect to find anti-foreigner references within the discourse of extreme right parties. These references typically emphasise the assumed homogeneous characteristics of the in-group (usually the national community, however ethnically defined) to exclude a targeted out-group (various types of foreigners). We expect the dichotomy between identity frames and oppositional frames to be important within the discourse of the extreme right party family. The us versus them distinction is used as a frame to present the discrimination of relevant out-groups and the inherent preference for the rights and privileges of the in-group. This negative conception of identity relies on cultural identity exclusiveness, which contrasts the true national community with its 'parasitic' foreign elements, be they influences, norms, values, institutions, or indeed people. This foreign out-group may refer to a foreigner within (e.g. minorities) or outside (e.g. other countries). Broadly defined xenophobic, racist, or anti-Semitic elements are perhaps the oldest aspect of extreme right politics to be identified by political scientists.

The BNP, for example, emphasises the in-group and out-group distinction of opposing the national community (however defined) and the targeted other. The party also refers to the national community as the 'indigenous peoples of these islands'. In addition, the BNP appoints itself as the spokesperson for the people of the national community, as we see in the following excerpt: 'we, as the sole political representatives of the Silent Majority of the English, Scots, Irish and Welsh who formed and were formed by our island home, have one overriding demand: We want our country back!'. In order to stress the distinction between the rights of the national community and that of others, the BNP states that 'when we talk of British democracy we do so in an ethnic as well as a civic sense'. This suggests that the BNP conceives democracy as a reserve for the national community and that it can be defined not only in a civic manner but also in an ethnic sense.

Furthermore, the BNP asserts that the country has been held hostage to the 'social experiment of multi-culturalism'. It also suggests that multicultural Britain is a product of a plan engineered by the elite: 'our Masters have spent decades giving our money away in pursuit of an unworkable imperial fantasy', and is part of the 'long-term cultural war being waged by a ruling regime'. The BNP believes that this will lead to the 'eventual liquidation of Britain as a nation and a people' and that 'Britain's very existence today is threatened by immigration'. A level of its scaremongering has an anti-Islamic slant: 'the accession of Turkey would at a stroke increase the EU's Muslim population by more than 75 million'. The BNP also indulges in some anti-American rhetoric such as 'US-led 'Clash of Civilisations' and 'the worldwide reach of US consumerist culture through film and television'.

The discourse contained within UKIP's manifesto has fewer references to the xenophobic conception of the negative identity dimension. UKIP demands that 'the first duty of the British government is to defend our country'. In addition, the party asserts that 'the first responsibility of a British government is to its own population, not to those who would like to settle here'. Here, there is little provision for immigrants and refugees: the party does not advocate forced repatriation of non-nationals, but does state that it wants to achieve zero immigration.

As we can see from the preceding examples taken from the two British extreme right parties, the xenophobic conception of the negative identity dimension has different interpretations and is of varying importance within the discourse of these extreme right parties. The BNP retains a clearly different line of xenophobic discourse than does UKIP.

We now turn our attention to the populist conception of the negative identity dimension.

The civic conception of the negative identity dimension: populist pillar

At the other end of the negative identity dimension lies the contrast between real people and an equally parasitic and devious influence: the elite, who are deemed to betray the nation's identity and interest. We expect the populist discourse of extreme right parties to target a variety of actors and institutions: political parties (with the extreme right parties implicitly presenting themselves as a non-party whilst often preferring the term of a popular movement), the media (seen as unified, hostile, and often controlled by other powers), and economic and bureaucratic elite. All are likely targets within this populist pillar, alongside pressure groups from trade unions to human rights organisations. All elite are accused of combining their forces and resources to share power and deprive the people of what is rightly theirs. The enemy is within and (broadly) institutional, and the extreme right party bestows upon itself the challenge to reclaim the people's power from the elite who have usurped it, only pretend to compete (a proper cartel), and are only interested in their personal professional and financial gains.

We now look at examples of the populist discourse within the manifestos of the BNP and UKIP. When speaking about the national parliament, the BNP refers to the 'rubber-stamping closed shops for rule by diktat from Brussels and Strasbourg'. Verbs such as blackmail and cajole can evoke allegations of corruption among the elites. In contrast, the BNP promises to restore honesty, integrity' and ,transparency to the civic and public institutions. The BNP also pledges to 'put an end to the blackmail and underhanded tactics' in which the elite engage. The out-of-touch liberal elite, left-liberal elite, or the tired remnants of the old ruling class do not understand the worries and insecurities of the common man on the street, and the 'handcuffs of bureaucracy' prevent them from listening to the people.

An element of paranoia and conspiracy theories abound in the discourse of the extreme right. This is indeed true of the BNP, which claims that the 'political elite are nearing the end of a process which will outlaw any expression of opinions deemed to be politically incorrect'. The party suggests that the political elite are engaging in a process that will ultimately subvert the freedom of speech. There are several references to the damaging influence of political correctness and that the elite use this to silence opposition from the BNP. The BNP promises to 'end the practice of politically correct indoctrination in all its guises'.

The populist conception of the negative identity dimension overwhelmingly dominates UKIP manifesto. UKIP emphatically criticises the existing political system and the mainstream political parties and their representatives, often alleging corruption against the establishment by the European Union. For example: 'the UK Independence Party exists because none of the old political parties are prepared to accept that the real government of Britain is now in Brussels' and 'the EU is undemocratic, corrupt and unreformable'. UKIP believes that 'the only way for Britain is UKIP's way: we must leave. Until this is done, individuals and our businesses will continue to be strangled by all the ill-conceived intrusive regulation'. This statement suggests that UKIP perceives itself to be different from all the rest and is the only party that can remedy the situation. The following extract exemplifies the simplistic rhetoric frequently iterated in the manifesto:

SAY NO to European Union. But we also say NO to the culture of paperwork, performance targets and spin, NO to uncontrolled immigration, NO to a society in which everything is regulated and dissent is suppressed by fear and political correctness. Only outside the EU will it be possible to begin rebuilding a Britain which is run for British people, not for career politicians and bureaucrats.

In addition, UKIP claims to represent honesty (in contrast to the allegedly corrupt and dishonest politicians and elite) and to voice the concerns of hard-working and law-abiding citizens. In the following excerpts, we can see these elements within the discourse of the manifesto: 'we are the party that speaks out and is prepared to confront our country's problems squarely and honestly' and 'decent, law-abiding British citizens feel increasingly vulnerable and personal safety is now a major concern, particularly for women and the elderly'.

Here again there are substantial differences within the populist discourse of the two British parties. UKIP leads the way in terms of populist references by identifying the elite as the main culprit of the 'mess'; the BNP is more interested in emphasising the xenophobic conception of the negative identity dimension. We now turn our attention to the authoritarianism dimension.

5.3   The authoritarian dimension:
social and institutional authoritarianism pillars

The conceptual map also posits that extreme right parties must choose a location on a second core ideological dimension: authoritarianism. In this respect, we expect extreme right parties to present themselves as the champions of order, if not the only ones capable of restoring it in countries vibrantly described as chaotic and anarchic. Many have argued that in the 2002 French presidential election the Front National had benefited from a campaign focused on 'insecurity'. Similarly, the Polish League of Polish Families and Self-Defence (Samoobrona Rzeczypospolitej Polskiej) largely build their campaigns on the idea that contemporary Poland has lost the yardsticks on which its order and cohesion relied. To recapitulate, we argue that the authoritarian stance of extreme right parties can take two distinct forms depending on the solution that they advocate to restore order. Fundamentally, these two conceptions represent either: (1) a return to a previously existing utopian order, whereby traditional society and values are deemed to be the answer to today's anarchy (reactionary pillar), or (2) a call for an empowered and strengthened state, expected to be able to atomise the elements that make society hell for good citizens (repressive pillar).

The social conception of the authoritarianism dimension: reactionary pillar

With regard to the authoritarianism dimension, we expect extreme right parties to distinguish between a social conception of authoritarianism that emphasises the traditional way of life and the sacralisation of an old and dominant culture, and an institutional conception based on a stronger state. We refer to these conceptions as *reactionary* and *repressive* forms of discourse, respectively. Reactionary discourse accentuates the traditional values and morals of an age long past in order to create a new revolutionary order. As a result, this national rebirth will require a collective and unitary effort. This reinstates the presumption that these goals can only be achieved if the national community works together as a whole. This type of group-oriented discourse has often been explained as a reaction to the erosion of traditional linkages such as the breakdown of family nuclei, loss of neighbourhood communities, or the collapse of social class solidarity. Reactionary discourse therefore emphasises a utopian vision of a higher social order that will overcome the alleged imperfections of contemporary civilisation in a bid to restore some kind of cohesion that is currently lacking in today's society. Within the discourse of reactionary types of extreme right parties, we would expect references to idealism, patriotism, belief in and respect for traditional values, the subordination of virtues such as efficiency and diligence to the national community, and the rejection of hedonism and the leisure society.

In the discourse of the BNP, the reactionary conception is expressed as a desire to return to an idealised past with utopian elements. The party wishes for a 'national and cultural regeneration'. The BNP stresses the importance of traditions and civic duties in order to create cohesive communities, stating, for example, that it wants a 'return to traditional standards of civility and politeness in British life', and the 'creation and maintenance of an undercurrent of national solidarity is one of the cornerstones of a true national democracy'. The BNP also states its 'obligation to pass on to generations yet unborn, the collected knowledge, wisdom and lore, which we ourselves have inherited'. Here, the emphasis is not on power and control but on preservation of traditions and ancestral heritage. The BNP demands 'a return of pride and purpose', a 'national revival' and measures to 'strengthen the traditional family'. It argues that 'tradition, heritage, and civility must be understood as goods in themselves, to be defended for their own sake'. The party also stresses the importance of heritage, patriotism, and pride in national identity: 'We demand the right to be proud of Britain again, and for the English, Scots, Welsh, Irish and Ulster peoples to be allowed to celebrate their identity and heritage with as much right as is accorded to other native peoples'. Similarly, they state: 'we demand the right to preserve our culture, heritage, and identity. Our national character and native institutions are a precious inheritance, for which our ancestors have paid a high price over the centuries'. Within the discourse of the BNP, the role of children and youth is crucial to the survival and preservation of national identity and cultural traditions. The following statements exemplify this notion. 'We believe that all children suffer when deprived of their right to an ancestral identity and contact with their cultural roots' and 'we will also seek to instill in our young people knowledge of and pride in the history, cultures, and heritage of the native peoples of Britain'. The next extract from the BNP manifesto highlights the BNP's self-proclaimed common sense approach and positions itself as the only one able to implement the changes required to bring society back from the brink of chaos: 'the British National Party with its comprehensive, articulated and common sense approach seeks to be the vehicle for that change. Our time is approaching'.

Within the discourse of UKIP we find a relatively significant number of references to the reactionary conception of the authoritarianism. For example, the following extract from the manifesto highlights the centrality of the family within society: 'when proper democracy is also restored, individuals, and particularly young people, will regain a stronger sense of belonging to a society with the family as the basic stable unit and a better set of values'.

The following example highlights the reactionary conception rather well:

> But too often, rights favour the criminal rather than the victim and the unruly pupil rather than the teacher. They create tension rather than relieve it, emphasise differences, set society against itself and diminish

the much more precious right to free speech. The reality is that all these rules and rights are killing off the virtues of trust, initiative, responsibility and respect that make society work. A change of mindset is necessary in order to move away from the regulatory culture, the dependency culture and the compensation culture.

The reactionary conception has its place in all three parties of the extreme right party family in Britain, but it seems to be most prominent and pronounced in the discourse of UKIP. In the final part of this section, we examine the repressive conception of the authoritarianism dimension within the manifestos of two British extreme right parties.

The institutional conception of the authoritarianism spectrum: repressive pillar

The repressive mode of the authoritarianism dimension relies on the exercise of state power to fight chaos and threatening anarchy. We expect extreme right parties to refer to the role of the strong state, the importance of restoring law and order within society, and the requirement of strong leadership. The references are not to lost values but to crime; the solution is not discipline but prison; the actors are not parents, priests, and teachers, but policemen, judges, and sometimes, the military. Fear of punishment and the restored authority of the state will ultimately re-establish order. As such, limitations are often imposed on personal and collective freedoms, and the only authorised collective identification is channelled toward achieving the great national destiny. We also expect references to a preferred hierarchical organisation of the community within the discourse of the extreme right. This hierarchy is determined by the party and often assumes the subordination of the individual to the state. Within extreme right discourse, the state is thus depicted as a strong and powerful institution that will employ its power to eliminate the disruptive elements in society.

Before we move on to discuss the examples of repressive discourse by the British extreme right parties, we note that it is predictably difficult to find references to and examples of repressive ideology in party manifestos. Extreme right parties may wish to minimise references to an omnipotent state or an autocratic leader in an official document such as a party manifesto, as this may inevitably restrict their potential electorate. This particular problem highlights the importance of combining the quantitative text analysis with the face-to-face interviews of extreme right party leaders and officials and triangulating the findings in order to gain a better understanding of the true ideological identities of extreme right parties.

Notwithstanding this cautionary note, the manifestos of the British extreme right parties did contain a few clear examples of the repressive conception. The BNP, for example, declares that the armed forces 'must take control of our national borders' and to 'defend our homeland and our independence'. They also aim to 'reintroduce the death penalty for terrorists'.

In terms of repressive discourse, UKIP does not wish to exert oppressive rule by force or strengthen the state: 'we need to relieve our forces from too much central direction, including performance targets, the mass of paperwork and politically-correct rules that ignore the realities of the job'. UKIP wants to see 'bobbies back on the beat' and the 'handcuffs on the criminals, not the police'. Again, we see the criticism of bureaucracy but this time it is preventing the police from doing its job.

Overall, these examples of discourse help us understand better the various ideological references common throughout the manifestos of the three British extreme right parties. The BNP seems to lead the way in its references to the xenophobic conception of the negative identity dimension; UKIP's discourse is predominantly populist and reactionary with few references to both the xenophobic and repressive pillars. This finding reinforces the tension between the two different conceptions of the ideological dimensions we propose in our conceptual map.

5.4   Exploring the conceptual map of extreme right ideology

In Chapter 3, we outline the overarching arguments guiding the research design and the empirical testing of the conceptual map of extreme right ideology. In Chapter 4, we use interviews with the extreme right elite to gain perspective into whether our conceptual map makes sense in the context of its discourse.

We now test whether the two founding strategic-discursive dimensions can be found within the official discourse of extreme right parties. The two dimensions create four possible sub-types of party within the extreme right party family: xenophobic-reactionary, xenophobic-repressive, populist-reactionary, populist-repressive. References to the four conceptions are coded, and we assign the parties a dominant ideological identity according to the conceptions they reference most often within the manifestos. With reference to communication theory, we expect extreme right parties to assume a dominant 'mode' on each dimension: to emphasise one of the two conceptions of each dimension in order to stake out their specificity and avoid ideological incoherence. Each party thus assumes an ideological identity within this specified and constrained ideological space.

In Chapter 3 we outline the general structure of our methodology for the text analysis of party manifestos. Our framework of analysis aims at capturing the salience given to the four strategic-discursive pillars in each manifesto to compare the ideological discourse of the 25 extreme right parties. Each manifesto was hand coded by native speakers. Informed by the interviews with extreme right leaders and the discursive illustrations of the four pillars from within the manifestos themselves, we considered all 25 manifestos before coming up with word lists. Individual coders were also given the opportunity to provide insight and mention the words and categories they thought were forgotten in the original word lists that represented the ideological discourse characterised by the conceptual map. Such proposed additions could either be made for all parties included in the analysis or represent country-specific issues (e.g. 'Padania' for Italy, or 'Joan of Arc' for France) which did not need to be replicated in other national contexts.

We used multiple coders on a selection of the word lists and a selection of the coding of a third of the manifestos. In those cases, the coding, including ascription to each of the four pillars, had a reliability of over 95 per cent. Instructions to the codes specified that all references were to be checked manually so irrelevant words could be discounted. The word occurrences were then systematically registered. We came up with a total list of 827 words, which were collapsed into 509 word categories that represented the two ideological dimensions of extreme right ideology. Full word lists appear in Appendix A.

Words and word categories across parties and countries were conceived to be equivalent rather than a mere translation. Total word occurrences for each pillar and each party were then expressed as two comparable proportions. Expressing occurrences as proportions of the total words in each manifesto would seem intuitive but would be linguistically unrealistic as shown by discourse analysts, as various languages use different proportions of 'wasted' grammatical words (e.g. prepositions, articles).

We thus created a variable expressing each word occurrence as a proportion of the total valid words in the manifesto, that is, the total words excluding neutral grammatical items. This Proportion of total Valid Words (PVW) is used when comparing gross word occurrences in party discourse (e.g. showing they appear more often in extreme right than non-extreme right parties). We created a second variable expressing word occurrences as proportions of the total coded words; that is, all the words that fit the xenophobic, populist, reactionary, and repressive pillars. This Proportion of total Coded Words (PCW) is used to compare the emphases of discourse and party types. The resulting patterns produce some provocative findings. On the whole the findings show that, in terms of proportions of total valid words, the word references corresponding to the four pillars are very significant: well over 30 per cent in most cases, and up to 59.7 per cent for the German Republikaner. This is approximately 6.5 times more than in the pilot mainstream left- and right-wing parties coded.

Table 5.1 gives another insight into the way these references are distributed across the two ideological dimensions. Overall, 58.0 per cent of total coded word counts (PCW) refer to the negative identity dimension and 42.0 per cent to the authoritarianism dimension. Indeed, for 24 of the 25 parties considered, the negative identity dimension takes precedence over ideological

Table 5.1 References to the two ideological dimensions in the twenty-five extreme right party manifestos

Country	Party	Negative identity		Authoritarianism	
		Xenophobic	Populist	Reactionary	Repressive
Bulgaria	Ataka	**34.0**	24.9	15.5	**25.5**
Russia	LD	20.2	**30.6**	22.4	**26.8**
Slovakia	SNS	**27.1**	26.0	16.3	**30.6**
Italy	FT	27.6	**29.6**	19.2	**23.6**
	AN	**30.4**	26.9	20.0	**22.6**
	LN	**52.8**	14.2	13.8	**19.3**
Greece	LAOS	24.3	**33.7**	**23.6**	18.4
Belgium	VB	34.2	**41.6**	10.5	**13.8**
	FNB	25.5	**32.2**	16.9	**25.5**
Netherlands	PVV	**27.0**	25.2	15.0	**32.9**
Denmark	DF	**28.6**	26.4	**30.0**	15.0
Austria	BZÖ	29.0	**34.6**	17.8	**18.7**
	FPÖ	23.0	**29.9**	23.2	**23.9**
Switzerland	SVP	23.4	**29.9**	**23.5**	23.1
Romania	PRM	**34.8**	25.8	15.0	**24.4**
France	FN	26.9	**29.7**	20.0	**23.5**
	MNR	27.8	**27.8**	20.1	**24.4**
	MPF	**32.1**	21.0	**29.8**	17.1
Great Britain	BNP	**33.4**	32.4	16.6	**17.7**
	UKIP	24.0	**38.3**	**26.6**	11.2
Germany	NPD	23.6	**31.0**	17.4	**28.0**
	REP	23.9	**24.3**	**26.4**	25.4
	DVU	**31.9**	31.7	16.5	**20.0**
Turkey	MHP	**29.0**	23.6	**20.8**	16.7
Sweden	SD	20.0	**32.2**	**29.9**	18.0
Overall		**28.7**	29.3	20.0	21.9

Notes: All figures are percentages. Figures in the first four columns represent proportions of total coded words (PCW) associated with each dimension for each party. The sum of these four figures in each row thus equals 100 (+/- rounding). The figure in the last column represents the total occurrence of words associated with the four dimensions (PVW) for each party. The average PVW for the 25 parties is 39.5% and for the six non-extremist parties, 6.1%.

discourse referring to the authoritarianism dimension. The exception to this is the German Republikaner, with 52 per cent of PCW dedicated to authoritarianism discourse, and only 48 per cent of PCW related to the negative identity dimension. The balance between negative identity and authoritarian dimensions varies quite a lot across countries and parties. For instance, the negative identity dimension seems particularly salient amongst British extreme right parties or extreme right parties in the Balkans. In contrast, extreme right parties in France and in Scandinavia tend emphasise more strongly the authoritarian dimension of discourse and proportionally less so the negative identity rhetoric.

Note that each dimension shows a relatively balanced division between the two possible pillars of rhetoric expression. In terms of negative identity, xenophobic references represent a total of 28.7 per cent of PCW on average whereas populist references represent 29.3 per cent of PCW on average. In terms of the authoritarian dimension, reactionary elements are slightly weaker on average (20.0%) than are repressive ones (21.9%). The even split between 'dimension ends' is also well illustrated by the predominant foci of the various parties. In terms of the negative identity, we have 15 predominantly populist parties, and 11 predominantly xenophobic ones. In terms of the authoritarian dimension, the balance is a little bit more unequal: 18 repressive parties and 8 reactionary ones.

Beyond the relative weight of each of the pillars and dimensions (Figure 5.1), we expected a tension between the two conceptions of each dimension. We test this by looking at the correlation between pairs of pillars for all of the extreme right parties in the analysis. We find negative correlations both between the parties' scores on the xenophobic and populist expressions of negative identity (-0.46) and between the reactionary and repressive conceptions of authoritarianism (-0.30).[1] This result emphatically confirms our expectation stated in Section 2.7 in Chapter 2 that each party will have a defining dominant mode of discourse that emphasises one of the two conceptions on each of the two ideological dimensions.

Our conceptual map acknowledges that extreme right parties can employ different strategies to choose their dominant ideological identity; therefore, we witness a diversity of ideological identities that combine different conceptions of the negative identity and authoritarianism dimensions. In order to differentiate themselves from their competitors in the same party system, extreme right parties are expected to emphasise different conceptions of the two structuring ideological dimensions. Indeed, Plate 1 shows how parties that are usually considered to belong to the same party family differ in their dominant discursive emphasis and are thus located in the four different quadrants created by the two structuring ideological dimensions. The results of this analysis confirm that the 25 extreme right parties competing in the three countries studied here occupy all four ideological quadrants. This finding echoes the core expectations of our conceptual model

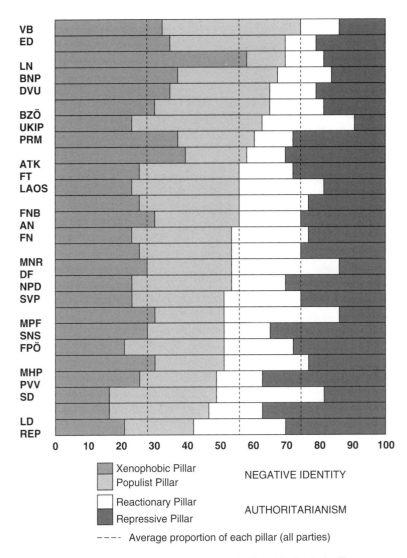

Figure 5.1 The distribution of discourse across the four ideological pillars

Note: Figures are proportions of total valid words (PVW) (percentage).

detailed in Section 2.7. All four types of strategic-discursive combinations are represented. In total, ten parties are populist-repressive (e.g. the Belgian Vlaams Belang, the Austrian FPÖ, and the French Front National), eight are xenophobic-repressive (e.g. the Romanian PRM, the Italian Lega Nord, or the British BNP), five parties are populist-reactionary (e.g. the Greek Laos,

Swiss SVP, and the British UKIP), and three parties fall into the xenophobic-reactionary category (Danish DF, French MPF, and Turkish MHP). This split into four uneven but distinct categories is an extremely important finding. As discussed in Chapter 1, the extreme right party family is traditionally believed to be either monolithically xenophobic or singularly populist in its very definition. The negative correlation coefficients between xenophobic and populist pillars on the one hand, and between reactionary and repressive pillars on the other hand, emphasise the logic of this distinction.

The majority of parties have a distinct location, with the exception of the MNR and DVU (on the negative identity dimension), the FPÖ, BZÖ, and SVP (on the authoritarian dimension), and the BNP and Republikaner (on both dimensions). These seven parties have a relatively unclear emphasis on either one or both dimensions (i.e. under 1 percentage point difference between the two pillars associated with one dimension). The confusion is likely to be mostly problematic for the BNP and the Republikaner, for which it concerns both dimensions, followed by the MNR and DVU, for which it concerns the most important dimension of extreme right discourse. In contrast, in the cases of the FPÖ, BZÖ, and SVP, the confusion only concerns the secondary dimension of extreme right discourse of the party. Plate 1 illustrates the ideological location of all 25 parties within the conceptual extreme right universe, based on their emphases, and location in one of the four quadrants of extreme right ideological discourse.

Our model and the resulting Plate 1 thus clearly show how European extreme right parties explicitly fit into four distinct categories. In the next four sections, we highlight briefly the nature of each of these four quadrants, or empirically supported prototypes, of extreme right political parties.

5.5   Populist-repressive parties

Ten of the 25 extreme right parties coded belong to the populist-repressive category according to their party manifestos, making it the largest category of extreme right party represented in our sample. These parties are the Russian Liberal-Democrats, the Italian Fiamma Tricolore, the Belgian Vlaams Belang and FNB, the Austrian FPÖ and BZÖ, the French FN and (marginally) MNR, and the German NPD.

Plate 2 shows how these ten parties are distributed in their discourse. As we can see, although populist-repressive parties are the most frequently found on the European extreme right scene, they can be found in most sub-regions of the continent. In terms of the negative identity dimension, of the group, the Belgian Vlaams Belang emphasises populism most with over 41 per cent of total coded words; only the French MNR puts little emphasis on populist discourse as opposed to xenophobic discourse. Most members of this quadrant moderately favour the repressive pillar over the reactionary one (very little, in the cases of the Austrian FPÖ and BZÖ), with the exception of the

NPD. This is interesting because, as we will see, xenophobic-repressive parties tend to emphasise the repressive pillar more strongly on average.

Finally, Plate 2 illustrates how the discourse of populist-repressive parties can assume two different diamond shapes: those with a strong populist predominance (e.g. VB, BZÖ) and those with an important repressive component as well (e.g. NPD, LD).

5.6 Xenophobic-repressive parties

After the populist-repressive type, the xenophobic-repressive category constitutes the second largest cluster of European extreme right parties, with eight members among the 25 manifestos that we coded:. They are the Bulgarian Ataka, Italian Allianza Nazionale and Lega Nord, the Dutch PVV, Romanian PRM, Slovakian SNS, British BNP and German DVU. Unlike the populist-repressive group, the xenophobic-repressive quadrant seems to be the preferred location of many Central European extreme right parties.

Plate 3 shows the strategic-discursive location of these eight parties and how they differ. As compared to populist-repressive parties, the xenophobic-repressive quadrant looks significantly more heterogeneous. In this case, the two main diamond shapes we encounter are radically more contrasted. Thus, parties such as the Lega Nord, Ataka, and the PRM have a very strong xenophobic predominance, while others such as the Slovak SNS and the Dutch PVV have repression as their dominant strategic-discursive focus. Within the quadrant, only the German DVU and the British BNP have a very narrow negative identity focus on xenophobia rather than populism, and the BNP is the only party within this quadrant to also have a very narrow focus on repression over reaction, while the other seven members of the quadrant are very distinctly repressive.

Overall, the strongest emphasis on xenophobia comes from the Lega Nord (52.75%) and the strongest focus on repression from the PVV (32.87%). The equilibrium points of the eight parties are clearly much more dispersed on Plate 3 than their equivalent in the case of populist-repressive parties (Plate 2).

5.7 Populist-reactionary parties

The third largest group of political parties in our sample are populist-reactionary organisations. The five parties within the populist-reactionary quadrant are the German Republikaner, British UKIP, Greek Laos, Swiss SVP, and Swedish Democrats. Their respective strategic-discursive positions are illustrated in Plate 4.

Within this group, the Swiss SVP has only a marginal emphasis on reactionary discourse over the repressive one; the Republikaner has a limited emphasis on both dimensions and remains the only party within our sample to emphasise the authoritarian dimension of its discourse more than its negative identity dimension. The other three parties in this quadrant all have a clear emphasis on both dimensions; indeed, UKIP is the second most emphatically populist party in our entire sample (38.3%) and the Swedish Democrats have the second most emphatically reactionary manifesto of all 25 coded ones (29.9%).

Note that the Republikaner has a fairly vertical diamonds that strongly emphasises authoritarianism, whereas Laos and UKIP have a strongly horizontal diamond predominantly emphasising negative identity discourse. The SVP and SD are somewhere in between.

5.8　Xenophobic-reactionary parties

The fourth and final category of extreme right parties in our sample, the smallest of the lot, consists of three xenophobic-reactionary parties: the Danish Dansk Folkeparti, the French MPF, and the Turkish MHP. The discourse used in the manifestos of these three parties is depicted in Plate 5. The MPF has a strongly focused discourse on both dimensions, whereas the Danish Folkeparti mostly emphasises the reactionary component of its discourse, which is the strongest of all the parties included in the analysis (30%).

Although the smallest group, the three parties that make the xenophobic-reactionary party family have some of the most distinctive strategic-discursive foci of all the parties included in our analysis. As such, they represent a very real fourth cluster of polarisation of extreme right political parties.

5.9　Summary

Our analysis of the 25 parties' manifestos reveals some extremely interesting patterns. The first concerns the conceptual geography of the extreme right. We show that the fundamental dimensions structure the extreme right territory into four quadrants where parties choose their strategic-discursive location (references to them are an extremely important 6.5 times more frequent in extreme right manifestos than in those of other parties). These two fundamental dimensions also structure the extreme right ideological territory into four quadrants: xenophobic-reactionary, xenophobic-repressive, populist-reactionary, and populist-repressive. Each extreme right party chooses specific strategies and emphasises different conceptions of its ideological discourse, giving the party a location on each dimension as well as its own ideological identity.

The implications of these findings are significant for our understanding of extreme right party politics. First of all, they explain why it is apparently so difficult to find common ideological traits across members of the extreme right party family. Indeed, our map of extreme right ideology shows that variations between xenophobic and populist attitudes on the negative identity scale and between reactionary and repressive positions on the authoritarianism scale are an intrinsic part of the very concept of extreme right ideology. The extreme right party is thus apparently difficult to define because a one-size-fits-all definition does not work when trying to understand the subtle complexities of this particular party family. Indeed, most extreme right party discourse refers to all four conceptions of the two ideological dimensions, but we show that they are negatively correlated by pair, and that at the extreme a pillar can be almost absent from a party's discourse as long as the alternative mode of expressing the same dimension is sufficiently emphasised.

This particular conceptual map of ideological discourse is tailored specifically to the extreme right party family, but could be replicated for other party families, albeit along with their own respective ideological dimensions. For example, a defining ideological feature in the discourse of the extreme right such as the xenophobic conception of the negative identity will not apply to the discourse of moderate parties. Each party family will therefore have its own structuring ideological dimension that can be used to define the sub-types of parties within it. Our findings suggest there is a difference between ideological dimensions that define the membership of a party family and policy dimensions that are important to a party's programme but are not essentially ideological. Political parties from all party families often change their policies, as they have far more freedom with respect to policy changes than to changes in ideological dimensions. Parties can decide to change their ideological identity (see Chapter 6 on the dynamics of party competition) and move their strategic-discursive position on the two dimensions, but the structuring ideological dimensions within the party family remain stable. Members of a given party family will therefore have to make fundamental choices between various conceptions or strategic-discursive expressions of their core ideological foundations.

As seen in this chapter, the axes of internal competition seem to vary across countries. In France, the main axis of opposition is between populist-repressive and xenophobic-reactionary parties; in the United Kingdom, a xenophobic-repressive party vies with a populist-reactionary one. In Germany, there is no predominant combination. This lack of correlation between the two dimensions of extreme right ideology emphasises their independence, and shows how both dimensions, and both pillars within each of them, participate equally in defining extreme right politics. If one were to argue, for example, that a xenophobic emphasis is a necessary pre-condition for membership in the extreme right party family, the French FN would be excluded from the family. This position would obviously be difficult to maintain, as the FN is widely referenced in prototypical definitions of extreme right parties. Similarly, the need for a repressive orientation would lead to the exclusion of Die Republikaner. If on both dimensions each possible pillar is a credible choice, one of the consequences of a party's chosen location is its likeliness to survive where several extreme right parties compete.

As a result, these strategic-discursive choices may have implications on the dynamics of internal party competition (see Chapter 6) and on the party's relative electoral success, depending on the match between the party's location within its own ideological territory and that of its potential voters (see Chapter 7). As we see in the next chapter, the dominant ideological emphasis and the corresponding specific location of a given party can also have repercussions on and implications for on the survival and existence of other parties from the extreme right party family; therefore, a party's ideological location will be influenced by the strategic-discursive choices of other competitors within and outside the extreme right party family. In addition, in Chapter 7 we highlight the impact of these strategic-discursive choices upon each party's relative electoral success. Their level of success may be determined, among other social, economic and political factors, by the relative match between the party's location within its own ideological territory and the ideological distribution of its potential voters.

6
Exploring the Extreme Right Universe: Patterns of Internal Party Competition

6.1 The phenomenon of multiple extreme right parties

In Chapter 5 we see that the 25 extreme right parties in the 17 party systems in our analysis can be defined according to their strategic-discursive choices and that the conceptual map of extreme right ideology adds to our understanding of the variation in ideological discourse within the party family. Each party occupies a unique position relative to its emphasis of the four ideological pillars, and some parties are located within the same ideological quadrant. This is true of the FN and the MNR in France and the BNP in the Britain. Germany is alone in that all three parties assumed different ideological identities.

The ideological position of each party within its respective party system undoubtedly casts interesting questions as to the impact of ideological position upon the internal dynamics of party competition and the relative openness to newcomers and challengers within the extreme right universe. This chapter focuses on the question of internal party competition within the extreme right party family and discusses the implications for success, coexistence, and survival amongst competitors, both as a member of the party family and a member of the national party system.

In several countries, including the party systems of Germany, Italy, the Britain, Poland, and France, several parties compete for the potential extreme right vote, hoping to conquer this increasingly lucrative electoral reservoir. On the basis of some successful electoral breakthroughs, the desire of an increasing number of parties to capitalise on the potential extreme right electoral reservoir is certainly not surprising; however, the coexistence and survival of multiple extreme right parties within the same party system has received little attention within the existing literature. This chapter builds upon the conceptual map of extreme right ideology exposed in Chapter 2 and the empirical party manifesto analysis of Chapter 5 that locates the respective ideological identities of the 25 parties. We argue that the key to understanding the survival and coexistence of multiple extreme right parties is to analyse their respective ideological locations within the extreme right ideological universe and decipher the dynamics of internal party competition within the party family. We consider the effect of each party's individual strategic-discursive choices on the dynamics of internal party competition in order to understand the logic underpinning the discursive variations within each party system.

In Chapter 5, we illustrate the ideological discourse of the 25 extreme right parties in Britain, France, and Germany. We see how a party's strategic-discursive choices determine its unique ideological identity, that is, its location in the xenophobic-repressive, xenophobic-reactionary, populist-repressive or the populist-reactionary quadrants. The empirical analysis shows how each party emphasises distinctive conceptions of the two fundamental ideological dimensions, and across all three of the party systems we witness parties that occupy each of the four quadrants. Although the ideological identity of each party is extremely interesting in terms of finding a suitable empirical definition of the extreme right party family, it also raises significant questions about which other factors might have influenced the strategic-discursive choices each party has had to make. Here, we focus on how the dynamics of party competition may influence these specific ideological locations and how it alters the extreme right ideological space within each party system.

6.2   Toward a 'within party family' model of party competition

Traditional spatial models of party competition that are based on the traditional left-right political spectrum do not predict the coexistence of two equally right-wing parties (Downs, 1957; Sartori, 1976); however, several party systems have witnessed the emergence of multiple extreme right parties that are undoubtedly competing for the same potential electorate and belong to the same party family. How can this be explained? We suggest that instead of looking at the global picture of party competition along the traditional left-right political spectrum, if we focus our attention on the bounded world of extreme right party competition we can further our understanding of these internal dynamics of party competition.

In this chapter we focus on the extreme right party family, concentrating on the ideological space these parties operate within in order to examine the underlying dynamics of party competition. In other words, the important distance between parties is measured not on a universal ideology scale but rather on dimensions meaningful to the parties and to their potential electorate. In the specific case of the extreme right party family, these are the two fundamental ideological dimensions of negative identity and authoritarianism.

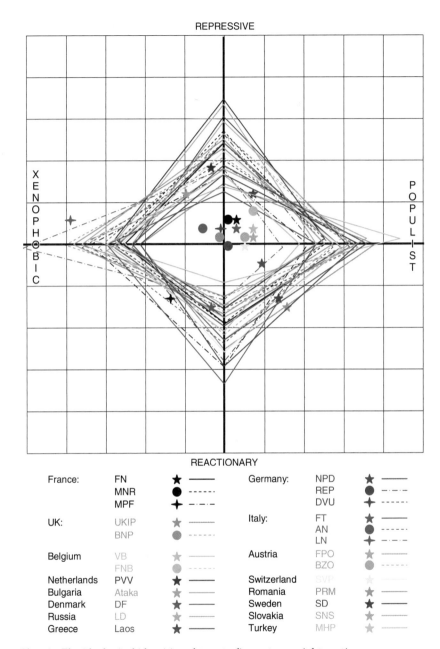

REPRESSIVE

X
E
N
O
P
H
O
B
I
C

POPULIST

REACTIONARY

France:	FN	★ ———	Germany:	NPD	★ ———
	MNR	● ------		REP	● —·—·—
	MPF	✚ —·—·—		DVU	✚ ------
UK:	UKIP	★ ········	Italy:	FT	★ ———
	BNP	● ------		AN	● ------
				LN	✚ —·—·—
Belgium	VB	★ ———	Austria	FPO	★ ———
	FNB	● ------		BZO	● ------
Netherlands	PVV	★ ———	Switzerland	SVP	★ ———
Bulgaria	Ataka	★ ———	Romania	PRM	★ ———
Denmark	DF	★ ———	Sweden	SD	★ ———
Russia	LD	★ ———	Slovakia	SNS	★ ———
Greece	Laos	★ ———	Turkey	MHP	★ ———

Plate 1 The ideological identities of twenty-five extreme right parties

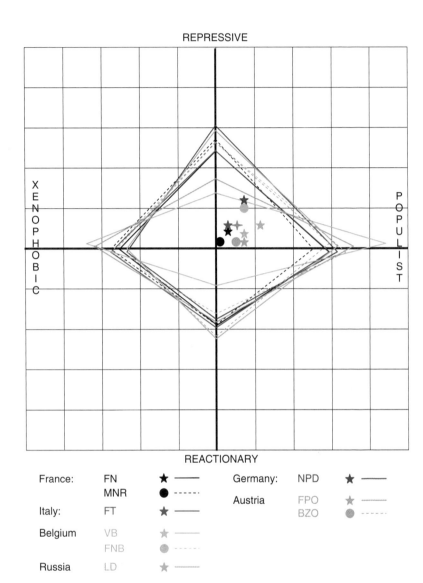

REPRESSIVE

XENOPHOBIC

POPULIST

REACTIONARY

France:	FN	★ ——	Germany:	NPD	★ ——
	MNR	● ------	Austria	FPO	★ -------
Italy:	FT	★ ——		BZO	● ------
Belgium	VB	★ ——			
	FNB	● ------			
Russia	LD	★ ------			

Plate 2 Europe's populist-repressive parties

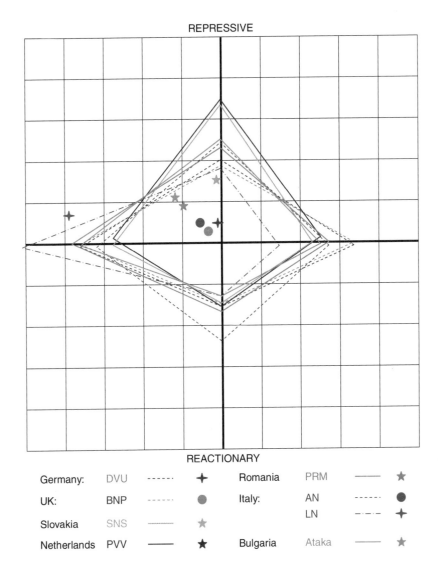

Plate 3 Europe's xenophobic-repressive parties

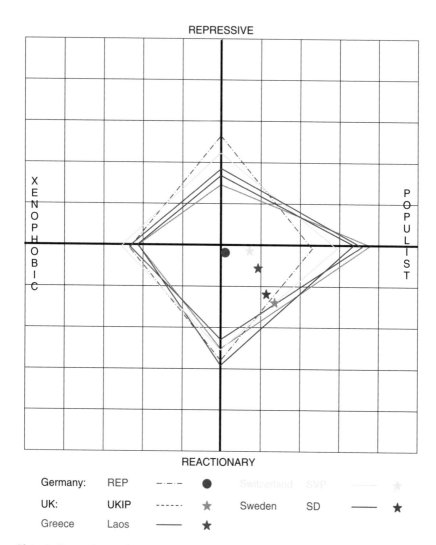

REPRESSIVE

X
E
N
O
P
H
O
B
I
C

P
O
P
U
L
I
S
T

REACTIONARY

Germany:	REP	—·—·—	●	Switzerland	SVP	————	☆
UK:	UKIP	- - - - -	☆	Sweden	SD	———	★
Greece	Laos	———	★				

Plate 4 Europe's populist-reactionary parties

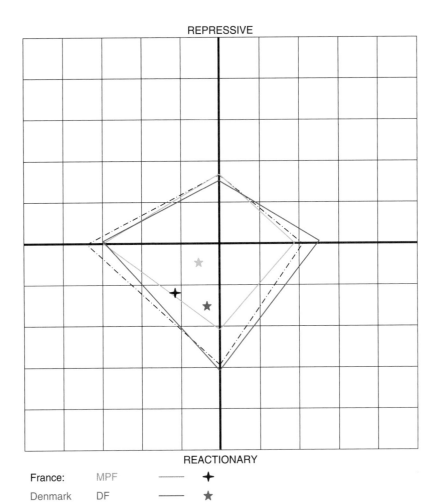

Plate 5 Europe's xenophobic-reactionary parties

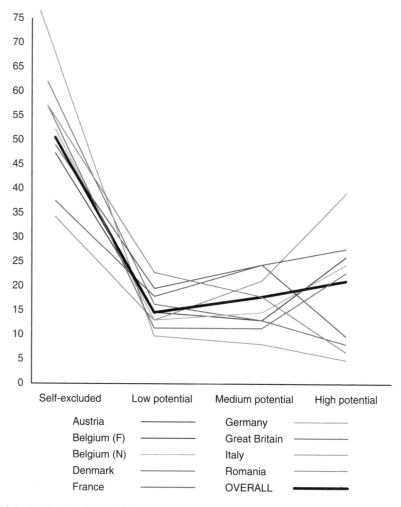

| Self-excluded | Low potential | Medium potential | High potential |

Austria	————————	Germany	·············
Belgium (F)	————————	Great Britain	————————
Belgium (N)	————————	Italy	————————
Denmark	————————	Romania	·············
France	————————	OVERALL	▬▬▬▬▬▬▬▬

Plate 6   Distribution of likeliness to vote for the extreme right by country

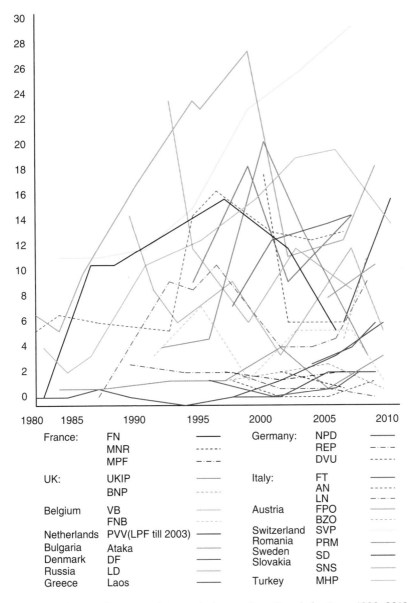

France:	FN	———	Germany:	NPD	———
	MNR	-----		REP	—·—·—
	MPF	—··—··—		DVU	-----
UK:	UKIP	———	Italy:	FT	———
	BNP	-----		AN	-----
				LN	—··—··—
Belgium	VB	———	Austria	FPO	———
	FNB	-----		BZO	-----
Netherlands	PVV(LPF till 2003)	———	Switzerland	SVP	———
Bulgaria	Ataka	———	Romania	PRM	———
Denmark	DF	———	Sweden	SD	———
Russia	LD	———	Slovakia	SNS	———
Greece	Laos	———	Turkey	MHP	———

Plate 7 Evolution of extreme right parties' scores in national elections, 1980–2010

We argue that the determinants of coexistence and survival of multiple extreme right parties within the same system are to be found in this 'within party family' model, where we analyse the ideological locations of each party and try to better understand their choice of location. In the following paragraphs, we outline some of our main arguments concerning the strategic-discursive choices of extreme right parties and the subsequent impact these locations have on the dynamics of party competition.

A clear and coherent ideological identity

In order to survive, particularly within a party system that is home to several extreme right parties, each party must communicate a clear, coherent, and understandable ideological identity to its electorate: it must adhere to a distinct location on each of the two dimensions and have a predominant emphasis on two of the four conceptions. Petrocik (1996) emphasised that certain issues can become synonymous or 'owned' by one party and that this party is often regarded as more credible or legitimate in the eyes of the electorate if it competes on this specific dimension. In multidimensional issue competition, parties may compete in party systems not by converging to similar positions but by emphasising the salience of the distinct issues that give them an advantage with the voters (Feld & Grofman, 2001). Similarly, Budge and Laver (1986) argue that political parties may decide to compete by accentuating issues on which they have an undoubted advantage, rather than by putting forward contrasting policies on the same issues.

One logical conclusion of the salience theory is that parties will try to differentiate themselves from other competitors by emphasising unique ideological identities. Because there is no reason to expect that any two parties will want to campaign on the same ideological location and thus attract the same sub-group of voters (i.e. either a clear winner, loser, or split vote), we expect parties to choose different ideological locations in order to maximise electoral success. Each party will therefore attempt to cultivate its own section of the ideological space or quadrant, usually one distinct from those of other existing extreme right parties.

Several parties can only coexist within one party system if they establish a clear ideological identity that enables them to appeal to sufficiently diverse electorates and differentiate themselves from their competitors; therefore, if a party is to be successful, it must emphasise different conceptions of the two ideological dimensions and have a unique location on the conceptual map. Two extreme right parties, regardless of relative radicalism, will not happily coexist within a party system if they are located too close to each other within the same quadrant of extreme right ideological territory. This would imply that their ideological identities are not sufficiently different, and the potential electorate for this specific type of extreme right party would be split between the two parties competing. In other words, a lack of ideological differentiation would mean that parties would be fighting for the same segment of their already small and restricted potential electorate. The key to successful cohabitation lies in the ability of extreme right parties to locate in different quadrants than their competitors, as illustrated by Figure 6.1.

The figure depicts a hypothetical scenario in which party X is the historic extreme right party within a given party system. This party has a predominantly populist-reactionary ideological identity. A new party wishes to emerge within the same party system and to challenge the electoral dominance of the historic party. The new party has several different choices as to where to locate within the extreme right ideological space, each of which has different risks and benefits. As the figure suggests, the optimal location would be the quadrant that is ideologically opposed to the historic party (that is, different conceptions of both dimensions) and the riskiest position would be to imitate the ideological identity of the historic party by emphasising the same conceptions on both ideological dimensions. In other words, the new party would have the highest chance of survival against the historic party if it chose a different strategic-discursive identity to that of the historic party; therefore, it would have to emphasise different conceptions of both ideological dimensions. In the hypothetical scenario here, the optimal ideological location would be the xenophobic-repressive quadrant.

This ideologically optimal location does not automatically ensure electoral success for the new party. For example, if the potential extreme right electorate does not find this quadrant electorally significant (i.e. the distribution of the potential extreme right electorate is not favourable to this particular quadrant), then the loyalty afforded to the historic party may reign and the challenger would ultimately fail to attract the extreme right electorate. Moreover, a party that fails to choose a distinctive position on either dimension (for example, a location that would take no distinctive position on the authoritarian dimension, with no clear emphasis on the repressive or reactionary conceptions) would be threatened by parties

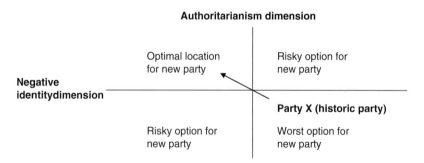

Figure 6.1 A strategic dilemma? The dynamics of internal party family competition

located in neighbouring quadrants, as these parties would have a stronger ideological identity.

No space at the inn…

New challengers wishing to capitalise on the potential extreme right vote must avoid choosing an ideological location that has been pre-selected by an existing party of the extreme right. If an existing party has communicated a clear ideological message and is the first party to settle within one of the four ideological quadrants (not straddling either conception of the two dimensions), then this party will be the historic party and will have to some extent a connection with the potential extreme right electorate. This existing party will have a fairly strong and stable electoral allegiance within its particular ideological quadrant. As a consequence, a new party may find it difficult to challenge this party on its own turf. Fiorina (1981) states that party supporters and voters develop a certain degree of brand loyalty based on past party performance. This is also consistent with Shepsle's (1991) findings, as he insists that parties will benefit when they campaign on previously staked-out party positions.

At any time, an existing extreme right party, whether alone in the party system or competing with ideologically close challengers, may wish to relocate to a different quadrant and change its ideological discourse. This move may be a good strategy if the party decides to locate in an ideological quadrant that is currently vacant (without an extreme right party's espousing that particular combination of discourse) and if the electoral potential of this location is high (i.e. there is a concentration of the electorate within this particular quadrant). Although this strategy may help a new or existing party surpass the electoral success of the historic party within that particular party system, it also risks alienating otherwise loyal existing supporters. A party should try to avoid making too many shifts across ideological territory in order to assume multiple ideological identities (i.e. changing the party's official ideological and discursive line). If a party is perceived as frequently changing its location on the core ideological dimensions, then it will cease to have a clear ideological identity and will not be trusted by its potential electorate. Moreover, a move from one quadrant to another will free up the ideological space previously occupied by the party and open it to potential competitors, so the party must be reasonably confident that the new position will have a greater reservoir of voters.

Keeping up with the times

A historic party could also lose out on a potential share of the extreme right electorate if it fails to keep abreast of new developments in voter preferences or if it simply occupies an ideological quadrant that is not attractive to potential extreme right voters in a given party system. For instance, if a new issue (such as opposition to European integration) suddenly becomes salient within the context of a particular election or campaign and the historic party fails to address it, then an entrepreneurial party or party leader may decide to incorporate it within their ideological discourse and benefit from higher levels of electoral success. In the Britain, UKIP emerged as a new and major challenger to the historic force of the BNP based on a virulent populist-reactionary location focused on anti-EU discourse. As a higher concentration of the potential electorate was within this quadrant compared to the xenophobic-repressive quadrant of the BNP, UKIP surpassed the electoral success of the BNP, especially in the European Parliament elections.

Distribution of the potential electorate

The relative electoral success of each party is thus dependent not only upon the appeal of the specific ideological identity that a party chooses to communicate to its electorate but also on the ideological distribution of the potential extreme right electorate across the four extreme right quadrants. In other words, it is logical to assume that some combinations of extreme right discourse are more attractive than others to a potential electorate (see Carter, 2005; Golder, 2003a; and the related discussion in Chapter 2). The distribution of the electorate across the two dimensions and the four conceptions are therefore not uniform but vary according to the preferences of the extreme right electorate. We discuss this further and analyse the consequences in Chapter 7.

In Chapter 2, we stated a series of arguments derived from the conceptual map that relate to each empirical chapter. To recapitulate, with regard to Chapter 6, we state that multiple extreme right parties can only coexist and survive alongside each other in a given party system if they choose different ideological locations within the four possible quadrants of extreme right ideology. A new competitor that chooses to locate in a quadrant already occupied by an existing party will struggle to survive, as a new challenger is at a comparative disadvantage to an existing occupant. A new competitor entering the field should try to locate in a distinctly different quadrant (ideologically opposed, that is, different conceptions of both dimensions) to the one occupied by the existing historic extreme right party. Moreover, each party must communicate a strong and coherent ideological message to its potential electorate. If a party's ideological identity is unclear it will be threatened by parties in neighbouring quadrants, rendering its chances of survival weaker.

We now present a brief overview of each party and its recent history within its respective party system. Then we discuss the impact of each party's ideological location on the dynamics of party competition within each party system. Finally, we outline how each party has had to find its own niche within the extreme right ideological territory and discuss whether each individual party's strategies have been successful or not.

6.3 The French extreme right party family: patterns of internal competition

The tradition of extreme right parties has long been established in France, with historical examples such as the personalised movements led by Boulanger in the nineteenth century and Poujade in 1950s, and the more global experience of the Vichy regime in the Second World War. Within the contemporary system, the historical continuity of extreme right representation in the party system has rested on the relentless presence of the Front National. The party, founded in the 1970s, obtained its first major success in the European Elections of 1984 where it secured its first national-level representation. It readily asserted its position as a serious contender on the French political scene in 1986, when a temporary introduction of proportional representation allowed the FN to acquire a seat in the national parliament. The Front National has grown stronger over recent years, culminating in the massive political earthquake that saw Le Pen access the second round of the 2002 presidential election. As a result, Le Pen has personified the party and doubts are expressed as to what the future of the FN will be when he steps down from power.

The FN is therefore the largest of the extreme right parties and has secured the most electoral success. Potential competitors from within the same party family need to challenge this historic party in order to have any chance of success in the French political system. Indeed, in recent years, the FN has been challenged over its overwhelming share of the potential extreme right electorate. The first contender was the Mouvement National Républicain, which was created when a group of former FN militants seceded from the mother party under the leadership of Bruno Mégret in 1998. Mégret's argument for secession was one of political and electoral efficiency. He and his supporters argued that the provocative rhetoric of Le Pen had become a liability and that his occasional xenophobic jokes had prevented the party from having any foreseeable chance of accessing government, whether in its own right or within a coalition. The MNR hoped that without the overzealous and autocratic Le Pen at its head it could tap into a more moderate and larger electoral reservoir within the extreme right electorate. In other words, the MNR wanted to emphasise a different conception of the two ideological dimensions and take the party in a different direction to that of the FN. Although the coup was severely resented within the ranks of the Front National and there was a lot of agitation between the two parties following the split, in 2006 Le Pen and Mégret entered negotiations regarding non-competing candidacies in the 2007 presidential elections.

In the mid 1990s another competitor emerged to challenge the FN for the potential extreme right electorate. The Mouvement pour la France primarily emerged from a scission of the moderate right on European issues.

Segments of the moderate right violently opposed the ratification of the Maastricht Treaty in 1993 (finally adopted by 51 per cent of voters by referendum) and concluded that the European issue was too important for them to remain members of a party endorsed by a majority of Europhiles. After being founded in 1994, the MPF hesitated for many years between staying within the moderate right camp or moving into new territory and attacking the extreme right potential based on the Eurosceptic theme. The 2002 French presidential elections were a turning point, and with the decisive takeover by de Villiers and sidelining (if not dismissal) of old Gaullist Pasqua, the party was ready to embrace a new direction toward the extreme right electoral territory. The party's new ideological identity became public when discussions were held between the National Front and the MPF on whether an alliance, favoured by many in both parties, would be feasible; however, a long series of disagreements and a fierce struggle for absolute power within the extreme right party family prevented any kind of alliance for the 2007 presidential elections. Nevertheless, in the general elections that followed, the support expressed by prominent MPF member Couteaux for the FN's Marine Le Pen in her second ballot battle against a socialist confirmed the party's ideological line.

With this multifaceted picture of the French extreme right party family in mind, this appears to be a perfect case study to explore the impact of ideological identities on intra-extreme right party competition. Both the MNR and the MPF have had to challenge the historic party of the FN for a share of the potential extreme right electorate. Our main arguments derive from the conceptual map, stated in Chapter 2 but also recapitulated at the beginning of this chapter, suggest that in order to challenge a 'pre-existing' party successfully, each party must choose a distinct and different ideological identity. As discussed later in this section, both the MNR and MPF employ different strategies and tactics to coexist alongside the FN.

The ideological locations of the FN, MNR, and MPF on the conceptual map of extreme right ideology are illustrated in Figure 6.2. The diagram illustrates that as the ideological location of the MPF is quite distinct from the two other parties it is not in direct ideological competition with the FN and MNR. In contrast, the ideological identity of the MNR mimics the discourse of the FN. Unfortunately for the MNR, the FN as the historic party has a significant advantage over the smaller party and thus is able to retain its position within the extreme right territory and obtain the lion's share of the vote. Indeed, the MNR is also hindered by its failure to give a clear ideological message to its potential voters because it straddles the two conceptions of the negative identity dimension.

As seen from the preceding discussion of the French extreme right party family, both the MNR and the MPF had to challenge the historical stronghold of the FN. In order to be successful, each party must choose a distinct ideological identity and locate in a quadrant that is different from that of

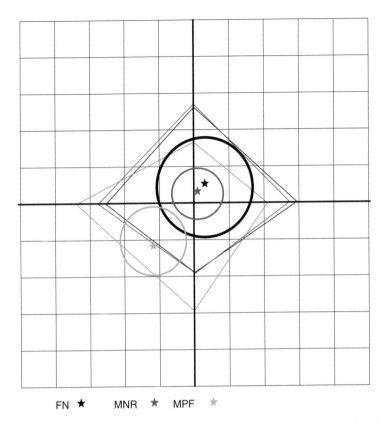

FN ★   MNR ★   MPF ☆

Figure 6.2 Patterns of competition within the French extreme right party family

Notes: The ideological dimensions are the same as in Figure 5.2. The thick circle corresponds to the historic party, the thin ones to its challengers. The diameter of the circles is relative to their electoral strengths.

the main historic party. Despite accusations of extreme xenophobia by the MNR, the FN's current dominant discourse is populist-repressive. This of course may be the result of recent ideological moderation, which has made the FN's core ideological positions less extreme than they were during the 1980s. Newcomers that challenge the historic party can only survive if they occupy a different quadrant than that of the pre-existing party. In this case, a challenger should theoretically choose to locate in the ideologically opposed quadrant of the FN, the xenophobic-reactionary quadrant, and as a result emphasise rather different conceptions of the two fundamental dimensions of extreme right ideology. This strategy ensures that the challenger to the historic party would be in the optimal position to exploit a yet-untouched potential of the extreme right electorate.

As the MPF retained an ideological influence from the moderate right, we would have expected the leadership to choose a soft populist discourse focusing on the Eurosceptic rhetoric when venturing into the newly sought-after extreme right territory. This strategy would have been the least effective to pursue, as the MPF's discourse would have been similar to that of the FN and the FN had a comparative advantage as the historic force. The analysis of the MFP's discourse shows, however, that this was not the strategy implemented by the MPF. Acknowledging that its Eurosceptic credentials would be worthless given the FN's dominant position on the populist dimension, the MPF after some initial hesitation finally decided to locate in the xenophobic-reactionary quadrant. This strategy was perhaps the most effective one the MPF could have pursued, as it was most radically opposed to the FN's ideological position.

By contrast, the MNR, which emerged as a dissident from the FN camp, clearly failed to pursue an effective strategy. Whilst the MNR accused the FN of being too xenophobic, fierce internal tensions erupted within the MNR. Factions of members wanting to push the MNR into adopting a more modern populist ideology clashed with the traditional ideologues within the party who wanted the party to adopt a stronger xenophobic line. As a result, the MNR became more extreme on the xenophobic conception of the negative identity dimension. In terms of its electoral prospects and chances of survival, this was a disastrous decision by the party leadership, as the MNR chose to replicate the same discourse (and located in the same quadrant) as the FN but with an accentuated ideological line, which proved too extreme for the majority of the extreme right electorate. As we outline, however, in our section on theoretical expectations derived from the model (Section 2.7), a that party fails to choose a clear ideological identity and communicates an incoherent message to the electorate (i.e. blurring the emphasis on the populist versus xenophobic conceptions of the negative identity dimension), which the MNR seems to have done, places itself in a highly vulnerable position and has little chance of survival.

Altogether, the MNR failed to distinguish itself from its old rival by replicating a similar discourse to that of the FN and sending mixed messages to its electorate. The MNR has little chance of electoral success whilst it is located in the same ideological quadrant as the historic force of the FN. The electoral implications of these strategic-discursive choices for intra-family party competition are highlighted by the circles representing the parties' electoral appeal in Figure 6.2. The FN occupies the populist-repressive quadrant, has secured a stronghold within the extreme right territory, and has the dominant share of the potential extreme right vote. The MPF has successfully adopted the optimal strategy and has located in the opposite quadrant to that of the FN. The MPF has therefore been able to tap into an unexploited extreme right electorate and has derived some electoral success from this new location in the xenophobic-reactionary quadrant. As a result, and as investigated more fully in Chapter 7, the MPF has obtained a few seats in the 2007 general elections and consistently scores above 3 per cent of the vote in other elections. By contrast, the MNR failed to present itself as a serious challenger for a share of the extreme right vote, as it chose to locate in the same quadrant as the FN, where it was suffocated by the dominance of the historic force.

Moreover, the MNR's fuzziness on the negative dimension undoubtedly handicapped its electoral progression. This failure to capture the extreme right electorate was confirmed in the general elections of 2007, when the MNR scored less than 1 per cent of the vote. On the whole, the theoretical expectations outlined in Section 2.7 seem to have stood the empirical test in the case of the three extreme right parties in France.

6.4 The British extreme right party family: patterns of internal competition

The British extreme right party family, although historically dissimilar to the French case just outlined, is also of interest with respect to the internal dynamics of party competition. Britain has few historical examples of the extreme right ideological tradition such as those of Boulangisme, Vichy, and Poujadisme in France. Few British parties espoused extreme right discourse until the 1970s. The main party that dominated the extreme right political scene in the Britain was the National Front, until it became the victim of a dissident coup in the 1980s, which slowly precipitated its death. In the face of the National Front's demise, the BNP arose as the new champion of the British extreme right. Although the BNP has been largely relegated to the peripheries of the party system, it had several local successes and managed to send two MEPs to the European Parliament in the 2009 elections.

Many believe that the extreme right potential in the United Kingdom is limited, but a challenger emerged in the 1990s that focused on vehement anti-European discourse. The Anti-Federalist League formed in 1993, quickly transformed into the United Kingdom Independence Party, and was readily competing in elections on a predominantly EU withdrawal agenda. Still predominantly a Eurosceptic force, UKIP has recently expanded its electoral appeal and campaigns in local elections on issues such as crime, law and order, and restrictions on immigration. These campaign issues are a direct threat and challenge to the traditional territory of the BNP. The BNP has attempted several times recently to form electoral allegiances in the local and European Parliament elections, but UKIP has so far resisted these attempts and has remained a challenger to the BNP for the potential extreme right vote.

In Britain, the BNP is the historic force new competitors have to face. In contrast to the French extreme right party family, which is structured by strong positions both on the negative identity and authoritarianism dimensions, the British extreme right party family seems to rely more on the negative identity dimension than on the authoritarianism dimension. As Figure 6.3 illustrates, this generates a more horizontal polygon compared to that of the French model. The BNP's ideological location on the conceptual map of extreme right ideology features a dominant tendency to emphasise xenophobic-repressive discourse and a weak reactionary pillar. UKIP had to challenge this position if it wanted to attack the extreme right potential vote. UKIP was in an enviable position, as it could locate in any of the three other ideological quadrants left vacant by the BNP. Obviously, the most logical strategy would be to locate in the quadrant most ideologically

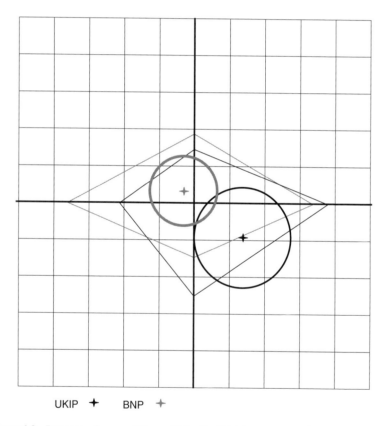

UKIP ✦   BNP ✦

Figure 6.3 Patterns of competition within the British extreme right party family

Notes: The ideological dimensions are the same as Figure 5.2. The thick circle corresponds to the historic party, the thin ones to its challengers. The diameter of the circles is relative to their electoral strengths.

opposed to the BNP's location. UKIP decided this was the most efficient strategy, and located in the populist-reactionary quadrant.

Similar to the French party system, each British extreme right party has a distinct ideological identity on the two ideological dimensions. In France, the MPF took a distinctive location within the xenophobic-repressive quadrant. The British UKIP, on the other hand, takes a distinctive location within the populist-reactionary quadrant, and is therefore not in direct ideological competition with the BNP.

Although UKIP is not the historic party within the extreme right party family, it has reached a stronger electoral position than the historic BNP, suggesting the distribution of the potential extreme right electorate is more favourable to UKIP's location within the populist-reactionary quadrant than that of the xenophobic-repressive discourse of the BNP. UKIP has almost no overlap between its electorate and that of the historic force.

Whilst the BNP was in the most favourable position of having the choice of all four quadrants, it failed to choose the most lucrative location in terms of electoral potential. Most of the potential electorate was in fact located in the ideologically opposed quadrant to the one chosen by the BNP. Fighting a pre-existing party in its own quadrant is a strategy doomed to fail, but a historic advantage never guarantees that an extreme right party will remain dominant when other parties start exploiting the quadrants left vacant. The historic party may be surpassed by a new competitor who exploits the electoral potential of another quadrant. In this case, as seen in Chapter 7, the BNP can hardly expect more than two to three per cent of the vote nationally in general elections. UKIP, on the other hand, excels in European Parliament elections (16.1% in 2004) and has had several successes at local elections.

6.5 The German extreme right party family: patterns of internal competition

In Germany, the Nationaldemokratische Partei Deutschlands has been the stalwart of extreme right ideology. Established in 1964 as a successor to the German Reich Party, the NPD has undergone several transformations including adopting several different names and competing under different guises. With links to several neo-fascist groups, ideological consistency, and the inheritance of key personnel from the German Reich Party, the NPD has faced a number of legal proceedings in the German constitutional court.

The NPD has been the dominant historic force of the German extreme right party family in terms of its history and ideological connections with the fascist legacy; however, Die Republikaner, a challenger from the south of Germany, had the first significant electoral success. Founded in 1983 by former Christlich-Soziale Union (CSU) members, the Republikaner secured an impressive six members of the European Parliament in the 1989 elections. Whilst struggling to gain federal representation, the Republikaner has obtained several successes at the regional level in Bavaria but finds the electoral threshold sometimes too high to surpass. Members of the NPD and the Deutsche Volksunion have attempted to form electoral alliances with the Republikaner but so far these efforts have been rebuffed. For the purpose of this analysis, we consider the Republikaner, not the NPD, as the historic force of the extreme right party family in Germany because it has a much more prominent electoral record and has been largely coherent in its organisation and structure as compared to the NPD.

The DVU was founded by publisher Gerhard Frey as an informal association in 1971 and established as a party in 1987. As of 2011, the party has never surpassed the five per cent threshold that is imposed as a minimum in federal elections, but has gained seats in several state parliaments. In 2004, the DVU entered a non-competition agreement with the NPD for the state elections in Brandenburg and Saxony. As a result, both parties passed the five per cent threshold in their respective states. (The DVU reached 6.1% in the Brandenburg state elections, and the NPD won 9.2% in the Saxony state elections.) After this relatively successful election, the parties formed an electoral alliance for the 2005 federal elections and consequently obtained 1.6 per cent of the total votes nationally. This is more fully examined in Chapter 8.

Historically, the NPD has been the major player on the German extreme right scene, but as stated earlier the Republikaner achieved the first real breakthrough in terms of reinventing the German extreme right. Figure 6.4 shows that Die Republikaner relies on a vaguely defined populist-reactionary stance. This hesitant location is almost symmetric to that of the French MNR. Consistent with our expectations, this position makes the Republikaner vulnerable to attacks from other potential parties within its quadrant as well as in neighbouring quadrants.

In the German case illustrated previously, the NPD has assumed a distinctive ideological identity to that of its two competitors. The weakest of the three parties, the DVU, is struggling to find its niche, although it is not entirely suffocated by its two competitors (unlike the case of the MNR in France). Despite being the only extreme right party within the German system to have a predominantly reactionary discourse on the authoritarian dimension, the Republikaner finds it difficult to define a clear ideological identity within the extreme right ideological spectrum and struggles to compete with the more ideologically defined NPD and DVU.

The NPD was resuscitated after German unification in 1990 with a new image and a strong presence in the former East Germany. The NPD chose a clear populist-repressive location within the extreme right ideological territory (similar to the French FN), whereas the DVU, which made several inroads in several of the Eastern Länder, chose a moderate xenophobic-repressive locate. The DVU's quadrant is opposite to that of the Republikaner, but the NPD is located in a quadrant neighbouring both the Republikaner

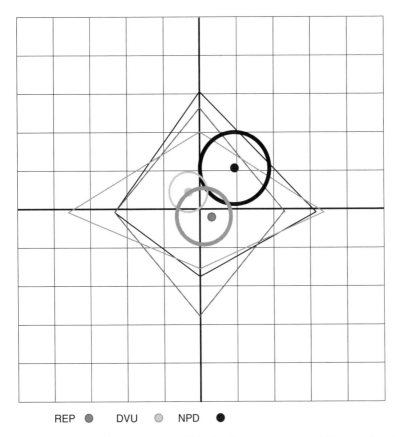

REP ● DVU ○ NPD ●

Figure 6.4 Patterns of competition within the German extreme right party family

Notes: Ideological dimensions are the same as in Figure 5.2. The thick circle corresponds to the historic party, the thin ones to its challengers. The diameter of the circles is relative to their electoral strengths.

and the DVU that made it a natural threat to both parties. Unlike parties of the extreme right party family in France and Britain, the three faces of the German extreme right have settled in three different ideological quadrants as they have chosen to emphasise different conceptions of the two dimensions. This may explain how they have managed to coexist and survive within the same party system. The pattern of competition illustrated by Figure 6.4 is clearly favourable to the NPD, which in the 2000s managed to encroach on some of the electoral potential of the Republikaner in its traditional stronghold in the southwest of Germany. The DVU, with its own distinct ideological identity, has also had space to develop its own niche and record several electoral successes. This confirms the central tenet of our model that if parties of the extreme right party family emphasise different conceptions of the two ideological dimensions then they can coexist successfully within the same party system, as the potential electorates associated with the four different conceptions are discrete and may only overlap at the boundaries of the four quadrants.

6.6　Broader implications: general party competition

In party systems where weak moderate right parties have led unsuccessful election campaigns or have failed to anchor their electorate, extreme right parties can quickly move in and capture an increased share of the vote (Swank & Betz, 2003). Mainstream parties are thus often faced with a dilemma: the choice of implementing accommodative or adversarial strategies (Koopmans & Kriesi, 1997). Using the emergence of the French Front National as an example, we can highlight the different strategies implemented and assess the dynamics of competition when an extreme right party emerges onto the political scene. With its strong anti-immigrant undertone, the FN would prove to be a direct competitor for the right-wing Rassemblement pour la République (Rally for the Republic, or RPR). In response to this threat, the RPR adopted an accommodative strategy, launching an intense campaign to convince voters of its ardent anti-immigrant position, and passed bills restricting the rights of immigrants in France (Pasqua Law of 1986, Debré Law of 1996) and halting further immigration (Pasqua law of 1993). In the 1980s and early 1990s, several RPR and FN candidates made electoral alliances in some local-level elections. The left-wing Parti Socialiste (PS), which was not immune to the threat of the radical right, responded with an adversarial strategy emphasising its opposition to the anti-immigrant policy. Using the strategic-voting logic (votes for the FN would split the right-wing vote, and to prevent a RPR-UDF (Union pour la Démocratie Francaise) victory), the PS hoped Le Pen would gain votes at the expense of the RPR if it implemented proportional representation. Indeed, the FN won 34 seats in the 1986 elections and as a result demolished the vote of the RPR.

Similarly, on 21 April 2002, Jean-Marie Le Pen, the leader of the French Front National, obtained a staggering 16.9 per cent of the vote in the first round of the presidential election. As a result, he was ushered into the second ballot alongside Jacques Chirac. This result caused massive mobilisation of the Left, and young people and demonstrations were organised across France in protest of the electoral result. Le Pen thus failed to garner enough support and lost the election to Chirac in the second ballot. Guiraudon and Schain (2002) note some of the consequences that followed from the shocking electoral success of the FN in 2002. The electoral breakthrough had a considerable impact upon the party system and the dynamic interaction among the mainstream political parties competing for votes. The electoral impact was manifested in a realignment of parties within the system in many voting districts. Le Pen's success also affected the distribution of issue priorities of voters across the political spectrum. The party was also able to gain increasing influence over the policy agenda, as parties of both the Right and the Left tried to combat the influence of the FN and realign themselves on the issues of immigration and the enforcement of law and order. The efforts of the mainstream parties to counterbalance the popularity of the FN by attempting to co-opt some of their policy stances turned out to be futile. Their efforts to offset the electoral success of the FN by directly addressing the issues of immigration and the enforcement of law and order were perceived by many as legitimising the concerns and demands of Le Pen and his party.

In the Netherlands, Pim Fortuyn's campaign centred upon the issue of immigration, particularly xenophobic discourse directed against Moslem migrants. Although this type of rhetoric was a sharp contrast to the traditional neo-liberal backdrop of the Dutch party system, this campaign was by no means something new. In 1989, the leader of the conservative Liberal VVD party (Volkspartij voor Vrijheid en Democratie), Frits Bolkestein, broke the Dutch elite consensus regarding immigration by calling Islam a deviant culture preventing the integration of Moroccan and Turkish immigrants, using terms similar to Fortuyn's pamphlet on 'the Islamization of Dutch culture' that deemed Moslems backward.

Throughout the 1990s, immigration and the integration of Moroccan and Turkish immigrants remained a key campaign issue that often capitalised on the anti-establishment backlash directed against incumbent governments. In the 1994 parliamentary elections, the Dutch Parliamentary Election Study panel survey revealed that almost 50 per cent of voters believed that foreign minorities were an important problem, a score higher than for any other issue.[1] Consequently, Hans Janmaat and two other Centruum Party members were elected. In the 1998 elections, with 24.7 per cent of the vote, the VVD became the second largest parliamentary group and joined the 'purple coalition'. Fortuyn's party was merely tapping into the existing extreme right vote potential and co-opting the policy agenda of the VVD, but this time with an extremely charismatic and flamboyant leader at its figurehead. The incumbent government attempted to reassure voters by introducing tough measures on illegal immigrants and restricting the number of applications for asylum. Rather than restoring confidence in its ability to keep the problem under control, the government's policies highlighted the issue further and gave yet more legitimacy to the claims of the LPF.

The strategy of co-opting issues of extreme right discourse has not always been dismissed as ineffective. The British and German cases seem to demonstrate that this strategy can work to hamper the progress of extreme right parties in given political systems. Kitschelt & McGann (1995) argues that the sharp shift to the xenophobic right by the Thatcher leadership was a key determinant in the demise of the British National Front in the later 1970s.

Minkenberg (1998) also comments that when the German mainstream parties co-opted the issue of immigration, extreme right parties lost out in terms of their electoral success. Despite the success of the strategy, he argues that 'at the sub-national level, these parties (extreme right parties) have demonstrated greater staying power than analysts were willing to concede' after their decline in the wake of the major parties' asylum compromise of 1993. Although periodic thrusts at the sub-national level have allowed the Republikaner, NPD, and DVU to influence immigration policy during the 1990s, the impact of these parties has been rather limited because of their fragmentation and inconsistent electoral success. On the other hand, in the context of the highly centralised French political system, decentralised structures are reinforced by strong local party units that enable parties such as the FN, MNR, and MPF to gain important policy-making roles. These local structures can sometimes magnify the influence of the extreme right onto the national political stage. On several recent occasions, mainstream parties entered into electoral alliances with the FN in some local and regional elections.

Extreme right parties often find they have the power to blackmail parties of the mainstream right by threatening to encroach upon their electoral territory or challenging them to take a stand on issues they would not have otherwise have approached. This was the case of UKIP, BNP, and Conservative Party in the United Kingdom during the 2005 general elections. The Conservatives were pushed into a tight corner by increasing pressure from UKIP about the question of immigration quotas in the United Kingdom. Michael Howard, the leader of the Conservative Party, was pushed into a tight corner until he eventually declared that it would indeed consider imposing immigration quotas. This move proved to be highly unpopular with the general public. It was interpreted as a legitimisation of the extreme right demands and delivered precious media attention and publicity into the arms of the extreme right parties. If mainstream parties react to the challenge of the encroaching extreme right party by incorporating elements of their discourse, they run the risk of normalising the extreme right's discourse and even its ideology. The Austrian, Swiss, and Italian governments have all been victims of such accusations after incorporating parties of the extreme right into national coalition governments. If the moderate right parties are perceived not to respond to the challenges posed by the extreme right, then they face the prospect that their campaigns may be overshadowed by the more provocative and attention-grabbing discourse of their competitors on the extreme right.

In any explicitly or implicitly spatial model whereby parties and voters can move along ideological lines, a question has to be raised as to whether parties are simply trying to catch up with voters or creating demand by aggregating some specific ideological preferences around a strategically chosen point in an almost entrepreneurial way (Schattschneider, 1957). This question is implicitly present in our strategic-discursive model: will parties move along the negative identity and authoritarianism dimensions to discover a statically optimal reservoir of votes, or by choosing a location will parties create an ideological magnet which will structure political demand to attract a potential electorate? As always in such cases, the answer invariably entails a bit of both movements. On the basis of the specific research design, we cannot fully evaluate the dynamics of reciprocal ideological influence between extreme right parties and their potential voters. This can be explored in other parts of our research that include a dynamic time component.

Within the framework of this book, we focus primarily on the race of extreme right parties for their voters for two reasons: First, in a multiple-party context, not in general, but even within the extreme right family, there is an analytical need to view the political world first through the eyes of the parties which maximise their appeal. Only in this way can we establish their real leeway in terms of movement on the two strategic-discursive dimensions developed earlier in Chapter 3. Second, as pointed out earlier, one of the puzzles of extreme right success in some European countries such as the United Kingdom is that the overall rate of success of the extreme right as a family sometimes seems bound to remain low until suddenly increasing sharply and rapidly, as has been the case with UKIP. Regardless of whether a party such as UKIP then shaped the political preferences of British extreme right voters, it thus seems conceivable to assert that the party discovered a ground which had real electoral potential and had not previously been exploited by other extreme right parties. Once again, the fact that an extreme right party will target the greenest possible electoral pasture should not make us forget that once the party settles down there, or indeed once any party moves from one ideological location to another, this will most likely also have an impact on voter preferences in that it can lead or shape ideological demand over time. Ideological demand should not be considered static. A strategic-discursive location that proved most fruitful at one time might well become obsolete, or one which was irrelevant might progressively become effective as citizens' preferences, worries, and problems evolve or as other parties offer changes.

We now summarise this chapter and draw upon some of its main conclusions.

6.7   Summary

Our findings in this chapter show that when it comes to understanding the coexistence and survival of multiple extreme right parties in a given party system, it is crucial to analyse the specific strategic-discursive choices each party has had to face when deciding where to locate. This is not just a simple question of whether there is enough room for several of them or indeed whether there are enough extreme right voters. Instead, the puzzle is multifaceted. We have to consider the location of the historic extreme right force and contemplate the best strategy for a competitor to secure an optimal position in order to challenge the dominant party for the potential extreme right vote. We must also consider the dynamics of competition outside the extreme right territory, for example, in the global universe of left-right party competition. The strategies of mainstream right-wing parties may also affect the location of an extreme right party because of accommodative or adversarial tactics.

We have shown that across three very different party systems similar patterns exist within the strategies of internal party competition in the extreme right party family. If two parties decide to locate in the same ideological quadrant, a comparative advantage will be given to the historic force; thus, a new party may fail to survive, as it risks being suffocated by the dominant extreme right party that has a pre-existing tradition of that particular ideological identity and an anchor within that specific extreme right electorate. Parties that do not communicate a strong ideological identity (i.e. that do not sufficiently emphasise one conception of the two dimensions) will find it hard to mobilise their potential extreme right electorate and are likely to be overshadowed by their competitors.

New parties that choose an ideologically opposed quadrant to that of the historic force and that communicate a clear and distinct ideological identity can coexist alongside the dominant party and may in some circumstances even surpass the dominant party's electoral success. In this respect, our findings present new perspectives on some of the paradoxes found within the existing literature concerning the heterogeneous electoral support of the European extreme right. Most studies that investigate the profile of an extreme right voter assume political competition is fixed by voter attitudes that are rooted in socio-economic experiences. The underlying model is one of demand for discourse or ideology that creates opportunities or dilemmas for political parties. This perspective prompted those studying the social composition of the populist vote to ask what voters' common grievances are and attempt to define new alignments. The demand model of political competition compensates for the void in Downs' spatial model (1967) that fails to define how the dimensions of political space are defined, or how they can be changed. As seen in this chapter, extreme right parties can and sometimes do change their strategic-discursive choices. They can often manipulate salient issues and change their direction because they are not tied to exclusive bases of electoral support. In contrast to many other mainstream parties, whose electoral bases are often supported by traditional socio-economic cleavages, extreme right parties are able to combine a discursive appeal that seduces voters from many different social categories.

The variety of strategic-discursive choices extreme right parties can make and the interdependence between internal and external party competition within limited dimensions transform a constrained ideological territory into a chessboard of partisan politics. In this way, we also need to consider the ideological distribution of the potential extreme right electorate over the four quadrants of ideology, as different ideological locations may offer variable electoral payoffs. This is indeed the question we set ourselves for the final empirical chapter.

Before addressing that question in Chapter 7, we analyse the long-term consistency and variations of the discourse of individual extreme right parties. If the strategic-discursive location of a given party influences patterns of competition, particularly in party systems where several extreme right formations compete against each other, do parties have an incentive to change their location over time, especially if they feel they are not realising their full potential? We now look at time-series strategic-discursive variations by analysing long-term press releases of five extreme right parties.

7
How Stable Is the Discourse of Extreme Right Parties over Time? Analysis of the Press Releases of Five European Extreme Right Parties

We have now explored the ideological diversity of extreme right parties across 25 parties in 16 different political systems. Extreme right party ideology varies along two complementary dimensions (negative identity and authoritarianism) and four different pillars (xenophobic and populist for the negative identity dimension, and reactionary and repressive for the authoritarian dimension). Parties are thus split into four clusters or quadrants, from the most frequent to the least frequent: populist-repressive, xenophobic-repressive, populist-reactionary, and xenophobic-reactionary parties.

Political parties' choice of quadrant to occupy within a given political system has a major effect on their internal competition. Indeed, we show that if several extreme right parties competing against each other in a single political system decide to occupy the same quadrant, they cannot co-exist successfully. They can potentially conquer different segments of the potential extreme right electorate if they choose to locate in separate quadrants, particularly if they choose 'opposed' quadrants.

We now turn to the dynamics of extreme right discourse. Considering that extreme right parties can vary their strategic expressions of negative identity and authoritarianism along the xenophobic-populist and reactionary-repressive axes, do they use this latitude to vary their discourse over time? Does extreme right party discourse differ depending on the period of the electoral cycle involved, particularly campaign periods versus non-electoral periods?

We answer these questions by looking at the quarterly press releases of five major European extreme right parties, the French Front National, the British BNP, the Swiss SVP, the Belgian Vlaams Belang, and the Danish Dansk Folkeparti, over periods ranging from five to nine years in the 2000s. Using the official press releases published by each of these five parties, we measure the relative occurrence (PCW) of xenophobic, populist, reactionary, and repressive references quarter by quarter.[1] Press releases are quite different from party manifestos. They are directed at the media and intended to publicise the party's views on specific events and issues. In the next few pages, we review each set of results party by party, then synthesise them in the concluding section of this chapter.

Based on the map of extreme right parties compiled in Chapter 5, we focus on five parties from all four quadrants: two from the main populist-repressive quadrant (the Front National in France and the Vlaams Belang in Belgium), and one each from the xenophobic-repressive (British BNP), populist-reactionary (Swiss SVP), and xenophobic-repressive (Danish DF) parties.

7.1 Tailoring discourse to elections? The Front National from 1999 to 2008

As discussed earlier in this book, for many the French Front National remains a typical example of the modern European extreme right party. Its structure, organisation, often provocative discourse and internal diversity as well as its ability to 'trouble' the electoral game of the French party system and its longevity have all been seen by many commentators and fellow European extreme right activists alike as both a potential model of success and a potential recipe for marginalisation. The FN is one of the most and longest established extreme right parties in Europe, and, as discussed in Chapter 5, is pivotally a populist-repressive party; that is, it is also a member of the largest cluster of extreme right parties in our dataset.

In this sense, it is useful to look at the evolution of the FN's as translated into its press releases over ten years, from 1999 to 2008. This period has been particularly critical for the Front National. The start of the period corresponds to the biggest schism in the history of contemporary European extreme right politics with the implosion of the movement and creation of the MNR, soon followed by a poor showing in the European elections of 1999 and numerous comments pointing towards the expected death of the French extreme right. Three years later, in April 2002, the phoenix was emerging from the ashes and Jean-Marie Le Pen created an earthquake in French politics by beating the French left to qualify for the second round of the French presidential election, where he subsequently lost to unpopular incumbent Jacques Chirac after the creation of a 'Front Republicain' against the FN leader. A few years of quiet stability followed for the FN, as did a moment of hope with the victory of the 'No' in the French referendum on a European Constitution in May 2005. Then came a new fear for the party's life (and financial sustainability) on the part of its members and leaders following the severe defeat of the party in the 2007 presidential elections where the FN was completely sidelined, not only by Nicolas Sarkozy from the right and Ségolène Royal from the left, but also by François Bayrou from

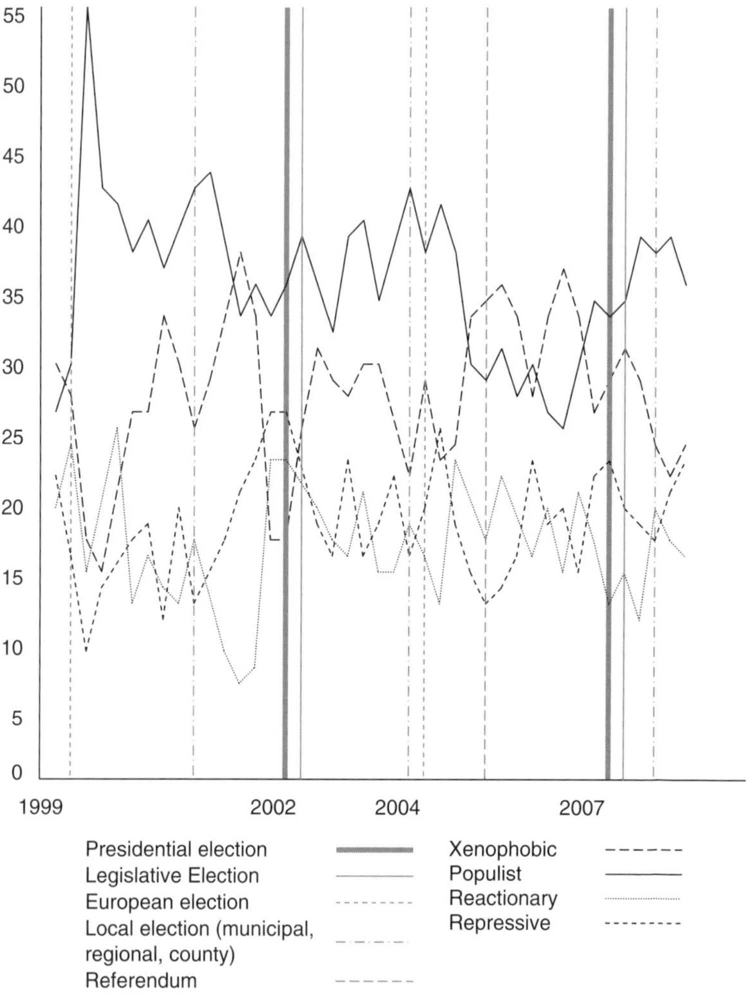
55
50
45
40
35
30
25
20
15
10
5
0
1999
2002
2004
2007
Presidential election
Legislative Election
European election
Local election (municipal, regional, county)
Referendum
Xenophobic
Populist
Reactionary
Repressive

Figure 7.1 Evolution of the discourse of the Front National from 1999 to 2008

the centre. This major counter-performance by the FN, followed by another poor showing in the June legislative elections, opened the door to the post-Jean-Marie Le Pen succession, which many commentators and journalists perceived as a succession war between the 'eternal no2' of the party, Bruno Gollnisch and Le Pen's own daughter Marine Le Pen, who aimed to incarnate a more modern and less provocative style within the party family. The succession war was ultimately won by the latter in January 2011. The period was also 'election rich' with two presidential elections (2002 and 2007), two legislative elections (same years), two European elections (1999 and 2004), as well as two municipal elections (1991 and 1998), two regional elections (1998 and 2004), three county elections (2001, 2004, and 2008) and one extremely salient referendum (2005).

Figure 7.1 represents the evolution of the discourse of the Front National in the context of these electoral challenges and of the periods of crisis and hope the Front National went through during those ten years. We see in the figure that the populist-repressive nature of the Front National is clearly confirmed by its press releases. Similarly, we confirm the negative correlation between the two negative identity pillars (xenophobic and populist) and between the two authoritarian pillars (reactionary and repressive).

Even more interesting is the way in which the focus of the Front National's discourse changes over time. Although over the ten-year period we witness no permanent switch from one type of discourse to another, The cyclical variations are truly interesting in that they represent significant forms of discourse adaptation around election cycles. They unfold as follows:

1. Most impressive is the way the balance between populist and xenophobic discourse is modulated in the run-up to all national and local elections. Every time an election approaches, xenophobic discourse is significantly toned down and populist discourse reinforced instead. After the election, xenophobic discourse picks up again. This phenomenon seems to correspond to a strategy whereby xenophobic references are perceived as provocative and election killers which must therefore be avoided in the run-up to elections in order to avoid alienating potential voters. In contrast, when the election is over, the cost of xenophobic references becomes much lower; they could be construed as attention-seeking in that they are far more likely to attract media coverage in periods when extreme right parties do not benefit from a natural salience.

2. The situation is a little bit different for European Parliament elections, even more so the French referendum on a European constitution. On these occasions, xenophobic discourse is heightened and in the case of the 2005 referendum even surpassed populist references fairly significantly. When Europe-related voting is to occur, xenophobic references are therefore not considered detrimental to electoral attractiveness; rather, such references would help capture a segment of the electorate which would be sensitive to such nationalist argumentation.

3. The balance between reactionary and repressive discourse is similarly affected by the election calendar. Most impressively, in the run-up to presidential elections the party significantly strengthens its repressive references. The repressive discourse represents a potentially fruitful choice for policy areas in which many extreme right parties such as the Front National arguably benefit from issue ownership; however, the repressive pillar is also the most propitious to an individual, charismatic

presentation of leadership which corresponds both to the tradition of extreme right parties (not least the FN, which had Le Pen as a strong leader for many years) and to the nature of candidate-centric presidential elections.

4. In contrast again, in the case of European Parliament elections and the 2005 referendum on the constitutional treaty, repressive discourse was toned down and partly replaced by a much stronger emphasis on the reactionary discourse which surpassed its repressive counterparts in both the 1999 elections and in the 2005 referendum.

5. Reactionary discourse also primes over a repressive one in the run-up to local elections and surpassed it every time in 2001, 2004, and 2008. Arguably, the reactionary end of the authoritarian dimension is more suited to elections which take place at a level at which citizens' identities and historical heritage are most naturally rooted.

The Front National is fundamentally a populist-repressive extreme right party, but seems to excel at tailoring its discourse to the fairly hectic electoral cycles of the political system in which it competes. For presidential elections, the main first-order elections in France and occasion favouring candidate-centric campaigns and inclusiveness, the Front National focuses on its trademark populist-repressive discourse and significantly tones down any xenophobic reference. When it comes to local elections, be they municipal, regional, or county-level (cantonales), the party retains its populist focus but replaces repressive references by reactionary ones which may be more suited to localist, heritage-centric levels of government. Finally, when it comes to European occasions (both European elections and referenda on Europe), the Front National openly switches its discourse from predominantly populist to primarily xenophobic, and associates these xenophobic references to reactionary references which are most susceptible to attract those 'losers of modernity' which have been considered by the literature to make up a large part of Eurosceptic crowds. Finally, outside of elections, the FN goes for more provocative and attention-seeking xenophobic references, which are more likely to attract media coverage than their populist alternatives.

7.2   Subtle changes: evolution of Belgian Vlaams Belang discourse from 2002 to 2008

According to our analysis of their manifesto, the Vlaams Belang is a second member of the populist-repressive sub-family of extreme right parties, although its profile is far different from that of the Front National. Vlaams Belang is more recent, and first and foremost emerged as a Flemish separatist party which generalised its discourse to become a prominent member of the European extreme right family according to most of the literature.

The party first emerged as the Vlaams Blok, then was judged (in first instance, in appeal, and again with a judgement upheld by the Supreme Court) to have breached the Belgian laws on racism and xenophobia by the Belgian court system. Facing a fine and a need to abandon part of its manifesto, the Vlaams Blok dissolved and re-emerged as the Vlaams Belang in 2004; however, voters and commentators alike widely perceived this new party to be a resurgence of the same party by despite its shedding the '70 steps' which had founded the Vlaams Belang since 1992. Indeed, the 'cordon sanitaire' formed by all other Belgian political parties to keep the Vlaams Blok away from power and illustrate its difference from the values of the rest of the Belgian parties was extended to the Vlaams Belang as well. As a result, consider the Vlaams Blok and Vlaams Belang's manifestos as a unified time series, and references to Vlaams Belang throughout the following material include the party itself as well as its predecessor the Vlaams Blok.

Since the early 1990s, the Vlaams Belang has rapidly progressed as one of the strongest political parties in Flanders. It competes in national, local (municipal, provincial, regional), and European elections in both Flemish and French-speaking parts of the countries even though its electoral basis is clearly strong in the former and marginal in the latter. In the period of interest, the Vlaams Belang fought two federal elections in 2003 and 2007, one European election in 2004, one regional election (held at the same time in 2004), and provincial and municipal elections (held concurrently in 2006). Variations in the strategic discursive emphasis of the Vlaams Velang, illustrated by Figure 7.2, are as interesting as that noted for the Front National but quite different in essence.

1. Like the Front National, the Vlaams Velang rethinks its discourse in electoral periods, decreasing xenophobic references and conversely increasing populist references.; however, unlike the Front National, the Vlaams Velang seems to treated all elections in the same way, with no significant variation of the party's discourse on the authoritarian dimension, which becomes largely secondary in the party's press releases.
2. The main difference with the Front National is that the Vlaams Belang seems to evolve in the long term. The authoritarian dimension is marginal and always dominated by the repressive pillar, but the dominant negative identity dimension switches progressively from a dominance of xenophobic references at the beginning of the period to a permanent preponderance of populist references from the middle of 2006.

The press releases published by the Vlaams Belang since 1998 show that an extreme right party can also progressively shift its position from the xenophobic-repressive positions that seemed dominant until 2006, to the

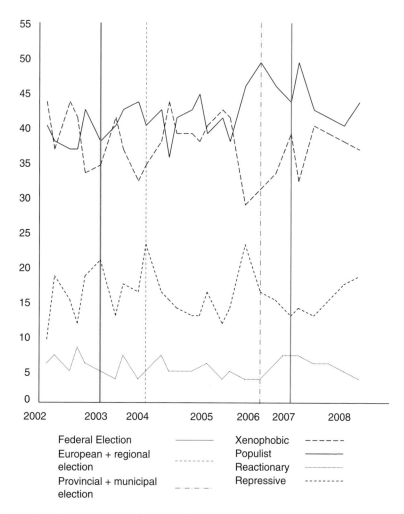

Figure 7.2   Evolution of the discourse of the Vlaams Belang from 2002 to 2008

populist-repressive positions that seem to characterise the late press releases of the party but also the manifesto we analysed in Chapter 5.

7.3   A change of focus: evolution of BNP discourse from 2004 to 2009

The British BNP remains one of the relatively less well-known members of the European extreme right family. Partly joined by a number of former members of the British National Front, partly new party, the BNP has been

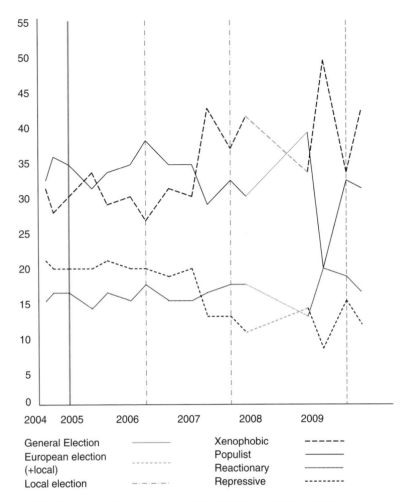

General Election	————	Xenophobic	– – – – –	
European election		Populist	————	
(+local)	- - - - - - -	Reactionary	··············	
Local election	–·–·–·–·	Repressive	- - - - - - - -	

Figure 7.3 Evolution of the discourse of the BNP from 2004 to 2009

Note: Greyed lines correspond to press release missing period.

perceived by the literature as relatively fragmented, with different sub-groups and politicians with diverging preferences and interests (and occasional significant internal crises, notably in recent months).

In the period of interest, the party competed in one general election (in 2005), one European election (in 2009), and yearly local and council elections.[2] The period also included one of the most notable successes of the party in recent years, when the BNP won two seats in the 2009 European

Parliament elections. The internal difficulties of the party, with some internal rifts, came after the end of the period covered by our analysis.

From the manifesto analysis in Chapter 5, we see the BNP emerge as a marginally xenophobic-repressive party with little emphasis on either dimension of discourse, which makes it particularly interesting to look at how the party's discourse evolves over time. Whether this rather narrow balance between xenophobic and populist pillars on the one hand and repressive and reactionary pillars on the other hand is permanent or the result of frequent changes in focus is another point of interest. In this context, Figure 7.3 summarises how the focus of the BNP's press releases evolves from 2004 to 2009, looking particularly at the four pillars of discourse highlighted by our model with some very interesting patterns.

1. The BNP's discourse does not seem to change consistently as elections near, unlike that seen with the Front National and the Vlaams Belang. The variations that transpire through the analysis of the five years of BNP press releases seem more related to long-term variations than to election cycles.
2. By contrast, the discourse of the BNP seems somewhat more volatile, and includes relatively frequent and significant changes of focus within the period as well as an apparent pattern of focus switches over time on both dimensions of extreme right ideology. By and large, the press releases of the party progressively switched from a predominantly populist-repressive focus to a predominantly xenophobic-reactionary one.

The change of focus of the BNP over time thus looks stronger than those of the BNP and VB, but without the sensitivity to electoral cycles that we noted in the other two cases.

7.4   The most volatile party? Discourse of the SVP from 2002 to 2009

The Swiss SVP is a relative newcomer to the European extreme right scene. Although it is a relatively old party, it was at the centre of Swiss politics before a significant change of its ideological stance, which currently makes most political scientists consider it part of the extreme right party family. In this context, the party has made quite an impact by managing a series of solid electoral successes, a strong entry in the Swiss council of ministers where it is now systematically represented within a new configuration of the 'golden formula' where it marginalised other previously stronger parties. The SVP also achieved significant national and international visibility through somewhat colourful and provocative campaigns, notably against minarets and for the expulsion of foreigners with crime convictions, media presence, and communication strategies, most famously embodied by

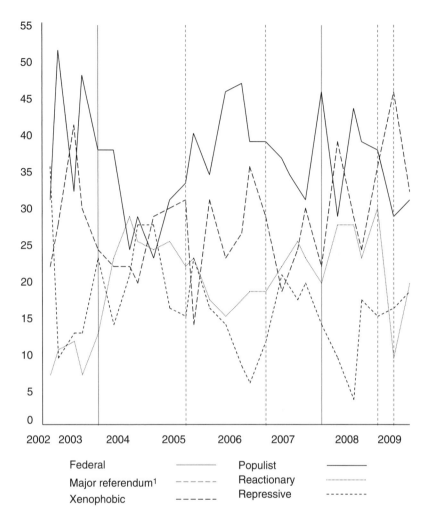

Figure 7.4 Evolution of the discourse of the SVP from 2002 to 2009

Notes: Switzerland has referenda several times each year. Only the most salient ones are depicted here.

posters involving a black and several white sheep, and a game involving questions on immigrants.

Unlike what most other political systems in Europe and the world, Switzerland has federal elections with relatively little impact on the national life of the country; by contrast, referenda ('votations') are frequent and can concern a large variety of legislative proposals, some of which have been prime ground for the SVP to formulate its positions (e.g. referenda on minarets in Switzerland, co-operation with the European Union, the expulsion of foreigners with crime convictions). The relatively minor impact of elections, despite two having taken place in the period covered in our analysis (2003 and 2007), and the occurrence of frequent and occasionally very salient referenda create an institutional context which is different from that of other European extreme right parties. These referenda are issue-specific and can create more volatility in press release topics, as they encourage voters to make a specific choice each time. The evolution of the party's discourse is represented in Figure 7.4. It confirms the notion that referenda can fragment and disturb the strategic discursive consistency of an extreme right party. Thus:

1. The SVP's scores on all four pillars are amongst the most volatile over time. Each of the four pillars has been the most salient in SVP discourse during at least one quarter in the period analysed.
2. Federal elections lead to a stronger populist rhetoric; major referenda lead to the abrupt strengthening of specifically relevant pillars of extreme right ideology. Their frequency leads to apparent inconsistencies in discourse.
3. It is difficult to draw definitive conclusions about long-term changes, but, over time, reactionary and xenophobic discourse seem to gain ground whereas repressive discourse has gone down.

The SVP thus presents a fascinating profile: that of a populist-reactionary party which needs to adapt its discourse constantly to the rapid rhythm of direct democracy in the country. This can give the impression of a more volatile and less readable discourse than that of most other European extreme right parties and makes it difficult to understand whether the party is going through a long-term change in strategic discursive focus or through incessant adaptations to nationally topical issues.

7.5   The most consistent party? Variation in Dansk Folkeparti press releases from 2001 to 2008

For a long time, political scientists have debated whether Scandinavian extreme right parties represent a specific sub-type within the party family. As a prime example, the Danish Folkeparti has been a significant long-term player within the Danish political scene and has sometimes become a necessary silent supporter of right-wing coalitions without entering government or being considered right wing by the Conservative or Liberal parties in the country. Since the beginning of the 2000s, the party has consistently polled between 12 and 15 per cent of the vote, presenting itself as a significant force in a country where the balance between centre-left and centre-right has always been narrow. The DF has neither been a coalition member, like

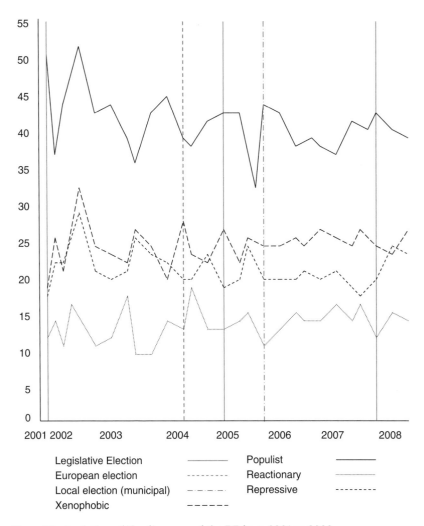

Figure 7.5 Evolution of the discourse of the DF from 2001 to 2008

some Italian and Austrian parties included in the analysis, nor openly ostracised and rejected by the rest of the party system, like its equivalents in France, Belgium, Germany, and the United Kingdom.

In this context, it is extremely interesting to see how the DF has progressively managed to find a place on the extreme right ideological map when looking at its press releases from 2001 to 2008. This period encompasses three legislative elections, one European election, and one local election. Denmark has also been the theatre of some fairly tight referenda on

European Union questions in recent years, but not in the period covered (a referendum on the euro took place in 2000 and another on royal succession in 2009, with an expressed intention to hold a new euro referendum in the country in the near future). Analysing the manifesto of the DF, the party clearly sat within the xenophobic-reactionary quadrant of the extreme right ideological map. Looking at press releases, we can confirm whether this is indeed the case of the party's day-to-day communication, and whether its ideological identity is stable or changed by electoral cycles. The results are represented by Figure 7.5. We note the following findings:

1. An analysis of the DF's party manifesto put it clearly into the xenophobic-reactionary quadrant, but the party's press releases put it clearly in the opposite populist-repressive quadrant. This comes as a surprise: the DF is the only one of the five parties whose press releases have showed such a discrepancy.
2. The DF is by far the most stable party in terms of the strategic- discursive focus of its press releases over the eight-year period. The predominance in both negative identity and authoritarianism dimensions never switches during the period, and only the balance between negative identity and authoritarian discourse changes a bit cyclically.
3. Notwithstanding the general stability of the party's press releases, electoral cycles do have an impact on the party's discourse by reinforcing the predominance of populist discourse in the run-up to all types of elections.

The DF is therefore as stably populist-repressive in its press releases as it was strongly xenophobic-reactionary in its manifesto. With the impact of election cycles confirmed, the DF thus shows a new pattern compared to the other four parties.

7.6   Conclusions and summary

After the analysis of party manifestos in Chapter 5, our focus on party press releases provides significant new insights, which help us understand better how extreme right party discourse varies in principle and over time, as well as the impact of electoral cycles on the parties' messages to media and citizens.

Having considered the press releases published by five different parties from each of the four quadrants of extreme right ideology over periods varying from five to ten years, we can now draw a number of conclusions which are potentially important to our understanding of extreme right politics:

1. Press releases are a different animal from party manifestos. They have different styles, targets, visibility, and objectives. This explains that although

most parties showed the same tendencies throughout their press releases and manifestos, one of them, the Dansk Folkeparti, has a significantly different strategic discursive focus in its press releases as compared to its manifestos.

2. When it comes to the ideological focus of extreme right parties press releases over time, it can be anything from highly stable to highly volatile, depending on the constraints of the institutional system, the ideological robustness of the party, and the impact of election cycles. We fundamentally have four different models, each represented in the case of the five parties whose press releases we have analysed:

a. Stability: Danish Folkeparti press releases vary relatively little over time regardless of short- and long-term constraints.

b. Inconsistency: The strategic discursive focus of the Swiss SVP's press releases seems to change all the time, with each of the four pillars dominating at one point or other. Institutional constraints, not least the changing pattern of policy salience imposed by frequent referenda on questions that can be key for the party, largely seem to create this situation.

c. Transformation: Some parties, such as the British BNP and to a certain extent the SVP, seem to have changed their main ideological focus over time. Over a relatively long period, the party migrates from one quadrant of extreme right ideology to another where it seems to settle down in a stable way.

d. Adaptation: In this final pattern, predominantly illustrated by the French FN but also to an extent by the VB and the DF, the party's discourse is adapted cyclically around the timing of various types of elections without necessarily incurring long-term changes. Typically, this means that in electoral periods the populist pillar is heightened and the xenophobic one toned down, although for the French FN xenophobic and reactionary pillars can also be mobilised in the context of elections and referenda related to European questions.

These four possible forms of time-series variation lead us to some important conclusions. First, the adaptation of discourse to election cycles is particularly noteworthy. A number of commentators have declared themselves surprised that such high proportions of voters will vote for parties which regularly make provocative comments. Extreme right parties seem to modulate their discourse strategically in the run-up to elections. These cyclical variations can also explain why many commentators suggest that the discourse of extreme right parties is not the same all the time (although we do not know whether similar variations exist amongst other types of parties). Party discourse does indeed change, because it gets adapted to electoral occasions; however, in such cases populist discourse is inflated and xenophobic discourse deflated. This could explain the relative predominance of populist parties over xenophobic ones in the manifesto analysis, as many parties write their manifestos in the run-up to major elections.

The second crucial point is about the possible migration of extreme right parties in the longer term within the extreme right conceptual map. Such movement takes time, and it may well be at least partly in reaction to patterns of internal competition as discussed in Chapter 6 (notably in the case of the BNP); however, consistent with our model, a party without a specific internal competitor can successively explore various positions within the extreme right ideological territory, probing different locations until it finds one that maximises its electoral appeal and the adequation between party discourse, members preferences, and electoral attractiveness.

Third and finally, the analysis emphasises the interdependence between extreme right parties and all forms of external constraint, including internal and external competitors as well as types and rhythms of elections. These elections affect the discourse of extreme right parties and their ability to develop some or other parts of their political preferences in order to signal to potential voters that their preferences are similar. Whether its position matches or does not matches the preferences of those potential voters largely determines the capacity of an extreme right party to be viable and electorally successful, and to make a lasting mark on its political system. The question of whether European extreme right parties can match potential voters or not and under what circumstances now occupies our attention in Chapter 8.

8
Match or Mismatch? Investigating the Match between Extreme Right Parties' Ideological Positions and the Ideological Preferences of Voters

8.1 Introduction

This chapter presents the final empirical component of the book. In the first section of this chapter, we discuss the various characteristics attributed to the social groups that are susceptible to vote for an extreme right party. The existing literature has often highlighted a few social groups consistently more likely than others to vote for parties of the extreme right. On the other hand, comparative analysis shows a remarkable heterogeneity within the social bases of extreme right parties. In the second part of this chapter, we conduct a quantitative analysis of some selected questions presented to respondents in a mass survey conducted in June 2009. A detailed description of the survey questions we selected and the methodology we used is presented in Chapter 3 and are outlined in Appendix C. Throughout this chapter, we look at the match between the parties' ideological locations as indicated by the elite interviews and the analysis of party manifestos, and the ideological distribution of these parties' actual and potential voters. Finally, the third section presents an analysis of the electoral success of the parties that we have studied in order to evaluate their relative success or failure in making a connection with their respective electorates.

8.2 The concept of potential extreme right voters

Many studies simply look at those who have voted (or say they will vote) for an extreme right party. This concept is problematic in a number of ways. Firstly, the notion of voting choice is a crude measure of citizens' partisan preferences and one which can be rather seriously affected by institutional differences between electoral and party systems (van der Eijk et al., 2006; van der Eijk &

Franklin, 1996); however, a number of voters are reluctant to admit they voted for extreme right parties. This problem, known as 'social acceptability' by social scientists is well known of survey companies, who widely admit they use ad hoc correction formulae to compensate for such voter reluctance. Although ad hoc corrective coefficients can be pragmatically understandable in the case of commercial survey companies trying to infer the likely level of electoral success of an extreme right party in a given election, we need to estimate effectively who the likely extreme right voters are, in order to explain their behaviour and perceptions, and how they differ from the rest of the citizenry.

In this context, using propensity to vote models (van der Eijk et al., 2006; van der Eijk & Franklin, 1996), we thus look into the concept of the potential extreme right voter. In a nutshell, we consider that for political and moral reasons a significant proportion of citizens would never consider voting for an extreme right party. Our understanding is that there is a significant difference between somebody who would fully exclude ever voting for an extreme right party in their life (a '0' on a propensity-to-vote question) and someone who would consider it (anyone else). Additionally, measuring propensity to vote for an extreme right party separately from an actual vote allows us to consider the important question of what leads some potential extreme right voters to choose an extreme right party in elections while other potential voters end up deciding neither to cast their vote for a competitor nor to vote at all.

We measured the propensity to vote for all major parties and extreme right parties in Austria, Belgium (French- and Dutch-speaking parts separately), France, Germany, Italy, and Great Britain, on a scale from 0 to 10. Although for the purpose of all of our statistical analysis we use the full scale of propensities to vote, we recoded the general results into four different levels of self-assessed probability for each voter to ever vote for an extreme right party:

1. Self-excluded voters (propensity to vote of 0 for all extreme right parties competing in the country, thus NOT a potential extreme right voter);
2. Low potential (propensity to vote for an extreme right party rated between 1 and 3);
3. Medium potential (propensity to vote for an extreme right party rated between 4 and 6); and
4. High potential (propensity to vote for an extreme right party rated between 7 and 10).

Table 8.1 and corresponding Plate 6 summarize the distribution of citizens of the different countries included in this section in terms of their likeliness to ever vote for one of the extreme right parties competing in their party system. The results show first and foremost that the proportion of potential extreme right voters is much higher than the proportion of actual voters (even more so than the self-identified proportion in mass surveys). Overall, one in two voters (49.8%) is a potential extreme right voter. These consist of 14.4 per cent of low potential (i.e. unlikely) voters, 16.9 per cent of medium potential voters, and 18.5 per cent of high potential voters. The average propensity to vote for an extreme right party in the seven systems is 2.77 on the 0 to 10 scale.

The table and plate show the proportion of potential voters varies significantly across the seven political systems. Indeed, these represent 78.7 per cent of total voters in Flanders, but only 24.4 per cent in Germany. Similarly, only 6.3 per cent of the German respondents appeared to be high potential voters, compared to 35.7 per cent in Italy and 33.6 per cent in Flanders. Overall, the highest propensities to vote for extreme right parties are to be found in Flanders (4.60), Italy (4.41), and Great Britain (3.70), and the lowest ones in Germany (1.14), French-speaking Belgium (1.75), and France (2.31).

The study of potential extreme right voters gives us a completely different insight on the people extreme right parties need to seduce in order to achieve electoral success. The self-claimed 'impossible supporters' for the extreme right are entirely out of their reach; by contrast, potential voters represent a reservoir which is sometimes significantly superior to the proportion of citizens who actually vote for the extreme right election after election. Most notably, the discrepancy between potential and actual voters

Table 8.1 Distribution of likeliness to vote for the extreme right by country

	Self-Excluded	Potential voter(low)	Potential voter (medium)	Potential voter (high)	Average extreme right PTV
Italy	33.2	12.4	18.6	35.7	4.41 (3.90)
Great Britain	35.6	16.7	21.8	25.9	3.70 (3.61)
Austria	47.1	14.4	13.9	24.6	3.21 (3.82)
Belgium (Ned)	53.0	13.0	13.2	20.8	2.74 (3.60)
Denmark	56.8	11.5	12.1	19.1	2.59 (3.59)
France	49.2	19.0	21.9	10.0	2.31 (2.92)
Romania	53.4	23.5	16.1	7.0	1.81 (2.61)
Belgium (Fr)	61.5	15.5	14.0	9.0	1.75 (2.79)
Germany	75.6	10.1	7.9	6.3	1.14 (2.52)
Overall	**51.5**	**14.6**	**16.2**	**17.6**	**2.66 (3.44)**

Notes: Maximal propensity to vote for an extreme right party:
Self-excluded =0
Low potential = 1–3
Medium potential = 4–6
High potential = 7–10
Results from 'Feeling European?' survey coordinated by M. Bruter (2009) following the 2009 European Parliament elections; 11,085 total valid answers in six countries.

for extreme right parties varies significantly from country to country, showing that some European extreme right parties are overwhelmingly better than others at successfully addressing their potential voters.

8.3 The actual vote for extreme right parties

Contrast these figures to respondent answers to questions about their actual vote in the recent European Parliament elections and their likely vote if a general election took place within a few days. Respondents who said they would probably vote were offered a choice of all the main parties competing in the party system (and all the lists actually competing in the elections for the European Parliament). In the following analysis, we simply give a score of 0 to respondents who did not choose one of the country's extreme right party in either election, a score of 1 to respondents who chose any of the country's extreme right party in one election but not the other, and a score of 2 for the respondents who chose one extreme right party for both elections. Respondents who answered that they had not voted in the European Parliament elections and would probably not vote in forthcoming general elections were excluded from the analysis; voters who answered that they had/would vote for only one were scored on the basis of their only answer.

The results of this coding are summarised in Table 8.2. We can see a clear difference between considering a vote for an extreme right party and actually voting for it. This time, the proportion of respondents claiming not to have voted for an extreme right party in the last European Parliament elections and not intending to vote for one in forthcoming general elections is even larger: 72.7 per cent in Austria and 73.6 in Britain, but 93.9 per cent in Romania and Germany and 95.1 per cent in French-speaking Belgium. Note, however, that social acceptability was likely to prove even more of a problem for these two questions than for the other. Indeed, when it comes

Table 8.2 Actual vote for extreme right parties

Chose an extreme right party	Neither election	Either European or General	Both elections
Austria	72.7	6.3	21.0
Great Britain	73.6	10.5	15.9
Italy	82.1	5.8	12.1
Belgium (Dutch)	82.8	3.7	13.5
Denmark	84.8	4.4	10.8
France	92.0	2.0	6.0
Romania	93.9	1.2	4.9
Germany	93.9	0.9	5.2
Belgium (French)	95.1	1.6	3.3
Average	*86.1*	*4.3*	*9.6*

to propensity-to-vote questions, one could consider a likely extreme right voter just lowering his or her score. When it comes to the actual vote, the only way to bow to the pressure of social acceptability would be to disguise an extreme right choice as a non-extreme right one (e.g. misrepresent vote as Unsure, Other, or a more respectable party). The consequence of this limited variance, which confirms that surveys do underestimate actual extreme right vote when we compare them to actual electoral results in the three countries, is that this question is harder for us to use in our analysis than is the case with the propensity-to-vote question, which is less skewed in its distribution.

Beyond these claimed non-voters, the proportion of respondents claiming to have/intend to vote for an extreme right party in both elections is 3.3 per cent only in French-speaking Belgium, but 21 per cent in Austria, 15.9 in Great Britain, 13.5 in Flanders, 12.1 in Italy, and 10.8 per cent in Denmark. If we intend to use propensity to vote as a more realistic proxy for extreme right voting, we need to understand better the relationship between the two variables.

8.4   The relationship between potential and actual extreme right vote

The next task at hand is therefore to look at the relationship between propensity to vote for extreme right parties and declared actual vote in just-past European Parliament and hypothetical future general elections. Table 8.3 summarises the way the average actual vote for the eight extreme right parties from France, Germany and Great Britain considered in the analysis increases for each extra point of average propensity to vote for extreme right parties within the party system in general.

Table 8.3 provides broadly interesting findings. First, in all eight cases at hand, a propensity to vote for extreme right parties of 0 results in an actual average vote of 0. In other words, there is a 'perfect match' between the two – potential and actual – questions when it comes to absolute extreme right non-voters, a finding worth stressing if only to emphasise the prima facie robustness of the propensity-to-vote question in the context of extreme right electoral behaviour. Second, in general terms, consistently with what one would expect, actual extreme right vote tends to increase when propensity to vote for extreme right parties increases as well. Some marginal exceptions exist. The MNR's voting scores are so low that such a pattern is almost unnoticeable, and in the case of the German Republikaner highest actual vote is in fact to be found amongst those with a propensity to vote for extreme right parties of 4, perhaps because the correlation between the propensity to vote for the Republikaner and other German extreme right parties is not high. In contrast, the progression of actual vote by propensity to vote is almost linear in the case of parties such as the BNP

Table 8.3 Increase in actual extreme right vote as propensity to vote for extreme right parties gets higher

Average extreme right PTV	UK		France			Germany		
	BNP	UKIP	FN	MNR	MPF	REP	NPD	DVU
0	0.00	0.00	0.00	0.00	0.00	0.00	0.00	0.00
1	0.01	0.02	0.00	0.00	0.01	0.01	0.01	0.00
2	0.00	0.05	0.01	0.00	0.01	0.02	0.01	0.00
3	0.01	0.16	0.05	0.01	0.06	0.09	0.05	0.01
4	0.10	0.25	0.11	0.01	0.02	0.19	0.11	0.00
5	0.05	0.22	0.04	0.01	0.04	0.02	0.01	0.03
6	0.10	0.35	0.07	0.03	0.10	0.10	0.25	0.00
7	0.15	0.37	0.34	0.00	0.09	0.18	0.24	0.09
8	0.31	0.21	0.06	0.00	0.17	0.06	0.33	0.06
9	0.15	0.23	0.44	0.00	0.06	0.15	0.20	0.10
10	0.33	0.06	0.06	0.00	0.00	0.15	0.27	0.04

or the NPD and very strong for the FN. Other parties tend to have cut-off points around an average propensity to vote of 3, 4, or 5, depending on the party, with the actual vote being high for UKIP, the DVU, or the MPF when this threshold is exceeded. Again, bear in mind that in this section we are looking at the relationship between an average extreme right propensity to vote and individual extreme right party choices, which certainly explains some of the marginal apparent inconsistencies of the table. Indeed, a very strong BNP voter may perfectly well want to stress that she will only vote for her party, and would not consider voting for competitors such as UKIP. This would in turn result in a lower average extreme right propensity to vote, particularly in systems where the tensions between competing extreme right parties are fierce. (To an extent, this is true in all three systems) Before looking at these differences, consider who the European potential and actual extreme right voters are.

8.5   A marked variation in the profiles of extreme right voters

The puzzle surrounding the variation in electoral scores of the extreme right across Europe is complicated by the fact that we know little about the voters of parties belonging to the extreme right party family. Because extreme right voters are extremely hard to identify and represent a small minority of the electorate, the characteristics of this sub-group are elusive to many scholars in this field. As a result, existing studies have had to cope with a low *n* even in the largest of national surveys and election studies. In addition, these parties are sometimes extremely small organisations and have little chance of accessing positions of responsibility; therefore, many comparative electoral studies have often failed to include extreme right parties in their survey questions. Electoral studies such as the European Social Survey and several National Election studies do include some parties of the extreme right party family but tend to focus on the relatively prominent and successful parties, excluding most of the other parties that fail to secure substantial electoral success but nevertheless belong to the extreme right party family.[1]

Despite these hurdles, several studies have analysed the extreme right electorate. Mayer (1998) for example has compiled an in-depth study of the characteristic voters of the French Front National. In an analysis of six elections from 1986 to 1997, Mayer (1998) found that the party's 'most solid support has come from two occupational groups – small shopkeepers and blue-collar workers' (1998:18). Similarly, scholars studying the Norwegian Progress Party and the Danish People's Party found that although these parties received a large proportion of tax-protest votes from owners of small businesses or the 'petit bourgeois' in the 1970s, they have received an increasing number of votes from blue collar workers since then (Svåsand, 1998; Andersen & Bjørklund, 2000). Although the marriage of these two radically different social groups seems contradictory at first, several parties of the extreme right have been increasingly able to tailor their strategic-discursive strategies in order to cater to the demands of these two social groups. In a study of the Swiss SVP and Austrian FPÖ, McGann and Kitschelt (2002) find that these two sub-groups of the population tend to be the most likely to be attracted to extreme right discourse. A similar pattern is reported in an analysis of the Italian Lega Nord voters in Northern Italy. Betz & Immerfall (1998) maintains that these small commercial and artisanal entrepreneurs and blue-collar workers in the Northern periphery accounted for much of the Lega's resurgence in 1996. Lubbers & Scheepers (2000a) found that unemployed people were more likely than most other groups to vote for an extreme right party. Similarly, Guiraudon and Schain et al. (2002) found that in 2002 Le Pen in his presidential campaign made gains with unemployed voters, obtaining 38 per cent of their vote in the ballot.

If we take the case study of France by Mayer (1998) as an example of the rapid changes in extreme right electorates, we can see that the steady rise of the extreme right in France from the mid-1970s to the early 2000s was to a large extent because blue collars defected from the array of left-wing parties. In the presidential election of 1988, support for Le Pen was higher than average among voters belonging to the working class. These voters were the largest bloc to move *en masse* to the FN. Alongside working-class voters, small business owners and farmers, drawn to the stridently pro-capitalist and anti-interventionist aspects of the FN strategic-discursive platform, have also regularly supported candidates of the Front National (Kitschelt, 1995). Extreme right parties clearly seem to draw upon a reservoir of support from a variety of stable social groups. Blue-collar workers, small and independent business people, and professionals all seem susceptible to the allure of the extreme right discourse, and this interesting mix of social groups dissects boundaries that are usually associated with the traditional left-right socio-political cleavage.

The Vlaams Belang (formerly known as Vlaams Block) has a slightly different profile amongst its key supporters (Ignazi, 1992). Although independent businesspeople are no longer overrepresented, blue-collar workers or what is described as lower classes are overrepresented within their electorate (Billiet & De Witte, 1995; Swyngedouw, 1998). With the exception of the Flemish case, then, the evidence is overwhelming that the support for the contemporary populist right rests on a coalition that disproportionately includes owners of small businesses and blue collar workers. As a result, Ivarsflaten (2005) argues that a simultaneous appeal to both blue-collar workers and owners of small businesses is difficult to achieve in Western Europe. She argues that these two sections of the electorate are 'deeply divided on the socio-economic dimension of politics, and they are, therefore, not a readily available coalition. The Flemish case is an example of how populist parties may easily fail to appeal to both these groups, while the French and Danish cases are examples where this difficult balancing act has been successfully pursued by the populist right.'

Gender

Existing studies often highlight that gender is one of the more defining characteristics of an extreme right voter, with male voters more likely than women to vote for an extreme right party according to many surveys. Simply put, Kitschelt (1995) argues that male voters tend to be more attracted than their female counterparts to the discourse and ideology of extreme right parties. Mayer (2005) finds strong feminist opposition to the ideology of the extreme right in her study of France; however, the Front National's electoral appeal although predominantly male (around 60%) is seen as cutting across class boundaries and extends itself across most social categories. This apparently simple notion of extreme right voting as a predominantly male phenomenon is sometimes questioned in the literature: for some authors, women, once unlikely to vote for the FN, have seen their leverage within the party's electorate increase (Schain et al., 2002).

In this context, the results of our study (illustrated in Table 8.4) are in fact quite extraordinary. We find that although men are slightly more likely than women to vote for an extreme right party according to their own declarations, a larger reservoir of potential extreme right voters exists amongst women than amongst men in many of the countries studied.

In many countries, women rather than men show the greatest propensity to vote for the extreme right, and men show the greatest propensity to exclude it, for at least four possible reasons.

Table 8.4 Gender and vote for the extreme right

Country	% Potential voters		Propensity to vote (mean)		Actual vote (mean)	
	Men	**Women**	**Men**	**Women**	**Men**	**Women**
Italy	**69.4**	64.2	**4.63 (3.91)**	4.19 (3.88)	0.16 (0.34)	0.14 (0.33)
Great Britain	64.7	64.0	**3.80 (3.69)**	3.59 (3.51)	0.22 (0.38)	0.21 (0.37)
Austria	50.2	**55.5**	2.93 (3.71)	**3.50 (3.92)**	0.22 (0.39)	0.27 (0.42)
Belg. (N)	**48.3**	45.8	**2.83 (3.63)**	2.66 (3.56)	0.16 (0.35)	0.15 (0.34)
Denmark	**49.8**	36.9	**2.94 (3.66)**	2.25 (3.49)	0.15 (0.34)	0.11 (0.30)
France	46.9	**55.2**	2.10 (2.88)	**2.55 (2.95)**	0.07 (0.25)	0.07 (0.25)
Romania	**50.5**	42.7	**1.82 (2.55)**	1.79 (2.68)	0.05 (0.22)	0.06 (0.22)
Belg. (F)	31.7	**45.1**	1.41 (2.59)	**2.09 (2.94)**	0.03 (0.17)	0.05 (0.20)
Germany	23.4	**25.3**	**1.15 (2.62)**	1.14 (2.42)	0.07 (0.24)	0.04 (0.20)
Overall	**48.9**	48.1	**2.70 (3.51)**	2.61 (3.39)	**0.12 (0.31)**	**0.11 (0.30)**

The first possibility is related to social desirability. As explained earlier in this chapter, we think propensity to vote is a particularly useful tool when studying the extreme right because of social desirability: a respondent would find it significantly more socially undesirable to admit he has voted for an extreme right party than to give a numeric score to the probability of ever voting for that party. Indeed, using propensity to vote scales, social desirability would be more likely to result in a slightly underestimated propensity score than into an actual '0' for someone who is a potential extreme right voter. If women are more affected by social desirability issues than men are, they may be more likely to be deceptive than men in admitting to extreme right voting. In such a case, the apparently greater likeliness of men to vote for extremist parties would be nothing more than an artefact, simply resulting from different levels of social desirability between women and men, while potential vote would re-establish the truth.

The second possibility has to do with the ideological value of the vote. Men are not necessarily less represented than women in the category of high probability extreme right voters, but they are significantly more likely to exclude it in most countries. A second hypothesis would therefore be that because men are on average more ideological than women in their voting preferences, they are more likely definitely to exclude a vote for extreme right parties as well as to be strong supporters when they consider it.

A third possibility is that although more women than men are potential extreme right voters, extreme right parties are somehow significantly better at addressing male voters in order to transform their potential support into an actual vote. There could be literally hundreds of reasons why this might be so. As explained in Chapter 7, many extreme right parties adapt their discourse to electoral cycles, with xenophobic references more frequent outside of election periods. It is perfectly conceivable that the impact of these references is either less negative or simply less long-lived in the perceptions of men than in those of women.

A fourth and last hypothesis, somewhat relating to the second and third possible explanations here, would be that although women are more likely than men to be potential extreme right voters, they place themselves differently in terms of their dominant strategic-discursive preferences. The reason an actual extreme right vote can also sometimes be higher amongst men or women could have something to do with the strategic-discursive preferences of the extreme right parties competing in a given party system. Some strategic-discursive positions would be more compatible with the dominant preferences of men or women, thus explaining why in some cases extreme right parties could be poor at transforming potential extreme right women voters into effective winning ballots.

We thus see that the relationship between gender and extreme right support is undoubtedly more complex than it appears at first. For reasons which may include social desirability artefact and measurement, ideological polarisation, or extreme right parties' strategy, women constitute a larger reservoir of potential extreme right voters but one which, apparently, extreme right parties find harder to convince on the day of the election. The literature seems even more certain that age has more effect than gender on extreme right support. Let us now consider whether this perception is more readily confirmed by our data in terms of both potential and effective support than is the case for gender.

Age

Existing studies have often shown that an age effect exists within the electoral base of extreme right parties, with both younger and older voters more likely than other age groups to support the extreme right. Perhaps the effects of a changing social structure have not affected all generations equally: young voters and pensioners are more likely to lack solid social ties. Greater social integration is likely to be reflected not only in higher levels of electoral participation but also in a tendency to refrain from voting for a party of the extreme right. Guiraudon and Schain (2002) conducted some extremely interesting individual-level analysis of voters for Le Pen. Surprisingly, Le Pen received the highest level of support among 18-to-24 year olds, with a massive 20 per cent of these young people casting their vote in his favour. This was almost double that of any other candidate (Jospin received 12% of the vote amongst this age group). Second only to Chirac, Le Pen also scored well amongst the 45-to-64-year-old category with 19 per cent of their vote. Interestingly, at the local level, Le Pen received some of his best results where the extreme left is strong and the abstention levels are high, suggesting that in these particular localities there is widespread dissatisfaction with the established parties and mainstream politicians.

In the survey, we thus explored how the proportion of extreme right voters, the average propensity to vote for an extreme right party, and the actual proportion of voters varied according to age, with the results reported in Table 8.5. Some of the literature contains contradictory statements about whether extreme right support is predominantly likely amongst the younger or older voters. In many ways, Table 8.5 does not arbitrate between these two alternatives. Although in a few countries older voters are more likely to be extreme right supporters (e.g. Denmark, Italy), in a majority, younger citizens are more prone to support such extremist parties (e.g. Germany, France). In Romania, the youngest and oldest voters are more strongly in support of extreme right movements which intermediary generations are less likely to embrace.

These apparently contradictory findings reinforce the plurality of possible explanations highlighted in the context of gender differences in support for the extreme right in Europe. This time, although social desirability seems a marginal possible explanation for the results at hand, the type of extreme right party involved is particularly likely to determine the age groups most likely to vote for the extreme right. Countries with a stronger potential support for the extreme right seem to be those in which the extreme right parties in competition have, according to the findings of Chapter 5, a strong xenophobic pillar; a greater base of potential supporters among young citizens is found in countries where extreme right parties emphasise populist discourse more.

Increasingly, our investigation into the profiles of extreme right potential voters thus suggests that the choices made by the extreme right parties themselves help determine which potential voters are likely to be mobilised. In the next sections, we consider how extreme right potential voters vary according to their education, income, and professional category.

Education

Studies of the extreme right have always shown that people with higher levels of education are less likely to support extreme right parties than are their less-educated counterparts. Indeed, DiGusto and Jolly (2008) find that higher skilled or educated respondents are consistently less xenophobic in their attitudes. This is consistent with expectations from economic models, such as the Heckscher-Ohlin theory, which suggests that higher skilled citizens have less to fear from more open trade and immigration regimes (Brinegar & Jolly, 2005). The likeliness to vote for an extreme right party will decrease as education levels increase. The argument maintains that through education, people are intensively exposed to liberal values and thus more likely to embrace them. Similarly, Mayer (2005) asserts voters of the FN tend to be less educated than other voters. A study carried out by Andersen and Evans (2004) reaffirms the importance of socialisation in determining authoritarian attitudes. They also found

Table 8.5 Age and vote for the extreme right

Country	% Potential voters				Propensity to vote (mean)				Actual vote (mean)			
	18–24	24–44	45–64	65+	18–24	24–44	45–64	65+	18–24	24–44	45–64	65+
Italy	73.1	66.6	64.8	74.3	4.47 (3.66)	4.37 (3.86)	4.37 (3.98)	4.84 (3.83)	0.17 (0.35)	0.17 (0.36)	0.13 (0.32)	0.13 (0.32)
Great Britain	65.8	64.2	65.4	61.1	3.19 (3.16)	3.50 (3.45)	4.00 (3.77)	3.72 (3.76)	0.12 (0.31)	0.20 (0.38)	0.24 (0.39)	0.21 (0.36)
Austria	60.0	58.9	48.3	44.2	4.16 (4.08)	3.68 (3.96)	2.79 (3.65)	2.45 (3.44)	0.37 (0.47)	0.29 (0.45)	0.20 (0.37)	0.16 (0.33)
Belg. (N)	48.9	50.0	46.8	39.5	2.84 (3.54)	2.98 (3.63)	2.65 (3.55)	2.67 (3.86)	0.12 (0.31)	0.16 (0.36)	0.15 (0.35)	0.16 (0.36)
Denmark	36.2	44.0	43.4	45.3	1.88 (3.05)	2.60 (3.57)	2.59 (3.61)	3.13 (3.93)	0.09 (0.28)	0.12 (0.30)	0.14 (0.33)	0.17 (0.36)
France	57.9	55.4	47.4	48.0	2.71 (3.05)	2.60 (3.05)	2.13 (2.84)	1.94 (2.64)	0.08 (0.25)	0.09 (0.28)	0.06 (0.23)	0.06 (0.22)
Romania	45.4	36.8	57.8	57.1	2.11 (2.95)	1.48 (2.61)	1.99 (2.37)	3.00 (3.32)	0.08 (0.27)	0.07 (0.25)	0.04 (0.17)	0.00 (0.01)
Belg. (F)	43.5	45.1	34.9	30.0	1.96 (3.09)	2.08 (2.95)	1.57 (2.66)	1.36 (2.53)	0.05 (0.21)	0.07 (0.25)	0.03 (0.14)	0.01 (0.11)
Germany	48.7	30.9	19.7	13.8	2.19 (3.07)	1.51 (2.75)	0.93 (2.38)	0.54 (1.73)	0.11 (0.30)	0.07 (0.25)	0.05 (0.22)	0.03 (0.16)
Overall	56.2	51.3	46.2	42.9	2.87 (3.35)	2.81 (3.45)	2.56 (3.47)	2.41 (3.45)	0.12 (0.31)	0.13 (0.32)	0.11 (0.30)	0.11 (0.29)

that blue-collar workers tend to be more authoritarian on all dimensions than people from other social classes, the traditionally right-wing authoritarian self-employed aside, which supports Lipset's working-class authoritarianism hypothesis. Moreover, Kitschelt (1995) argues that people employed in non-manual jobs who enjoy a small degree of autonomy in their work are likely to develop authoritarian preferences, similar to those ascribed to working-class voters. Our analysis looks into the details of the impact of education on extreme right potential vote as illustrated by Table 8.6.

Our results confirm that education is clearly a powerful deterrent of extreme right voting. Overall, there is a statistically significant (at 0.01 level) negative correlation of –0.17 between education and propensity to vote for the extreme right. The negative correlation holds in all countries, the highest of which is French-speaking Belgium (–0.19), followed by Austria (–0;18), Denmark (–0.15), Romania (–0.14), Great Britain and Flanders (–0.13), France (–0.10), Germany (–0.09), Italy (–0.05). The results are confirmed at every level both comparatively and nationally within most countries. The results of Table 8.6 are fairly straightforward and confirm the negative correlation highlighted earlier. This time, comparative differences are minimal with the relative exceptions of Germany and Flanders, where education seems to have relatively little impact except for the most highly educated respondents. Note that there seems to be relatively little difference between respondents with low and medium low education levels in many countries; higher education degrees ('high') seem to have the strongest negative impact everywhere on citizens' likeliness to vote for extreme right parties.

Income

Does income have the same impact as education on citizens' likeliness to become potential extreme right voters? The literature has often been more sceptical about the logical effect of income on extreme right voting; indeed, our results suggest that income has probably no impact on the likeliness of respondents to be potential extreme right voters overall, with a non-significant negative correlation coefficient of 0.01. The country-specific story is rather different, and several countries show statistically significant correlations between propensity to vote for the extreme right and income, albeit negative (–0.17 in French-speaking Belgium, –0.11 in Austria and Romania, –0.09 in Germany, –0.08 in France). Table 8.7 gives further details about how likeliness to consider voting changes with income.

Table 8.7 shows little coherent relationship between income and propensity to vote for the extreme right. For instance, in Austria and the whole of Belgium, the least wealthy voters tend to be the most likely to vote for an extreme right party; in Italy and Germany, the wealthiest people are most

Table 8.6 Education and vote for the extreme right

Country	% Potential voters				Propensity to vote (mean)				Actual vote (mean)			
	Low	Med Low	Med High	High	Low	Med Low	Med High	High	Low	Med Low	Med High	High
Italy	68.2	70.2	59.3	61.8	4.50 (3.89)	4.71 (3.89)	3.68 (3.82)	4.76 (4.25)	0.18 (0.36)	0.16 (0.35)	0.11 (0.29)	0.17 (0.36)
Great Britain	69.0	63.6	60.8	55.4	4.36 (3.77)	3.38 (3.41)	3.77 (3.88)	2.58 (2.95)	0.30 (0.43)	0.16 (0.33)	0.24 (0.39)	0.07 (0.22)
Austria	64.8	41.8	51.1	42.9	4.25 (4.07)	2.73 (3.85)	3.09 (3.73)	2.14 (3.34)	0.35 (0.46)	0.17 (0.36)	0.23 (0.40)	0.14 (0.33)
Belg. (N)	52.2	66.7	54.0	36.0	3.09 (3.79)	3.83 (3.89)	3.40 (3.76)	1.90 (3.10)	0.20 (0.39)	0.17 (0.34)	0.18 (0.38)	0.09 (0.27)
Denmark	58.3	36.5	49.3	35.6	3.70 (3.89)	2.16 (3.42)	2.92 (3.67)	2.07 (3.34)	0.21 (0.40)	0.14 (0.33)	0.12 (0.32)	0.10 (0.27)
France	53.4	54.0	45.5	33.3	2.57 (3.06)	2.49 (2.98)	1.93 (2.70)	1.52 (2.84)	0.07 (0.25)	0.08 (0.26)	0.05 (0.22)	0.13 (0.33)
Romania	76.5	64.3	49.3	42.9	3.06 (2.54)	3.18 (3.19)	2.12 (2.86)	1.49 (2.35)	0.18 (0.40)	0.07 (0.23)	0.06 (0.23)	0.04 (0.20)
Belg. (F)	42.4	51.3	43.8	30.4	1.91 (2.84)	3.07 (3.19)	2.15 (2.98)	1.09 (2.11)	0.04 (0.19)	0.08 (0.27)	0.05 (0.23)	0.03 (0.15)
Germany	24.6	26.8	27.2	15.4	1.23 (2.65)	1.30 (2.73)	1.25 (2.53)	0.60 (1.88)	0.07 (0.25)	0.06 (0.23)	0.05 (0.20)	0.05 (0.21)
Overall	53.5	55.2	44.5	33.7	3.14 (3.66)	3.11 (3.57)	2.33 (3.28)	1.55 (2.79)	0.17 (0.36)	0.12 (0.31)	0.10 (0.28)	0.07 (0.24)

Table 8.7 Income and vote for the extreme right

Country	% Potential voters				Propensity to vote (mean)				Actual vote (mean)			
	Low	Med Low	Med High	High	Low	Med Low	Med High	High	Low	Med Low	Med High	High
Italy	66.2	61.6	70.1	65.9	4.35 (3.93)	3.96 (3.94)	4.83 (3.98)	4.41 (3.92)	0.16 (0.35)	0.12 (0.29)	0.20 (0.39)	0.13 (0.31)
Great Britain	63.3	67.8	69.6	58.6	3.75 (3.80)	4.00 (3.65)	4.05 (3.66)	3.20 (3.39)	0.26 (0.42)	0.25 (0.40)	0.23 (0.39)	0.14 (0.31)
Austria	57.5	53.8	46.9	46.4	3.86 (4.15)	3.15 (3.76)	2.85 (3.67)	2.72 (3.67)	0.34 (0.46)	0.25 (0.42)	0.21 (0.38)	0.18 (0.37)
Belg. (N)	46.0	43.9	49.3	43.2	2.94 (3.81)	2.50 (3.48)	2.81 (3.60)	2.39 (3.44)	0.18 (0.37)	0.15 (0.34)	0.13 (0.32)	0.14 (0.34)
Denmark	37.5	40.0	40.9	44.4	2.19 (3.45)	2.41 (3.57)	2.23 (3.49)	2.73 (3.64)	0.14 (0.34)	0.12 (0.30)	0.12 (0.31)	0.13 (0.32)
France	53.3	53.6	48.3	44.1	2.62 (3.20)	2.28 (2.69)	2.02 (2.70)	1.99 (2.85)	0.10 (0.29)	0.06 (0.22)	0.06 (0.24)	0.06 (0.23)
Romania	50.7	55.5	44.8	39.2	2.01 (2.62)	2.39 (3.04)	1.66 (2.47)	1.41 (2.33)	0.06 (0.22)	0.08 (0.27)	0.05 (0.22)	0.02 (0.15)
Belg. (F)	50.0	40.2	39.1	26.7	2.45 (3.12)	1.98 (3.05)	1.85 (2.93)	1.06 (2.14)	0.08 (0.26)	0.05 (0.20)	0.01 (0.11)	0.02 (0.13)
Germany	28.5	21.8	23.0	19.7	1.43 (2.80)	0.96 (2.33)	0.99 (2.39)	0.83 (2.14)	0.08 (0.27)	0.05 (0.20)	0.05 (0.22)	0.04 (0.20)
Overall	47.1	49.8	51.7	45.3	2.62 (3.51)	2.65 (3.40)	2.76 (3.48)	2.53 (3.43)	0.13 (0.33)	0.12 (0.30)	0.13 (0.32)	0.10 (0.28)

likely to do so. In Denmark and France, there seems to be no relationship between income and extreme right voting. Note that one of the problems with assessing the impact of income on potential electoral support is that a significant proportion of respondents choose not to answer questions on income; therefore, the results are somewhat skewed, with up to a quarter of respondents appearing as missing values.

Professional categories

Table 8.8 illustrates the variation in the occupational profiles of extreme right voters across countries. It highlights the main social bases of extreme right parties in Germany, Belgium, France, Austria, Britain, and Italy.

Bearing in mind that sample sizes vary, Table 8.8 shows that in the Britain and in Germany, the main reservoir of support for the extreme right is represented by middle management; self-employed business owners and independent farmers primarily affiliate with the extreme right ideology in France. In Belgium, the main supporters are top-level managers; in Austria, the leftist populist origin of the extreme right electorate is highlighted by the primary support of blue-collar workers. Employees are the largest groups to sympathise with extreme right parties in Italy but most other categories, including students, also feature highly. In Germany, there is broad support amongst the self-employed, middle management, and manual workers. This diversity could be explained by the individuality of each of the three main extreme right parties in Germany. We have seen in previous chapters that each party retains a distinct ideological line and discursive identity. In addition, few attempts have been made to form a union across the three parties despite the fact that the extreme right vote is split amongst the three parties. Moreover, in the general European context, it is interesting that no socio-professional category truly escapes the tentacles of the extreme right party family.

Table 8.8   A comparison of extreme right support in six European democracies

	Self-empl.	Top-mgr	Mid-mgr	White-collar	Manual worker	Unempl. Retired	Student	ALL
Germany	11.4	9.4	**12.8**	7.6	11.6	8.7	4.8	**9.3**
Belgium	6.2	**25.0**	12.9	7.0	8.9	8.9	6.0	**9.1**
France	**28.3**	10.6	14.0	8.8	6.1	11.1	2.5	**9.8**
United Kingdom	10.3	8.5	**11.6**	4.6	7.0	10.6	8.3	**8.7**
Austria	7.9	1.4	5.9	8.6	7.7	**13.3**	6.4	**9.0**
Italy	17.2	18.2	10.7	**19.2**	10.9	15.1	16.4	**15.8**

Notes: Data is from Eurobarometer 53 (April–May 2000). Figures in bold represent the primary category of support for the extreme right in the country.

8.6   Match, set, and game?

Does the ideological positioning of extreme right political parties across the three countries on which we have focused matter when it comes to the attitudes of their potential voters? The results of a mass survey run in the aftermath of the June 2009 European Parliament elections help us investigate this.[2] In this context, we want to tackle a number of questions regarding public attitudes toward the extreme right:

1. What is the relationship between the actual and potential vote for extreme right parties in the three countries we are studying?
2. How are the public opinions in these three countries ideologically distributed when it comes to the four pillars of extreme right ideology that we define in the conceptual map?
3. How does the likeliness to vote for an extreme right party increase as citizens become more radical on these four ideological pillars?

Let us now consider these three questions in turn.

8.7   Extreme right voting and ideological positioning on the four pillars of extreme right ideology

The ideological stances of parties traditionally classified as belonging to the extreme right party family vary significantly. The Scandinavian Progress Parties, for instance, have been characterised as Right-libertarian (Harmel & Gibson, 2007); even voters for hard Right parties such as the Vlaams Belang are not entirely homogeneously authoritarian (Evans et al., 2001), but over time have converged toward a more similar authoritarian stance (Andersen & Evans, 2004). Voters who share authoritarian, ethno-nationalist, and xenophobic attitudes were more likely to support the Front National. Although van der Brug et al. (2000) and van der Brug and Fennema (2003) argue that the principal motivation for voting for extreme right parties is the presence of an authoritarian ideology, Mayer (1995) insists that extreme right voters tend to express a lower degree of trust in France's cultural and political institutions, except the trust invested in the police and the military. Mayer (1995) also finds that FN voters are far more xenophobic than supporters of other right-wing parties. Kitschelt (1995) states in contrast that FN voters are only marginally more racist than are other right-wing party supporters. More specifically, Rydgren finds that xenophobia, law and order, personal security (for example death penalty), anti-European Union sentiments, and a belief that politicians do not care about the opinion of ordinary people were of particular importance (Rydgren, 2005).

In summary, creating a profile of a standard extreme right voter is not straightforward. There does seem to be some consensus that blue-collar workers, small business owners, and the unemployed are amongst the occupation groups most likely to vote for a party belonging to the extreme right party family. Education seems to matter, with lower-educated voters more likely than others to sympathise with extreme right ideology. Young male voters are also more prone to vote for an extreme right party. Some attitudinal dispositions make people more likely to confirm their ideological sympathy with an extreme right party; for example, citizens who retain authoritarian, xenophobic, populist, or reactionary values are expected to be amongst voters of the extreme right. There are many comparative differences not only across countries but also within party systems. In an attempt to shed more light upon the preferences of extreme right voters, we move on to investigate the match between the strategic-discursive positions of the 25 extreme right parties included in the analysis and the ideological preferences of potential and actual voters.

Let us now consider the relationship between extreme right voting – both in terms of actual vote and of extreme right propensity to vote, and respondents' positions on the four strategic-discursive pillars of extreme right ideology defined in Chapter 2: xenophobic, populist, reactionary, and repressive.

Are all countries equal in the face of extreme right ideology? When it comes to explaining the overall success of extreme right parties in various European party systems, the argument that some countries are more predisposed than others to consider extreme right arguments is far from rare, and the survey data that we analyse gives us an opportunity to verify whether this is indeed true. As explained in Chapter 3, all respondents were asked to situate themselves on eight attitudinal scales, two for each of the four pillars of extreme right ideology that we wanted to target. The scales used asked respondents the extent to which they agreed with given statements, using an agreement scale that varied from 0 to 10. Each time, one of the statements was phrased positively and one negatively to avoid problems of acquiescence.

8.8 Ideological predisposition to vote for extreme right parties in Britain, France, Germany, Italy, Austria, Belgium, Denmark, and Romania

Based on the model developed in Chapter 2, we defined extreme right ideology on the basis of the relative combination of four ideological (or, in the case of parties, 'strategic-discursive') pillars: xenophobia and populism as expressions of negative identity, and reactionary attitudes and repression as forms of authoritarianism. Conversely, when it comes to voters, we therefore expect citizens who score highly on some of these four pillars to be more predisposed to vote for extreme right parties.

We contrasted the aggregate level of adhesion to these four pillars in Britain, France, and Germany versus the average adhesion level in the eight countries in which the questions on extreme right ideology were asked: Britain, France, and Germany, of course, but also Austria, Denmark, Italy, Romania, Northern Ireland, Belgium (with French- and a Dutch-speaking samples). The relative adhesion to the four extreme right pillars is summarised by Table 8.9 for the examples of France, Germany, and Great Britain.

Table 8.9 shows interesting variations across the three countries included in the analysis. The gross results need to be taken with caution, however, as the eight items were not distributed similarly, and some distributions were therefore more skewed than others across countries. British citizens score higher on average than the eight countries included in the analysis on all four pillars, particularly in terms of xenophobic, repressive, and reactionary attitudes. By contrast, Germany, which has the lowest combined extreme right vote out of the three countries studied here, scores lower than average, particularly in terms of xenophobic and reactionary (and to some extent repressive) attitudes. France is far more reactionary than average, but scores lowest on the repressive pillar of the three countries at hand.

In short, the first finding could be rephrased by saying that overall levels of ideological predisposition to extreme right voting seems to be high in the Britain, average in France, and low in Germany. The second finding suggests that the three electorates have different specificities, with the British being mostly xenophobic and repressive, the French reactionary, and the Germans rather populist and repressive. Note as well that the populist pillar seems to vary least across the countries studied, certainly in part because of the rather skewed distribution of the two populist items.

Both findings are obviously quite important at face value. The different levels of predisposition are interesting because for many years Britain was considered a country with a relatively low propensity to vote for the extreme right; however, our results show that the ideological potential is high, which may explain why the emergence of new parties that were more in tune with

Table 8.9 Relative support for the extreme right ideological pillars (compared to the average of eight European democracies)

	Reactionary	Repressive	Xenophobic	Populist
Britain	6.96	7.69	7.21	8.10
	(2.53)	(2.49)	(2.88)	(2.16)
France	7.15	6.91	6.27	8.02
	(2.36)	(2.86)	(3.02)	(2.29)
Germany	6.26	7.00	5.97	8.04
	(2.57)	(2.70)	(3.06)	(2.29)
Average 8 countries	*6.59*	*7.40*	*6.53*	*8.00*
	(2.52)	*(2.64)*	*(3.00)*	*(2.30)*

Notes: Figures are on a 0–10 scale. Figures in brackets are standard deviations of the means.

the aspiration of potential extreme right voters ended up revealing the extreme right reservoir of Britain. In contrast, although the extreme right does not poll highly in Germany, our results suggest that its potential based on the ideological predisposition of its citizens is in fact not much superior to its actual results at the moment. As this is the first time these questions were asked in a survey, we do not know how robust or volatile this ideological predisposition remains over time. Finally, although there is potential for extreme right voting in France, it does not poll as highly as in Britain and currently seems to favour the ideological positions of the MPF more than those of the FN and the MNR.

We also need to understand how the four fundamental pillars of extreme right ideology highlighted by our model work together and how different demographic, social, and cultural groups are likely to adhere to these four pillars.

Most notably, Table 8.10 highlights a contrast between the situation of parties and voters. indeed, while parties' discourses are marked by negative correlations between xenophobic and populist references, as well as between reactionary and repressive ones in their manifestoes, for voters, all four pillars of extreme right ideology are positively correlated. This part is interesting, because it suggests a discrepancy between party strategy and voter consistency. Indeed, although strategically there is a tension between the use of the xenophobic pillar on the one hand and populist one on the other hand, and between the reactionary pillar and repressive one by extreme right parties in their discourse, when it comes to voters, the two dimensions and four pillars tend to reinforce each other in an important way.

Table 8.11 suggests that among the possible predictors of adhesion to the four major pillars of extreme right ideology identified by our model, the most useful by far is education and the least useful, gender. On the whole, women tend to be a little bit more repressive, older people more reactionary and more xenophobic, wealthy people less reactionary and less populist, and more educated people significantly less convinced by every single pillar of extreme right ideology, especially xenophobia.

Table 8.10 Correlations between four fundamental pillars of extreme right ideology

	Xenophobic	Populist	Reactionary	Repressive
Xenophobic	1			
Populist	0.40	1		
Reactionary	0.50**	0.46**	1	
Repressive	0.58**	0.49**	0.52	1

Notes: *: statistically sigfnificant at 0.05 or better; **: statistically significant at 0.01 or better.

Table 8.11 Correlates of the four cardinal pillars of extreme right ideology

Correlate / Pillar	Xenophobic	Populist	Reactionary	Repressive
Gender	0.01	0.02*	0.03**	0.05**
Age	0.10**	0.06**	0.12**	0.05**
Education[3]	−0.21**	−0.13**	−0.18**	−0.17**
Income	−0.06**	−0.08**	−0.10**	−0.01

Notes: *: statistically significant at 0.05 or better; **: statistically significant at 0.01 or better.

Table 8.12 Correlations between extreme right ideology pillars, propensity to vote, and effective vote for extreme right parties

	Propensity to vote for Extr. Right				Actual vote for Extr. Right			
	Xeno	Pop	Reac	Repr	Xeno	Pop	Reac	Repr
Austria	0.43**	0.25**	0.30**	0.36**	0.33**	0.23**	0.31**	0.30**
Belgium (F)	0.23**	0.12**	0.17**	0.19**	0.15**	0.11**	0.11**	0.08*
Belgium (N)	0.44**	0.28**	0.32**	0.25**	0.31**	0.21**	0.23**	0.16**
Denmark	0.50**	0.16**	0.30**	0.36**	0.39**	0.17**	0.28**	0.26**
France	0.34**	0.10**	0.17**	0.27**	0.24**	0.10**	0.10**	0.17**
Germany	0.26**	0.07**	0.16**	0.12**	0.26**	0.12**	0.16**	0.13**
Italy	0.43**	0.11**	0.12**	0.27**	0.27**	0.06*	0.10**	0.16**
Romania	0.21**	0.08*	0.18**	0.00	0.07*	0.07*	0.15**	0.07*
Great Britain	0.36**	0.23**	0.28**	0.25**	0.33**	0.23**	0.23**	0.20**
ALL	0.38**	0.10*	0.22**	0.26**	0.30**	0.13**	0.17**	0.18**

8.9   Adhesion to the four pillars of extreme right ideology and likeliness to vote for the extreme right

Let us now look at this at the individual level. After looking at the mood of the three nations we want to analyse, it is crucial as a test of the worth of our model to understand whether voters who are more reactionary, repressive, xenophobic, or populist end up being more likely to vote for extreme right parties. For this particular part of the analysis, we look at the link between pillar scores and the potential and actual vote for extreme right parties.

The correlations between extreme right voting and each of these four pillars are shown in Table 8.12. Are people with strong xenophobic, populist, reactionary, and repressive beliefs more likely to consider voting for the extreme right? Are they effectively more likely to put a ballot with the name of an extreme right party in the ballot box on election day?

Table 8.12 provides an extremely clear picture of strong and significant positive correlations between each of the four pillars of extreme right ideology highlighted by our model and (potential as well as actual) extreme right vote. Overall, potential vote is more highly correlated with pillars of ideology than is actual vote, but this could be an artificial consequence of the more strongly skewed distribution of actual vote as well as its less subtle (3-point) scale.

The correlations are also strongest with the xenophobic and repressive pillar on the whole; however, here again the perceived impact of the populist pillar is bound to be limited by a fairly skewed distribution of the variable. Moreover, interestingly enough, the negative-identity pillar that best predicts extreme right voting varies between countries: the repressive pillar appears to be a dominant predictor of extreme right voting in Italy, France, Austria, and Denmark; the reactionary pillar seems to have the stronger impact in Romania, Flanders, and Germany.

This relationship between ideological pillars and the extreme right vote is shown in Tables 8.13 and 8.14 and Figure 8.1. These illustrate how different levels of extreme right vote and propensity to vote correspond to the increasing strength of the four extreme right ideological pillars highlighted in our model.[4]

Tables 8.13 and 8.14 as well as Figure 8.1 confirm in great detail what the correlation table showed: as adhesion to the four pillars of extreme right ideology progresses, propensity to vote for extreme right parties strongly increases, as does the likeliness that citizens will actually vote for extreme right parties. In the context of the actual vote, there is little difference between hard-core extreme right voters who claim that they voted for an extreme right party in the European Elections and would vote for one in forthcoming first-order national elections, although both categories are very different from people who vote for other parties instead.

8.10   Toward a unified model of extreme right voting

We have now looked into some of the major specificities of adhesion to the four cardinal pillars of extreme right ideology, potential vote and propensity to vote for the extreme right, and, ultimately, actual extreme right voting. Let us now see how these elements fit together into a unified theory of extreme right voting tested by multiple regression. In other words:

1. Does the inclusion of variables measuring voters' adhesion to the four core pillars of extreme right ideology add explanatory power to a model; and
2. Does the match between party choice of strategic-discursive location and local voter preferences also play a role?

Throughout this book, we claim that four major pillars, two forms of negative identity (xenophobic and populist) and two forms of authoritarianism (reactionary and repressive), serve as the foundations of extreme right ideology. We also hypothesise that as extreme right parties can vary

Tables 8.13 Evolution of extreme right ideological pillars scores as the propensity to vote for extreme right parties increases

Xenophobia Country/Propensity to vote	Excluded	Low	Medium	High
Austria	5.71 (3.30)	6.94 (2.60)	7.73 (2.36)	8.89 (1.81)
Belgium (F)	6.60 (2.93)	6.82 (2.66)	7.70 (2.30)	8.62 (1.72)
Belgium (N)	6.39 (2.81)	7.34 (2.24)	8.22 (1.81)	9.28 (1.32)
Denmark	4.55 (3.03)	6.79 (2.05)	6.97 (2.26)	8.56 (1.97)
France	5.35 (3.17)	6.45 (2.67)	7.22 (2.38)	8.40 (2.36)
Germany	5.57 (3.09)	6.76 (2.47)	6.81 (2.49)	8.53 (2.32)
Italy	5.25 (3.42)	6.15 (2.83)	6.94 (2.57)	8.23 (2.12)
Romania	4.85 (2.53)	5.59 (2.48)	5.74 (2.45)	6.50 (2.31)
Great Britain	6.28 (3.22)	6.46 (2.75)	7.45 (2.48)	8.79 (1.89)
All	**5.47 (3.16)**	**6.42 (2.65)**	**7.09 (2.49)**	**8.45 (2.12)**

Populism Country/Propensity to vote	Excluded	Low	Medium	High
Austria	7.36 (2.51)	7.47 (2.24)	7.89 (2.33)	8.68 (1.74)
Belgium (F)	8.03 (2.20)	7.93 (1.76)	8.14 (2.15)	9.00 (1.74)
Belgium (N)	7.69 (2.17)	7.72 (2.17)	8.53 (1.66)	9.02 (1.47)
Denmark	5.86 (2.78)	6.07 (2.43)	6.30 (2.34)	6.91 (2.42)
France	7.91 (2.41)	7.84 (2.32)	8.14 (1.97)	8.64 (2.19)
Germany	8.02 (2.32)	7.88 (2.19)	7.81 (2.16)	8.83 (2.06)
Italy	8.91 (1.90)	8.97 (1.55)	8.16 (2.19)	8.40 (1.87)
Romania	8.78 (1.97)	7.74 (2.70)	7.49 (2.88)	7.16 (2.41)
Great Britain	7.70 (2.50)	7.79 (2.01)	7.98 (2.00)	8.94 (1.56)
All	**7.89 (2.46)**	**7.87 (2.28)**	**7.91 (2.20)**	**8.51 (1.99)**

Reactionary Country/Propensity to vote	Excluded	Low	Medium	High
Austria	5.21 (2.78)	5.92 (2.58)	5.96 (2.39)	7.20 (2.37)
Belgium (F)	7.03 (2.48)	6.94 (1.99)	7.64 (1.85)	8.40 (1.76)
Belgium (N)	5.88 (2.49)	6.39 (2.05)	7.04 (2.20)	7.75 (2.24)
Denmark	4.94 (2.67)	5.63 (2.01)	5.95 (2.22)	6.97 (2.60)
France	6.80 (2.47)	7.24 (2.13)	7.45 (2.15)	8.49 (2.16)
Germany	6.07 (2.57)	6.45 (2.35)	6.67 (2.26)	7.69 (2.75)
Italy	6.74 (2.41)	6.63 (2.17)	6.59 (2.21)	7.28 (2.20)
Romania	5.87 (2.41)	6.09 (2.49)	6.49 (2.20)	7.16 (2.41)
Great Britain	6.31 (2.77)	6.50 (2.22)	7.11 (2.29)	8.04 (2.19)
All	**6.19 (2.62)**	**6.59 (2.29)**	**6.91 (2.27)**	**7.58 (2.36)**

Repressive Country/Propensity to vote	Excluded	Low	Medium	High
Austria	5.79 (3.08)	6.48 (2.56)	7.03 (2.35)	8.26 (2.18)
Belgium (F)	7.57 (2.74)	7.91 (2.12)	8.47 (1.75)	9.04 (1.83)
Belgium (N)	7.06 (2.28)	7.36 (2.06)	7.90 (1.86)	8.38 (1.82)
Denmark	5.96 (2.97)	7.09 (2.04)	7.35 (2.22)	8.53 (2.08)
France	6.23 (3.13)	7.08 (2.39)	7.58 (2.42)	8.49 (2.16)
Germany	6.84 (2.77)	7.42 (2.27)	7.09 (2.39)	8.09 (2.59)
Italy	7.56 (2.68)	8.00 (2.21)	8.07 (2.09)	8.97 (1.74)
Romania	8.08 (2.32)	7.24 (2.86)	7.30 (2.62)	8.61 (2.06)
Great Britain	7.11 (2.87)	7.42 (2.29)	7.80 (2.24)	8.59 (1.92)
All	**6.84 (2.89)**	**7.36 (2.38)**	**7.65 (2.32)**	**8.66 (2.01)**

Notes: Figures are on a 0–10 scale.

Xenophobia

Country / Effective vote	No	European or National	Both
Austria	6.33 (3.17)	8.57 (1.97)	8.74 (2.00)
Belgium (F)	6.83 (2.76)	8.42 (2.28)	8.81 (1.76)
Belgium (N)	7.02 (2.65)	8.88 (1.47)	9.24 (1.46)
Denmark	5.39 (3.04)	7.80 (2.43)	9.10 (1.49)
France	6.00 (2.98)	8.19 (2.56)	8.86 (2.20)
Germany	5.63 (3.03)	8.17 (2.41)	9.12 (1.71)
Italy	6.40 (3.08)	7.70 (2.61)	8.81 (1.80)
Romania	5.25 (2.53)	6.38 (2.43)	5.99 (2.10)
Great Britain	6.70 (2.97)	8.53 (2.13)	9.07 (1.66)
All	6.02 (3.03)	8.17 (2.41)	8.89 (1.88)

Populism

Country / Effective vote	No	European or National	Both
Austria	7.42 (2.39)	8.63 (1.78)	8.65 (1.97)
Belgium (F)	8.01 (2.11)	9.38 (1.43)	9.00 (1.85)
Belgium (N)	7.87 (2.08)	8.68 (1.68)	9.10 (1.53)
Denmark	5.93 (2.70)	6.67 (2.24)	7.33 (2.16)
France	7.85 (2.32)	8.45 (1.82)	8.78 (2.17)
Germany	7.94 (2.31)	9.20 (1.56)	9.11 (1.76)
Italy	8.53 (1.97)	8.52 (1.65)	8.90 (1.60)
Romania	8.18 (2.39)	8.00 (2.10)	8.99 (1.89)
Great Britain	7.88 (2.17)	8.78 (1.66)	9.11 (1.52)
All	7.84 (2.37)	8.48 (1.88)	8.80 (1.86)

Reactionary

Country / Effective vote	No	European or National	Both
Austria	5.32 (2.71)	6.32 (2.55)	7.41 (2.28)
Belgium (F)	7.11 (2.30)	8.21 (1.80)	8.35 (1.90)
Belgium (N)	6.22 (2.44)	7.56 (2.38)	7.79 (2.15)
Denmark	5.22 (2.60)	6.58 (2.21)	7.53 (2.34)
France	7.02 (2.32)	7.63 (2.12)	7.95 (2.30)
Germany	6.08 (2.56)	7.80 (2.40)	7.78 (2.46)
Italy	6.79 (2.27)	7.03 (2.40)	7.46 (2.12)
Romania	6.09 (2.45)	6.19 (2.10)	7.79 (2.19)
Great Britain	6.72 (2.51)	7.89 (2.11)	8.16 (2.26)
All	6.41 (2.51)	7.42 (2.29)	7.78 (2.30)

Repressive

Country / Effective vote	No	European or National	Both
Austria	6.06 (2.96)	7.65 (2.36)	8.18 (2.31)
Belgium (F)	7.80 (2.50)	9.00 (1.85)	8.73 (2.28)
Belgium (N)	7.37 (2.19)	8.10 (1.86)	8.33 (1.88)
Denmark	6.47 (2.81)	7.45 (2.78)	8.80 (1.79)
France	6.68 (2.87)	8.59 (2.26)	8.51 (2.31)
Germany	6.85 (2.74)	8.30 (2.10)	8.31 (2.33)
Italy	8.07 (2.32)	8.78 (1.96)	9.12 (1.69)
Romania	7.75 (2.52)	6.63 (2.00)	8.76 (1.85)
Great Britain	7.42 (2.58)	8.66 (1.72)	8.58 (2.01)
All	7.15 (2.72)	8.47 (2.09)	8.67 (2.05)

Notes: figures are on a 0–10 scale.

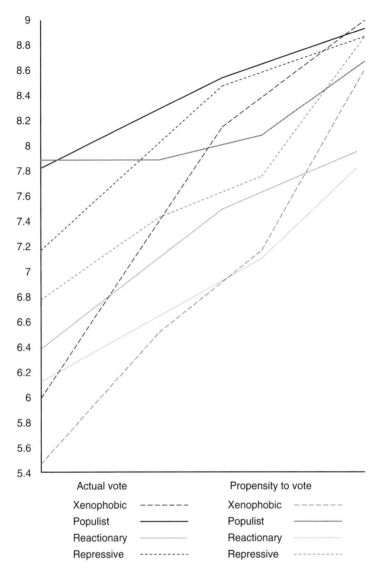

Figure 8.1 Ideological pillars, propensity to vote, and actual vote for the extreme right

their discourse along these two dimensions of negative identity and authoritarianism, the choice of strategic-discursive location by an extreme right party will affect its ability to seduce a smaller or larger proportion of potential extreme right voters depending on the match achieved between the

party's strategic-discursive location and the ideological preferences of its potential voters.
The logical progression of our model is that:

1. Adhesion to various pillars of extreme right ideology should largely explain why individuals are more or less likely to be potential (and indeed likely) extreme right voters;
2. The match between the parties' strategic-discursive choices and the potential voter's ideological focus will explain some further variation within the model.

Let us therefore first consider models of extreme right potential voting.

Table 8.15 shows that our model of propensity to vote for the extreme right accounts for 20 per cent of the total variance in propensity to vote for the extreme right. This is a high result considering how skewed the dependent variable is. Even more importantly, however, all the relevant parts of our model, importance of individuals' adhesion to the four cardinal pillars of extreme right ideology, parties' strategic-discursive choices, and match between voters' and parties' ideological foci, conceived as an interaction between the negative identity and authoritarian dimension 'balances' of respondents and parties. These effects are confirmed when controlling for such variables as gender, age, education, and income.

Let us first consider adhesion to the four pillars of extreme right ideology. All four pillars have a statistically significant effect, but xenophobia is the highest determinant of potential extreme right voting, and in the case of

Table 8.15 Regression of propensity to vote for extreme right parties

	b (s.e.)	β
Xenophobic	0.40 (0.01)	0.34**
Populist	−0.09 (0.02)	−0.06**
Reactionary	0.08 (0.02)	0.06**
Repressive	0.04 (0.02)	0.03*
Parties (negative-identity focus)	0.09 (0.01)	0.17**
Parties (authoritarianism)	0.03 (0.01)	0.05**
Match (negative identity)	0.1 (0.00)	0.07**
Match (authoritarianism)	0.00 (0.00)	0.01
Gender	−0.18 (0.06)	−0.03**
Age	−0.02 (0.00)	−0.06**
Education	−1.23 (0.12)	−0.10**
Income	0.56 (0.12)	0.04**
Intercept	1.37 (0.21)	
R^2		0.19

Notes: *: statistically significant at 0.05 or better; **: statistically significant at 0.01 or better.

populism, the relationship is in the wrong direction. Note that this anomaly may come from multi-collinearity problems and the strong pulling power of the xenophobic variable, which is correlated with populism at a 0.40 level. Reactionary and repressive pillars, although less strong than xenophobia, both have a statistically significant effect in the right direction. As for the other pure individual-level variables, they all have a statistically significant effect: negative for age and education (the latter being of some magnitude) and positive in the case of income (suggesting that once controlling for education, higher incomes mean a higher propensity to vote for the extreme right). The effect of gender is small but also statistically significant and points to a slightly higher likeliness to vote for the extreme right for men as compared to women, consistent (if limitedly so) with the rest of the literature.

In terms of the variables that correspond to the effect of party strategies, there is again a statistically significant effect of some magnitude for both dimensions. In terms of negative identity, there is a strong bonus to parties which focus on a predominantly xenophobic rhetoric as opposed to a populist one and thus increase citizens' propensity to vote for extreme right parties in the long term. This is interesting considering that Chapters 5 and 7 show that most extreme right parties seem to consider it more effective to choose a populist (rather than xenophobic) focus, but also that many parties with strong xenophobic references only switch to populist discourse in electoral periods. As for the authoritarian axis, it seems to give a bonus to parties choosing a reactionary approach over a repressive one, which is again at odds with the dominant choice of most extreme right parties, but rather consistent with the way the extreme right parties included in our analysis tailor their discourse to electoral cycles.

This time the model is partly successful, with a statistically significant and important effect of the match between the negative identity preferences of voters and the party(ies) competing for their vote. By contrast, the match on the authoritarian pillar does not have a statistically significant effect on the individual voter's propensity to vote.

Beyond the general model, it also seems interesting to consider how the individual-level components of our model work within each of the nine party systems included in the analysis. The results are summarised in Table 8.16, focusing on the overall explanatory power of the model as well as the ideological pillars which are statistically significant in each country.

The country-by-country results show that the model works better in some countries (e.g. Denmark, Italy, Flanders, Austria) than in others (French-speaking Belgium, Romania, Germany). It also shows that the ideological pillars that matter most in explaining who will have a higher propensity to vote for extreme right parties varies across countries as well. Xenophobia remains the dominant pillar in most countries, with the exception of Romania where populism is a stronger predictor of extreme right vote.

Table 8.16   Explanatory power of individual-level multivariate predictions of propensity to vote for the extreme right by country

Country	R^2	Significant ideological pillars
Denmark	0.27	Xeno** Reac** Pop** Repr**
Italy	0.25	Xeno** Pop** Repr**
Belgium (Dutch Speaking)	0.22	Xeno** Reac** Repr*
Austria	0.21	Xeno**
France	0.15	Xeno** Pop*
Great Britain	0.15	Xeno** Reac**
Belgium (French Speaking)	0.12	Xeno**
Romania	0.10	Pop** Reac** Xeno**
Germany	0.10	Xeno** Reac** Repr*

Notes: R^2 for each country based on individual-level predictors only
Significant ideological pillars in order of magnitude (beta). ** = sig<0.01, * = sig<0.05

Adhesion to reactionary ideology matters in many countries, but populism also matters in France and repressive ideology in Denmark, Italy, Flanders, and Germany.

Whether our four-pillar, bi-dimensional model also explains actual vote for the extreme right and not only propensity to vote for extreme right parties is also important to understand. Here again, we use the same model, which includes individual, parties, and 'match' interactive variables to explain actual voting for extreme right parties in national and European elections.

In many ways, the test of actual vote for an extreme right party is more extreme than that of propensity to vote for the extreme right. Fewer people actually vote for the extreme right (for European, national, or both elections) than would actually consider doing it, resulting in a highly skewed dependent variable. Although propensity to vote for the extreme right is measured as an absolute potential vote for the extreme right in the future, actual vote is obviously a significantly more complex issue with a large number of exogenous factors, including those relating to other parties' candidates, campaigns, and records.[5]

Table 8.17 presents some insights into how much of the decision to vote for the extreme right or not our model can explain in two different contexts. the first represents voters in general, and the second, corrects for the skewedness of voters' distributions, whereby in most countries, a clear majority of voters would completely exclude ever voting for an extreme right party, with their inclusion in the sample introducing `error' in the models. Therefore, under the second scenario, we correct for this error by excluding these non-voters.

We run a regular model of actual vote for the extreme right, which by and large confirms every finding from the propensity-to-vote model, but with a slightly lower ability to explain variance overall (with an R^2 of 0.11). As for

Table 8.17   Regression of actual vote for extreme right parties

	Model 1: All		Model 2: Including potential vote	
	b (s.e.)	*β*	*b (s.e.)*	*β*
Xenophobic	0.03 (0.00)	0.27**	0.1 (0.00)	0.16**
Populist	0.01 (0.00)	0.02	0.1 (0.00)	0.05**
Reactionary	0.01 (0.00)	0.05**	0.1 (0.00)	0.01
Repressive	−0.00 (0.00)	−0.02	−0.01 (0.00)	−0.04**
Parties (negative-identity focus)	−0.00 (0.00)	−0.03**	−0.01 (0.00)	−0.15**
Parties (authoritarianism focus)	0.01 (0.00)	0.07**	0.01 (0.00)	0.04**
Match (negative-identity focus)	0.00 (0.00)	0.02*	0.00 (0.00)	0.07**
Match (authoritarianism focus)	0.00 (0.00)	0.01	0.00 (0.00)	0.02*
Gender	−0.01 (0.01)	−0.02*	−0.01 (0.01)	−0.01
Age	−0.00 (0.00)	−0.08**	−0.00 (0.00)	−0.02*
Education	−0.08 (0.01)	−0.07**	−0.01 (0.01)	−0.00
Income	0.02 (0.01)	0.02	−0.02 (0.01)	−0.03*
Potential extreme right voter	0.03 (0.02)		0.06 (0.00)	0.61**
Intercept			−0.04 (0.02)	
R^2		0.11		0.43

Notes: *: statistically significant at 0.05 or better; **: statistically significant at 0.01 or better.

models of propensity to vote for the extreme right, in terms of ideological pillars, xenophobic values are the strongest predictor of effective extreme right vote, followed by reactionary values. In this general model, populist and repressive values are not statistically significant. In terms of the parties' positions, the parties' foci on both dimensions appear important and statistically significant, but this time the most vote-enticing negative-identity focus on the part of parties is one which is primarily populist and not xenophobic. This state of affairs seems to validate strongly the strategy of many extreme right parties, which develop xenophobic rhetoric away from elections (thus stimulating the propensity to vote for the extreme right in the long term) but focus on populist rather than xenophobic discourse in election periods as shown in Chapter 7 (thus boosting actual extreme right vote in specific electoral periods). Respondents' reactions seem to confirm that the extreme right discursive strategies on the negative-identity dimension are intuitive and potentially successful. As for the 'match' variables, it proves an important consideration again but only on the negative-identity dimension in the general model of extreme right actual vote.

Clearly, however, the results of model 1 are completely blurred by the fact that 86.1 per cent of the sample consists of non-extreme right voters and the remaining 13.9 per cent are shared between occasional and consistent electoral supporters of the extreme right. This strong skew, which we simply cannot avoid because it corresponds to the reality of support for political parties only a small portion of the population effectively votes for, encourages us to develop a second model where we also control for potential extreme right voting (based on propensity-to-vote results) in explaining why some people effectively vote for the extreme right or not in an election. As we know, 51.5 per cent of our sample claimed they would never in their life consider voting for an extreme right party. Controlling for whether a respondent is part of this small but important majority or is part of the population which would potentially consider voting for the extreme right in their life seems to make great sense. The results of this new model are extremely telling.

Once we control for the fact that a respondent is a potential extreme right voter or not, our model explains 43 per cent of the total variance in effective vote for the extreme right: nearly half of the final decision whether to vote for an extreme right party.

Not only is the model a powerful explanation of effective extreme right voting, but the inclusion of potential voting as a control variable also strengthens the importance of the main explanatory variables in our model when it comes to explaining citizens' actual vote. Three of the four ideological pillars of extreme right ideology become statistically significant, xenophobia, populism, and repression, although the latter with the wrong sign (but bear in mind multi-collinearity issues here as the pillars 'fight' for explained variance with potential voting, which already reacts to it). Party positions have a much stronger statistically significant effect favouring once again the choice of populist and reactionary discourses. Finally, the match variables become statistically significant for both dimensions and their effect is substantially increased, demonstrating that a potential extreme right voter is far more likely to vote for an extreme right party which matches his or her ideological focus in the context of negative identity (xenophobic or populist) and authoritarianism (reactionary or repressive).

8.11   From seducing individual voters to achieving global success: aggregate level fortunes of extreme right parties over time

In this last section of the chapter, we look at the evolution of the aggregate level of success of the eight extreme right parties that have consistently competed in national and other elections in the United Kingdom, Germany, and France in contemporary years. In traditional Downsian theory (Downs, 1957), the very definition of a political party is that it aims to achieve political power, and thus, by extension, to win elections. Since then, particularly in the case of multi-party systems, it has been theorised that political parties may try to achieve different types of success, not only by office seeking, vote seeking, or policy seeking (Lijphart, 1984; Luebbert, 1986), but also by sometimes exerting a nuisance power or indirect influence that may be tailored to an individual institutional context. One thing remains clear: by and large, it is accepted that political parties will want to achieve the best possible results in elections in order to maximise their power and influence. Extreme right parties, as seen in Chapter 1, tend to be secondary actors in most party systems. When assessing the success of extreme right parties, it is therefore important to look not only at national elections, where dominant parties may hope to obtain the key to government, but also at European Parliament elections, where smaller parties may hope to use the second-order election phenomenon (Reif & Schmitt, 1980) to benefit from the willingness of electorates to punish government parties and often large parties in general.Let us now discuss how the eight parties in our analysis evolved over time in both national and European Parliament elections. We also investigate how this evolution seems to matches the patterns we theoretically proposed earlier in this book by looking in particular at national intra-extreme right party competition.

In this section, we consider the evolution of the fortunes of extreme right parties across the countries included in our manifesto analysis, before focusing more specifically on three case-studies: France, Germany, and the United Kingdom.

Plate 7 charts the progress of extreme right parties in general, legislative, and parliamentary elections in Europe over the past 30 years. The general trend is one of: (1) multiplication, and (2) general progression. This is particularly and consistently true of some parties such as the Swiss SVP, the Swedish Democrats, or the Greek Laos. Other parties, such as the German Republikaner and the French MNR, have been consistently declining over the period. For many other European extreme right parties, the story of the past 30 years has been one of normalisation, with significant progression interrupted by periods of decline, and falls which have proved everything but final with the parties re-emerging a few years later; thus, parties which seemed to have consistently progressed, such as the Belgian Vlaams Belang or the French FN, have ended up losing ground in some elections but are already hoping for the sort of resurgence that the Austrian FPÖ and the Dutch PVV have experienced of late after surviving some significant crises.

The next step needed in our analysis is to understand whether the evolution of the extreme right parties over time is at all related to their strategic-discursive choices. The question encompasses several aspects: (1) Are extreme right parties from some quadrants more successful than others over time? (2) Have the four sub-types of extreme right parties evolved similarly?

Table 8.19 partly answers the first question and shows that, on the whole, only xenophobic-reactionary parties obtain significantly higher levels of adhesion than the three other sub-types of extreme right parties over the past 30 years. The other three categories have remarkably similar average results, with an overall average electoral score of 6.92 across all parties.

Apparent similarities, could of course obscure some differences across the period of over three decades. Figure 8.2 maps the evolution of the average

Table 8.18 Extreme right parties' scores in national elections, 1980–2010

Country	Party	1979–82	1983–84	1985–86	1987–88	1989–90	1991–92	1993–94	1995–96	1997–98	1999–2000	2001–02	2003–04	2005–06	2007–08	2009–10
Austria	FPÖ	6.1	5.0	9.7		16.6		22.5	21.9		26.9	10.0		11.0	17.5	
	BZÖ													4.1	10.7	
Belgium	VB*	2.3		1.4	1.9		6.6		7.8		9.9		11.6		12.0	7.8
	FNB*				0.1		1.1		2.3		0.4		2.0		2.0	0.5
Bulgaria	Ataka													8.1		9.4
Denmark	DF									7.4		12.0		13.2	13.9	
France	FN	0.2		9.9	9.8			12.4		14.9		11.3			4.3	
	MPF									2.4		0.8			1.2	
	MNR											1.1			0.4	
Germany	Rep					2.1		1.9		1.8		0.6		0.6		0.1
	NPD	0.2	0.2		0.6	0.3				0.3		0.4		1.8		1.8
	DVU									1.2		0.2		***		1.0
Greece	Laos												2.2		3.7	5.6
Italy	LN				0.5		8.7	8.4	10.1			3.9	3.9	4.6	8.3	
	AN	5.3	6.8		5.9		5.4	13.5	15.7			12.0	11.5	12.3	~	
	MSI								0.9			0.4		0.6	2.4	
Nethds	PVV**											17.0	5.7	5.9		15.5
Romania	PRM						3.9	22.9	4.5		19.4		13.0		3.2	
Russia	LD								11.2		6.0				8.1	
Slovakia	SNS					13.9	7.9	5.4		9.1		3.3	11.5	11.7		5.1
Sweden	SD									0.4		1.4		2.9		5.7
Switzd	SVP	11.1			11.0		11.9		14.9		22.5		26.6		28.9	
Turkey	MHP								8.2		18.0	8.4			14.3	
UK	BNP	0.5			0.6		1.2			1.3		3.9		0.7		3.1
	UKIP									1.1		1.5		2.3		1.9

Notes:

*Scores for the VB and FNB are at the national level. Representation in Plate 7 is as a proportion of Dutch- and French-speaking electorates. (To convert, in late 2000s, multiply VB score by 1.56 and FNB by 2.84.) VB scores include first Vlaams Blok, then Vlaams Belang.

**Note that score is that of the List Pim Fortuyn till 2003, then PVV.

***In 2005, NPD and DVU ran common lists

~In 2008, the AN ran common lists with the Popolo della Liberta

Election years:

Austria (1979, 1983, 1986, 1990, 1994, 1995, 1999, 2002, 2006, 2008);
Belgium (1981, 1985, 1987, 1991, 1995, 1999, 2003, 2007, 2010);
Bulgaria (2005, 2009);
Denmark (1998, 2001, 2005, 2007);
France (1981, 1986, 1988, 1993, 1997, 2002, 2007);
Germany (1980, 1983, 1987, 1990, 1994, 1998, 2002, 2005, 2009);
Greece (2004, 2007, 2009);
Italy (1979, 1983, 1987, 1992, 1994, 1996, 2001, 2004, 2006, 2008);
Netherlands (2002, 2003, 2006, 2010);
Romania (1992, 1996, 2000, 2004, 2008);
Russia (1993, 1995, 1999, 2003, 2007);
Slovakia (1990, 1992, 1994, 1998, 2002, 2006, 2010);
Sweden (1998, 2002, 2006, 2010)
Switzerland (1983, 1987, 1991, 1995, 1999, 2003, 2007);
Turkey (1995, 1999, 2002, 2007);
UK (1983, 1987, 1992, 1997, 2001, 2005, 2010)

Table 8.19   Average electoral score of extreme right party by quadrant

	Reactionary	Repressive
Xenophobic	9.07 (5.79)	6.79 (5.07)
Populist	6.78 (8.52)	6.65 (6.88)
All	*6.92 (6.54)*	

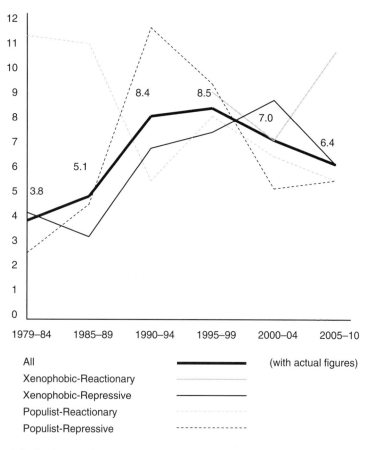

Figure 8.2   Evolution of extreme right parties over time by quadrant

support for the four types of extreme right parties for each half-decade between 1979 and 2010. The first finding of the decade is confirmation of the
overall trend of extreme right party fortunes over the period. The general
pattern seems to suggest that extreme right parties kept progressing till the
end of the 1990s before starting to lose ground. At the peak of their form in

the late 1990s, the 25 parties included in the analysis gathered an average 8.5 per cent of the vote in a typical election, which is much more than the 3.8 per cent they managed to attract in the early 1980s but also quite a lot more than the 6.4 per cent of the vote they declined to by the end of the 2000s. Most interestingly, the figure also suggests that different sub-types of extreme right parties have followed different patterns over time and peaked at different periods. Populist-reactionary parties were the most electorally successful sub-type of extreme right parties throughout the 1980s but have consistently declined since then. Populist-repressive parties progressed fast at first to become the strongest type of extreme right party in the early 1990s. They peaked during this period but suffered a steep fall until the early 2000s, after which they stabilised, remaining nevertheless the least successful type of extreme right party. Xenophobic-repressive parties have been much slower starters, but consistently progressed until the early 2000s when they emerged as the new leaders of the extreme right camp. In the later part of the 2000s, they lost some ground and converged towards the central tendency of the extreme right family. Finally, xenophobic-reactionary parties started emerging much later than the other three types of extreme right parties, but have managed a strong showing since the late 1990s, progressively becoming the leading electorally successful type of extreme right party of recent years.

These findings are confirmed by Table 8.20, which suggests that, over the whole period, parties choosing a reactionary focus have progressed faster each year on average than those choosing a populist one. At the same time, to a lesser extent, extreme right parties that chose a xenophobic focus of negative identity have also progressed faster than those which chose a populist strategic-discursive angle.

Overall, the European extreme right party family has certainly strengthened in the past 30 years, but it also seems to have ended the period of non-stop and apparently unstoppable growth that seemed to characterise it in the 1990s to lose a little bit of ground in the 2000s. Whether this is only a temporary threshold that some extreme right parties will surpass or they have reached a natural level of stabilisation remains to be seen. We have seen that the four sub-types of extreme right parties have seen different

Table 8.20 Evolution of the aggregate level success of European extreme right parties by strategic-discursive quadrant

	Average change between two consecutive elections	
	Reactionary	Repressive
Xenophobic	2.67 (5.46)	1.26 (5.85)
Populist	1.76 (2.71)	0.97 (5.23)

dynamic curves of success, and comparative differences remain significant in some cases. In order to get a clearer and more refined picture, we thus focus on the progression of extreme right parties in three countries with a long and diverse experience of extreme right politics: France, Germany, and the United Kingdom. According to the findings of Chapter 5, these parties represent all four quadrants of the extreme right ideological map.

8.12   Spotlight on three countries: France, Germany, and the United Kingdom

Evolution of extreme right party success in France

As explained in Chapter 3, the Front National emerged as the historical extreme right party in France, born in the 1970s before becoming a true political force in the mid-1980s. It was later joined by the MPF, which split from the moderate right in the mid-1990s, and the MNR, which split from the FN itself in 1998. We also saw in Chapter 5 that although the MPF progressively occupied a strategic-discursive position radically different from that of the FN, the MNR failed to differentiate itself in any significant way from its former big brother and simply assumed a slightly more blurred ideological identity than that historic comparator. According to our theory, the MNR should therefore have had difficulty coexisting successfully alongside the FN, unlike the MPF, which carved out its own ideological breathing space.

Table 8.21 looks at the historical results of all three parties in French general elections. After a timid start, the FN emerged as a strong political party in 1986, when France used proportional elections as a one-off departure from the fifth Republic tradition of two-ballot majority-plurality elections in single-member districts. (First ballot requires an absolute majority of the vote; if not, all candidates obtaining over 12.5 per cent of registered voters are allowed to run again in a second ballot, after which the candidate with the highest proportion of the vote is elected.) The limit of the institutional analysis is that a return to majority-plurality elections did not impede the

Table 8.21   Election results of French extreme right parties in general elections since 1978

		1978	1981	1986	1988	1993	1997	2002	2007
FN	%vote	0.8	0.2	9.9	9.8	12.4	14.9	11.3	4.3
	Seats	–	–	34	1	–	1	–	–
MPF	%vote						2.4	0.8	1.2
	Seats	–	–	–	–	–	2	1	1
MNR	%vote							1.1	0.4
	Seats							–	–

Notes: FN: National Front; MPF: Mouvement pour la France; MNR: Mouvement National Republicain.

progress of the FN in terms of the vote, despite condemning it to having between zero and one elected member of Parliament in all subsequent elections. The FN remained strong in general elections, apart from a disastrous result in the 2007 legislative ballot(Figure 8.3).

From the point of view of internal competition, the arrival of two trouble-makers (MNR and MPF) made electoral races far more interesting in terms of extreme right rivalry. Although the MPF still ran as part of the presidential majority in 1997, its first truly independent showdown in 2002 made for a timid electoral score. The party picked up more support in 2007, in a generally difficult election for smaller parties. The MNR followed a completely different curve. When it split from the FN in 1998, it was promised a bright future by many analysts; indeed, many French political commentators expected the new party to outshine the FN by embracing a similar discourse without the embarrassing blunders of FN leader Jean-Marie Le Pen. Although the 1.1 per cent of the vote obtained in 2002 was probably disappointing for leader Bruno Mégret and his troops, who had secured some major electoral successes in the municipal elections of 1999, the party's results continued to collapse steadily, reaching a negligible 0.4 per cent of

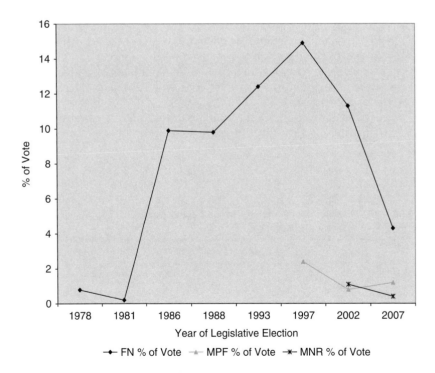

Figure 8.3 Extreme right electoral success in France

the vote in 2007. Thus, between the late 1990s and the late 2000s, the new extreme right party expected to do well collapsed, whereas the one expected to do poorly managed to build a strong enough reservoir of independent support to survive.

According to our model, this largely resulted from the fact that the MPF managed to find a distinctive strategic-discursive position to make it unique within the French extreme right scene; however, the MNR never managed to emerge from the shadow of the FN, whose ideological discourse it merely echoed. In terms of European Parliament elections, the picture is partly similar and partly different. The similar component is that, as was the case on the national political scene, the MNR started with a promising result of 3.3 per cent in 1999 before collapsing and remaining under 0.5 per cent in subsequent elections(see Table 8.22). The different aspect is that the MPF started its existence as a front runner in European Parliament elections, trumping the Front National, before a change of fortune in 2004, when the party declined in support and fell second to the FN. From this point of view, remember that the MPF first emerged as a splinter group of the Gaullist (moderate) right in the mid-1990s. At that time, it predominantly campaigned with a strong Eurosceptic focus, and even managed to get the support of prime traditional right-wing politicians such as Charles Pasqua. In the early 2000s, the party completely changed its ideological placing to focus primarily on xenophobic rhetoric, which emphasised its ideological independence from the FN but also came at a cost when it was trying to attract the disappointed moderate right-wing voters. Moreover, the new tone of the party revealed its extreme right identity and as a result many of the non-extremist politicians, including Pasqua, decided to withdraw their support.

In the following section, we turn our attention to the electoral success of the extreme right party family in Germany.

Table 8.22 Evolution of French extreme right parties' electoral success in European Parliament elections

		1979	1984	1989	1994	1999	2004	2009
FN	%vote	1.3*	11.2	11.7	10.5	5.7	9.8	6.3
	Seats	0	10	10	11	5	7	3
MPF	%vote	–	–	–	12.3	13.1	6.7	4.8
	Seats	–	–	–	13	6	3	1
MNR	%vote	–	–	–	–	3.3	0.3	0.5**
	Seats	–	–	–	–	0	0	0

Notes: * PFN was a predecessor of the FN. ** The French party MNR ran under the title of Parti de la France.

Evolution of extreme right party success in Germany

As explained in Chapter 3, the historical genesis of the German extreme right scene is somewhat less straightforward than in the French case. Under different names and in different forms, the NPD is probably the oldest component of the modern German extreme right; however, with several judicial condemnations and even dissolutions, for several lengthy periods the party did not have a presence, including in the 1980s, when the Republikaner emerged as a strong new extreme right party. As for the DVU, it mostly first emerged as a one-man populist party in 1987 (despite the pre-existence of a looser form of association since 1971), before rooting itself in its extreme right positioning throughout the 1990s.

In Chapter 5 we conclude that all three parties occupy distinct strategic-discursive positions, whereby the NPD is predominantly populist-repressive, the DVU xenophobic-repressive, and the Republikaner populist-reactionary. Despite some overlaps between each of these parties, they all have a form of ideological specificity that would normally give them a protected core electorate. In federal elections, it is interesting to note that the NPD, the true historical party, tended to lose ground in the early years until 1994, before slowly rebuilding its electoral strength. The party almost completely disappeared from its original Western heartlands to re-emerge primarily as a strong player in East Germany as soon as the unification honeymoon was over in the mid-1990s. By contrast, the Republikaner, which had a relatively strong showing in the 1990 elections, progressively lost ground to almost collapse towards the late 2000s. Finally, the DVU, which did not do well in 2002, started to pick up support again in subsequent elections, partly through some implicit partnership agreements with the popularising NPD (see Table 8.23). Altogether, by the late 2000s, the federal extreme right scene therefore looked poly-partisan, albeit with a consistent fading of the Republikaner whose support in wealthy Southern Germany (e.g. Bayern, Baden-Württemberg, Sachsen-Anhalt) seemed to erode for good.

When it comes to European Parliament elections, which were the first to witness a strong Republikaner party in 1989, the state of affairs is slightly different and the three parties' fortunes rather harder to compare. The main reason for this is that the NPD and DVU never ended up competing against each other. In some cases, the two parties gave some more or less explicit electoral advice to their voters; in other cases, they did not. As a result, neither party could be seen shining in European Parliament elections where they also tended to invest truly minimal effort and resources. The Republikaner saw its score consistently erode as it did for federal elections. The party obtained a modest 1.3 per cent in the 2009 vote(Table 8.24).

The most interesting conclusion we can derive from these European Parliament elections results, consistent with our model, is that even when a dominant extreme right party does not compete in an election, its support is in no way transferred automatically to other extreme right competitors.

Table 8.23 Election results of German extreme right parties in federal elections since 1949

		1949	1953	1957	1961	1965	1969	1972	1976
REP	%vote								
	Seats								
NPD	%vote	1.8	1.1	1.0	0.8	2.0	4.3	0.6	0.3
	Seats	5	–	–	–	–	–	–	–
DVU	%vote	–	–	–	–	–	–	–	–
	Seats								

		1980	1983	1987	1990	1994	1998	2002	2005	2009
REP	%vote				2.1	1.9	1.8	0.6	0.6	0.1
	Seats				–	–	–	–		
NPD	%vote	0.2	0.2	0.6	0.3	–	0.3	0.4	1.8	1.8
	Seats	–	–	–	–	–	–	–		0
DVU	%vote	–	–	–	–	–	1.2	0.2	1.8*	1.0
	Seats									

Notes: REP: Die Republikaner; NPD: Nationaldemokratische Partei Deutschlands (1949: German Right Party, DRP; 1953–1961: German Reich Party, DRP. *In the 2005 Federal Election, the NPD and the DVU (Deutsche Volksunion) ran under the same list. DVU candidates appeared on the NPD list.

Table 8.24 Evolution of German extreme right parties' electoral success in European Parliament elections

		1979	1984	1989	1994	1999	2004	2009
NPD	%vote	–	0.8	–	0.2	0.4	0.9	–*
	Seats	–	0	–	0	0	0	–*
DVU	%vote	–	–	1.6	–	–	–	0.4
	Seats	–	–	0	–	–	–	0
REP	%vote	–	0.8	7.1	3.9	1.7	1.9	1.3
	Seats	–	0	6	0	0	0	0

Notes: *The NPD and DVU had some electoral alliances and only the DVU ran in the 2009 European Parliament Elections.

In the case of the 2009 elections, the most fashionable extreme right party of the moment, the NPD, did not compete; however, the NPD's absence benefited neither the Republikaner nor the DVU, both of which achieved rather poor showings overall. In other words, the ideological differences between the three parties clearly seem to impede the transfer of electoral support from one to the other, regardless of whether an absent party tries to influence its voters.

Evolution of extreme right parties' success in Great Britain

The third country included in our comparison is the United Kingdom (or rather, in practical terms, Great Britain, as Northern Ireland has a different

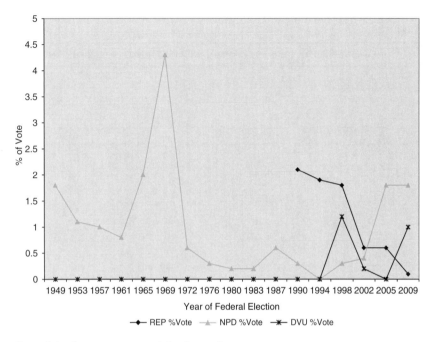

Figure 8.4   German extreme right electoral success

core structure and is not aligned on the left/right spectrum in the usual sense). The historic British extreme right party was the National Front, which slowly lost some ground to be replaced by the British National Party, a splinter group which became a fully-fledged party in 1982. In the 1990s, the UK Independence Party emerged as a Eurosceptic party before progressively mutating into a more broadly encompassing extreme right political party. In Chapter 3, we highlight some elements of proximity and tension between these three parties, including their history of prime politicians' moving from one party to the other, and mostly failed attempts at electoral agreements. In Chapter 5, we find that the BNP tends to occupy mostly the xenophobic-repressive quadrant in our conceptual map. The UK Independence Party has located in the completely opposite quadrant, the populist-reactionary quadrant. According to our model, this position would make it easier for UKIP to survive alongside its rival, as compared to the scenario in which it would try to replicate the ideological identity of the BNP and thus compete with the historic party on its own ground.

Table 8.25 shows how the fortunes of the three parties in general elections have evolved over time. Although the modern BNP never managed to equal the strong results of the National Front in the 1960s, since it re-emerged as an independent political party in 1982 and apart from a weak showing in 2005, its electoral strength has consistently progressed. Conversely, the

Table 8.25   Election Results of British extreme right parties in general elections since 1964

	1964	1966	1970	1974	1974	1979	1983	1987	1992	1997	2001	2005	2010
BNP	9.1*	5.3*	–	–	–	–	0.5	0.6	1.2	1.3	3.9	0.7	3.1
	–	–	–	–	–	–	–	–	–	–	–	–
UKIP										1.1	1.5	2.3	1.9
											–	–	–

Notes: *1964 and 1966 results are those of the National Front, the BNP only emerging as a party in 1982.

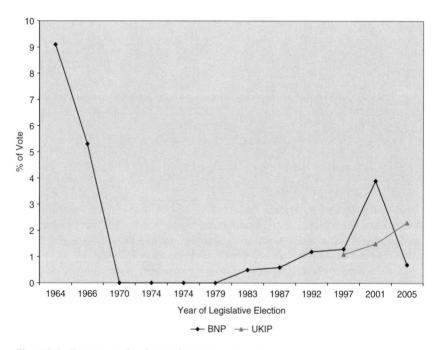

Figure 8.5   Extreme right electoral success in Britain

UKIP was always portrayed in the media as a Eurosceptic party despite its increasingly generalist rhetoric, but since it first ran for general elections in 1997 its electoral support has consistently progressed, and it overtook the BNP as the top extreme right party in the general elections of 2005 (Figure 8.5). This seems to confirm our understanding that extreme right political parties mostly encroach on each other's electorate when they are situated in close strategic-discursive proximity; extreme right parties situated in

Table 8.26 Evolution of British extreme right parties' electoral success in European Parliament elections

		1979	1984	1989	1994	1999	2004	2009
BNP	%vote	–	–	–	–	–	4.8	6.0
	Seats	–	–	–	–	–	0	2
UKIP	%vote	–	–	–	1.0	7.0	16.0	16.1
	Seats	–	–	–	0	3	12	

different quadrants on our conceptual map may attract new types of potential extreme right voters.

Table 8.26, which looks how the British extreme right parties' European Parliament election results evolved over time, seems to confirm this broad tendency, but the way the parties approached elections make their results more difficult to compare. Before 2004, the BNP invested no effort into European Parliament elections, preferring to focus all its resources and energy into the local elections that always took place at the same time. Conversely, the BNP would also leave the field entirely open to UKIP, which already emerged as an important player in these elections in 1994 and 1999. When the other two parties joined the race in 2004 and 2009, they clearly confirmed that this did not, in any way, affect the electoral support basis of UKIP. Both the BNP and UKIP managed to thrive at the same time, and their fortunes progressed synchronically, confirming that the types of potential voters they were seducing were probably parallel rather than overlapping.

Throughout the 1990s and 2000s, British extreme right parties managed to progress in electoral terms in parallel, without having the success of one affect the electoral potential of the other, either in general or in European Parliament elections.

8.13 Summary

In the first section of this chapter, we examine the profile and characteristics of an extreme right voter. As we know from other areas of our study, it is extremely hard to conduct empirical analyses of extreme right voters because of the relatively small number of voters in each country and the fact that most electoral studies exclude smaller parties such as those belonging to the extreme right party family. The existing literature highlights certain social groups believed to be more susceptible to vote for an extreme right party. For example, the typical profile of an extreme right voter tends to be blue-collar worker or unemployed, with a low level of education, between the age of 18 and 25, and predominately male. Although these social groups are more likely to vote for an extreme right party, there is a relative amount of variance across countries. These variations show that few social categories are left untouched by the allure of the extreme right discourse and that the electoral base of extreme right parties often dissects boundaries that are usually tied to the traditional left-right socio-political cleavage. With this in mind, the next section endeavours to understand the ideological preferences of the voters in each of the three countries included in our analysis. We attempt to find a match between the ideological position of a party (ascertained by the empirical testing of the conceptual map via elite interviews and analysis of party manifestos) and the preferences of the party's targeted electorate. In order to do this, we analyse the ideological preferences of potential and actual voters on the four main pillars. First, we look at the average propensity to vote across countries. In Italy, only 33.2 per cent of the voters would never consider voting for any of the three extreme right parties competing for their vote, but this proportion increases to 51.5 per cent of the electorate across the eight countries, and even to 75.6 per cent of voters in Germany. Second, the proportion of respondents claiming never to vote for an extreme right party respectively reaches 72.7 per cent in Austria, 86.1 per cent across the eight countries, and 95.1 per cent in French-speaking Belgium. The proportions claiming to vote for extreme right parties in both elections are 3.3 per cent in French-speaking Belgium and 28.0 per cent in Austria while averaging 9.6 per cent across the eight countries and nine political systems.

When comparing the results of the two questions there is a perfect match between potential and actual voters when it comes to absolute extreme right non-voters; with some minor exceptions, the actual vote tends to increase when the propensity to vote for extreme right parties increases as well. Overall levels of ideological predisposition to extreme right voting also change significantly across countries. This variation in the distribution of the national electorates across the four ideological pillars undoubtedly affects the chances of electoral success for each individual party and confirms that some of their electoral success will depend upon their strategic-discursive choices and their consequent location on the conceptual map.

In analysing how the electoral success of extreme right parties has evolved, we encounter some interesting results and findings. Consider systems in which multiple extreme right parties compete against each other. Regardless of national context (in some countries, the extreme right was globally on the 'up', in others, on the 'down'), the emergence of new internal extreme right competitors has different consequences depending on whether they invest a pre-occupied strategic-discursive ground or a previously abandoned one. As predicted by our model, in the former case, as with the emergence of the MNR on the grounds already occupied by the FN in France, the new entrant will find it hard to prosper unless it can actually fight the historic party to death. In the latter case, as with the emergence of UKIP in a quadrant completely opposed to that of the BNP within the extreme right conceptual map, the two parties will be able to prosper alongside each other;

they may even benefit from a new dynamic of extreme right voting that they may jointly generate.

Despite the differentiation often made between true extreme right parties and single-issue, notably Eurosceptic – parties, ultimately the fortunes of extreme right parties tend to be parallel in national and European elections. A given party may do much better in one type of election than in the other, but on the whole they do not tend to improve in one type of election if they collapse in the other.

More generally, however, we show that the four sub-types of extreme right parties have had different types and patterns of dynamics of electoral success over time. Populist-reactionary parties peaked first in the 1980s but also declined fastest soon afterward. Then, populist-repressive parties progressed fast to become dominant in the early 1990s but fell steeply later on before stabilising in the late 2000s; they nevertheless remain the least successful type of extreme right party of the current period. Xenophobic-repressive parties, which had a slow start, took over as the most successful type of extreme right party in the early 2000s; however, they regressed toward the main average of the party family in the late 2000s, when recently emerged xenophobic-reactionary parties finally took over as the most successful current type of extreme right competitor

9
Summary of Findings, Conclusions, and Discussion

9.1 Introduction

Mapping extreme right ideology over the past eight chapters, our book casts a spotlight on parties, manifestos, press releases, leaders, and voters to get a sense of the shape, tensions, and variations within the extreme right universe. Throughout the book, we confirm the founding statement of Chapter 1: far from being a monolithic and unified concept, the European extreme right constitutes a varied and complex multidimensional universe, with its tensions, hesitations, transformations, and challenges on how to match the preferences of parties, leaders, members, and potential voters over time.

The notion of multidimensionality is both fundamental and multi-leveled in our model. Much of the literature has already highlighted differences and inconsistencies amongst extreme right parties, leaders, and voters. Our goal is to understand analytically and demonstrate empirically how, far from being oddities or anomalies, these variations follow specific patterns along two strategic-discursive dimensions: negative identity, which can be expressed in a xenophobic or populist way, and an authoritarian dimension, which itself can assume a reactionary or a repressive mode.

This concluding chapter has two main goals:

1. Highlight how our main findings fit together to draw a clearer map of the European extreme right.
2. Grasp the broader consequences of our findings for our general understanding of the evolution of party ideology and party families in a largely dealigned context, as well as the way we envision the evolution of party competition and voter choices within and across party families.

Before we look at the empirical findings, note that the extreme right family is a fast-changing political section of a fast-changing world. This book is a study of contemporary extreme politics, and our findings are relevant to specific times and data sources. By the time the book is published, or within days, weeks, months, or years, new parties will have emerged on the extreme right scene while others will have clearly ceased to belong to the extreme right. For example, at the beginning of this volume we could note that although the Alleanza Nazionale clearly was an extreme right party according to most of the literature at some point in its life, a majority now consider that it has slowly but successfully escaped that category. Conversely, much of the literature considers today's Swiss SVP as an important member of the extreme right party family, but some decades ago the party could not have been associated with extreme right politics by any commentator. Further such complications are bound to occur, and we insist again on the necessary relativism in associating any party or voter to any party family whatsoever in a world where these families are neither clear-cut nor positively defined.

When it comes to the timing of the data used, a few points need to be borne in mind. The party manifesto we analysed were dated between 2006 and 2008, anchoring this book to that specific snapshot in time. The press releases used in Chapter 7 date back to 1999 in some cases and were collected until either 2008 or 2009, depending on the case involved. The interviews were conducted over a period of a year and the survey data was collected in 2009, on the days that followed that year's European Parliament Elections. For these reasons, our findings refer to these specific time points and any conclusions drawn from these results should be viewed within this time frame.

9.2 Key findings: ideological match and mismatch between European extreme right parties and their voters

Throughout this study, we theoretically develop and empirically test a conceptual map of the extreme right ideological world, based on two dimensions: (1) a negative identity dimension that can take two predominant forms of expression, which we respectively define as xenophobic and populist, and (2) an authoritarian dimension, of which the two founding modes are respectively reactionary and repressive. We show that the first dimension concerns the way an extreme right party, leader, or voter tends to identify the simplified source of the problems faced by the nation and that the second concerns the equally simplified universal and utopian solution that they propose to fix it.

In order to test our model, our research design embraces multiple empirical tests starting with interviews of some extreme right party leaders and high-ranking politicians from France and Britain. We also systematically analyse the party manifestos of 25 extreme right parties across 17 party systems, and look at the dynamic evolution of the discourse of five extreme right parties from as many different countries, over several years using their press releases. Finally, we spotlight the voters and potential voters of the extreme right, considering various attributes of their demographics and ideological stances, and looking at the impact of party positions and the match between party and voter ideological foci on their individual decision whether to vote for an extreme right party, before considering the evolution of the aggregate-level support for the parties from 17 political systems whose manifestos we coded and analysed in Chapter 5.

Let us now summarise some of the most intriguing findings derived from this battery of coordinated empirical tests. In Chapter 4, we attempt to understand the spontaneous forms of discourse used by extreme right leaders and high-level representatives, and how they correspond to the four ideological pillars identified in our conceptual model. In order to do so, we interviewed 92 leading politicians from four French and British parties (the FN and MPF in France) and (UKIP and BNP in Britain). These politicians included top party leaders and executives, locally elected representatives, MEPs, and young party organisation leaders. We use these interviews to confirm how the references these politicians make vary along the two highlighted dimensions of negative identity and authoritarianism. The interviews also enable us to understand qualitatively the specific types of xenophobic, populist, reactionary, and repressive references made by extreme right party leaders in their everyday discourse.

Different politicians tend to emphasise different pillars in their discourse. For instance, the BNP and MPF interviewees tend more to use xenophobic discourse, whereas the FN and UKIP leaders place a stronger emphasis on a populist alternative. Similarly, the MPF and UKIP show a clear tendency to stress reactionary references; the FN and the BNP politicians are clearly more enthusiastic when suggesting repressive solutions to the ills of their respective societies. Some examples of discourse that we highlight include populist discourse referring to a glorious past or golden age. Leaders advocate a return to traditional morals and values and demand respect of the family, the sacred nucleus of society. Within the domain of the repressive discourse, we hear leaders speak of enforcing law and order, calls for the reintroduction of the death penalty, a strengthened state that can eradicate delinquency and deliver 'proper' sentences to criminals. Similarly, on the negative identity dimension, we hear leaders refer to measures to stop mass immigration, the importance of preserving the nation, the imminent danger posed by foreigners to national identity and the nation's very existence. Finally, in reference to the populist conception, leaders cite the corruption and betrayal of the politicians and institutional elite and claim to represent the man on the street, stating that their party is the only true voice of the people and therefore different from all the rest of the parties and politicians that are only in it for what they can get out of it.

Chapter 4 uses the qualitatively and more spontaneous approach to capture the four types of discourse that structure the two dimensions of our extreme right conceptual universe, whereas Chapter 5 embraces a quantitative and more systematic methodology to evaluate the party manifestos of 25 extreme right parties that compete in 17 political systems. We simply count the total references to words embodying the four pillars of interest in our conceptual map of extreme right ideology, measure them as proportions of the total word count in each party manifesto, and finally compare them across parties.

One of our first key findings in Chapter 5 is that the total global references to words belonging to the four pillars number quite high in the discourse of extreme right parties, averaging 39.5 per cent of total valid words for the 25 extreme right parties analysed. Again, this does not mean 40 per cent of the party manifestos; rather, this is the proportion of references that a reader can effectively *associate* with notions of cultural identity (e.g. nation, minority, foreignness), civic identity (e.g. parties, elite, partisan cartels), the past (e.g. history, heritage, transmission), and state-controlled order (e.g. crime, justice, punishment), regardless of their connotation.

Within the framework of our model, these references, regardless of the connotation actually provided within manifesto discourse, will resonate within the minds of potential extreme right voters and echo their ideological preferences. In exactly the same way, social democrats' talking of inequality, even without any explicit connotation, will ring a bell in the minds of their potential voters, as will liberals when the word freedom is repeated in their manifesto.

Direct references to the two dimensions, by their strong presence, seem to confirm their role at the heart of the extreme right ideology. This finding supports our core theoretical expectation that the negative identity and authoritarianism dimensions of discourse are indeed the structuring backbone of the extreme right ideology and distinguish the extreme right from neighbouring party families. That is, even though non-extreme right parties can also refer to a xenophobic, populist, reactionary, or repressive ideology, these references added together will simply not compare to the total negative identity and authoritarianism emphasis of an extreme right party. Our findings also show a clear and important negative correlation between xenophobic and populist discourse on the one hand, and between reactionary and repressive discourse on the other hand.

The next equally important finding from the perspective of our conceptual map is that the 25 party manifestos coded in our analysis confirm that different parties can occupy any one of the four quadrants of extreme right ideology defined by our model: xenophobic-reactionary, xenophobic-repressive, populist-reactionary, and populist-repressive. Overall, the 25 parties consist of ten populist-repressive parties (e.g. the FN, the FPÖ, or the VB), eight xenophobic-repressive parties (e.g. the BNP, the Lega Nord, the PVV or the Russian Liberal-Democrats), five populist-reactionary parties (e.g. the SVP and UKIP) and three xenophobic-reactionary parties (e.g. the DF and the Turkish MHP). This finding is extremely significant because much of the literature tends to claim that one given pillar (e.g. xenophobia for the proponents of the anti-immigration party model or populism for the supporters of the right-wing populist definition) is a prerequisite for admission into the extreme right club. Our results suggest, however, that you can be a fully fledged member of the extreme right party family even with relatively marginal xenophobic references if you make up for them in terms of populist discourse and authoritarianism or vice versa. To add to the more quantitative analysis of word frequency, we also highlight numerous extracts from the party programmes that typified the ideological discourse of the two British extreme right parties: the BNP and UKIP. This allows us to understand further the discursive context of the ideological word references and helps us validate the quantitative analysis.

From this confirmation of the organised multifaceted nature of the extreme right, it intuitively follows that one should examine the effects of this model on party competition, be it internal (between multiple extreme right parties within the same party system) or external (between an extreme right party and its non-extreme right competitors). This is the object of Chapter 6, with a few important findings. We confirm the theoretical expectations that we outline in Section 2.7: when several extreme right parties coexist within the same party system, as in the three case studies covered by our analysis, it seems inefficient to focus only on their relative placement on broad left-right scales. Instead, it is more relevant to look at their respective locations within the confines of the extreme right conceptual map.

The key to the parallel survival of multiple extreme right parties within a specified system becomes their location in different quadrants of the conceptual map so that each party retains an independent reservoir of potential voters who will ensure its continued electoral existence. The supposedly doomed MPF survived alongside the FN until some unforeseen non-political circumstances put a question mark on its future. In contrast, even when a party is promised some electoral fortune, if it locates itself in the same quadrant as a pre-established party, only one of them will probably survive. Still in France, this was the case of the MNR, which many commentators originally expected to do well by but ended up suffocating electorally after failing to find an ideological niche, any distance at all from the FN. These contradictory tales emphasise the need for extreme right challengers to occupy different and vacant quadrants from their internal competitors. In fact, in the case of the United Kingdom, we show that the quadrant first invested in by an extreme right party may not be the most electorally rich; thus, UKIP, while settling itself in the opposite quadrant to the BNP, found itself uncovering an apparently much stronger electoral mine.

In the same chapter we look at patterns of external competition, showing that the type of quadrant occupied by extreme right parties unveils different possible strategies for their mainstream right- and left-wing opponents. These include a broad choice between pre-empting areas of focus of extreme right parties or trying to marginalise them. Of course, the strategic-discursive choices of extreme right parties themselves will affect the best possible response of mainstream competitors as well as their credibility in terms of issue ownership. Thus, for example, in the case of the populist-repressive FN, the repressive response of right-wing Sarkozy was clearly more threatening to the historic French extreme right party than the reactionary discourse of a similarly right-wing Chirac was, even though it also provided greater latitude to respond to the MPF with its predominantly xenophobic-reactionary manifesto.

We then move on to Chapter 7, where we look at how the discourse of five extreme right parties from five different countries evolved dynamically over time. The chapter confirms the negative correlation between the xenophobic and populist pillars of negative identity, and between the reactionary and repressive alternative forms of authoritarianism. The chapter also shows that most extreme right parties have significant variation in the focus of their discourse over time. In most cases, these changes are cyclical: populist references increase during electoral periods, and xenophobic references increase away from elections. Some parties also seem to have a long-term progressive switch from one type of discourse to another. For instance the BNP's discourse progressively changed over the 1990s and 2000s. Finally, a few extreme cases of complete consistency (DF) or continuous change and apparently inconsistent variations (SVP) complete the possible models of cyclical or permanent consistencies and inconsistencies of extreme right party discourse over time.

Finally, in Chapter 8, we focus on the extreme right's potential electorate. In this chapter, we first empirically introduce the notion of potential extreme right voters which we analytically develop in Chapter 2. We show that, overall, respondents in the nine political systems included in our analysis are shared almost equally between those who would never ever consider voting for an extreme right party, and those who would consider doing so. We demonstrate that it is difficult to find common social demographic traits of extreme right voters that work across countries and historical contexts. For instance, variations across gender and age do not work in the same way in different countries, and although education clearly has a negative impact on the likeliness of a citizen to vote for the extreme right, the impact of income is far more volatile.

We contrast these limits of the political sociology approach to the clear specificity of potential extreme right voters in terms of how they score on xenophobic, populist, reactionary, and repressive scales. Indeed, we demonstrate that as the propensity to vote for extreme right parties increases so do the scores of voters on all four scales, and the relationship between propensity to vote and these scales is in fact not only statistically significant but also substantively strong. The relationship is equally strong when it comes to looking at respondents' actual/planned vote for extreme right parties in terms of both European and national (general) elections. We then show that two party-related types of variables also have a strong impact on the vote. The strategic-discursive choices of extreme right parties on the negative identity and authoritarianism dimension have a statistically significant impact over propensity to vote for the extreme right and actual vote for the extreme right alike. Moreover, the actual match between the position of the parties competing in elections and that of the actual individual voter also has a strong and statistically significant effect on propensity to vote for the extreme right and on actual extreme right vote, especially when we control for potential vote. All the multiple regression models show statistically significant effects of the relevant independent variables included in our theoretical model, and successfully explain considerable proportions of variance in the propensity of citizens to vote for the extreme right and their actual vote overall.

In the last section of Chapter 8 we examine the long-term electoral success of all 25 parties from 17 systems, whose manifestoes we first analyse in Chapter 5. The section allows us to move back from the individual level and the decision process of individual potential extreme right voters to the aggregate-level success of parties, emphasising the effects of strategic discursive 'match and mismatch' between extreme right parties and their potential voters over time. We show that the dynamic curves of the electoral success of extreme right parties vary across parties and political systems. Nevertheless, the overall tendency of the parties included in our analysis was one of steep progress till the late 1990s followed by a slight decline over the 2000s. We also demonstrate how the four different types of extreme right parties highlighted in our model have had different fortunes over time. Populist-reactionary parties were first to peak and dominate the extreme right scene in Europe in the 1980s but have declined since the early 1990s. Populist-repressive parties took over in the early 1990s but declined steeply afterward. Xenophobic-repressive parties, which emerged more slowly at first, became the most successful type of extreme right party in the early 2000s before stabilising at a time when the most recently emerged xenophobic-reactionary parties became the most successful sub-type of extreme right party in the late 2000s.

We then focus more specifically on three case studies: France, Germany, and the United Kingdom, looking at their extreme right parties' results in general and European parliament elections. We confirm quantitatively the results of Chapter 6 that concern the need for a new extreme right party to: (1) choose a clear position in one given strategic-discursive quadrant, and (2) ensure that this quadrant be distinct from those already occupied by pre-existing historic extreme right parties. We even show that when this is indeed accomplished and two parties spread over two significantly differentiated sub-parts of the extreme right conceptual universe, as is the case for the BNP and UKIP in Great Britain, then, far from threatening each other's survival, these ideologically complementary parties may create an extreme right momentum that could lead to their parallel electoral growth. This result clearly challenges a simplistic interpretation of Sartori's (1987) analysis of the spatial model of the vote and party dynamics in the context of multiparty systems.

We obviously acknowledge the fact that the political science literature on party support has made tremendous progress over the past 60 years and we draw upon their findings and conclusions here in this book. Traditional explanations of extreme right support successfully include sociological determinants (e.g. Lipset & Rokkan's 1967 four cleavages), socialisation (e.g. Greenstein, 1960; Butler & Stokes, 1974), utility maximisation (the entire rational choice literature starting with Downs, 1957), economic perceptions (e.g. van der Brug et al., 2007; Wlezien & Anderson, 1997), short-term factors such as policy, personality, or incumbents' evaluations and records.

In this particular context, it was not possible to propose a fully integrated model as the data is not based on a voting behaviour dataset and therefore did not include all these variables. When looking at the impact of citizens' positioning on all four pillars as a possible source of support for extreme right parties in general or individual parties in particular, one should therefore take our results with a certain caution if positions on these four pillars could likely be highly correlated with any of these traditional explanations of voting behaviour. Because of this limit of our model, we restrict our interpretation of the findings as 'correlations' and 'patterns' between support for xenophobic, populist, repressive, and reactionary statements and propensity to vote for extreme right parties, without claiming that the model necessarily explains every aspect of such behaviour, for which a model that would also include exogenous forces of context and competition is obviously needed.

With this note of caution in mind about the limitations of our analysis, we have, however, proposed a conceptual model that seems largely confirmed by the discourse and behaviour of extreme right parties, leaders, and potential voters. The broader implications of our findings on the more global fields of partisan politics, party competition, and electoral behaviour must also be considered in a European context of significantly dealigned politics.

9.3 Broader implications: towards a new generalisable model of partisan competition and ideologically coherent dealigned electoral behaviour

Some of this book's findings prompt a question about the extent to which our model and its implications might be generalisable to other countries, party families, and aspects of electoral choice and electoral change. In terms of countries, we can only re-emphasise that although some aspects of our analysis were applied to a large European extreme right universe, some countries or parties were excluded for practical reasons; and other aspects of the analysis focus on smaller sub-samples of case studies. Any extension of the universe in which any sub-question is tested would help us to test more refined hypotheses on why certain extreme right parties choose specific quadrants and on patterns of internal and external party competition. Ultimately, a larger potential extreme right voter sample may result in more statistically significant findings about different types of potential extreme right voters.

Whether our model is generalisable to other party families when it comes to the party family ideological theory is, however, a significantly more complex issue. Our model posits that ultimately, although any political party will make a number of policy proposals on multiple issues (an extreme right party may of course make numerous proposals on tax policy, foreign policy, pensions, or the environment), a limited number of discursive themes may create structuring ideological dimensions relevant to a specific party family but not to others. Thus, socialist parties will certainly make policy proposals about crime, law and order, or immigration, but the fact that these do not constitute their own structuring ideological axis will give them a completely different value than when extreme right parties develop their own proposals in these areas. The model – we used – which claims that in a party's discourse, seeding the seeds of ideological association might be sufficient without any use of actual connotation is also important and worth investigating further in the context of our model which claims that parties do not just try to convince 'everyone' in the nation but more specifically their 'potential voters' with a certain pre-disposition to react to mere evocation of core themes.

Conversely, our model begs the question of whether all other party families may be structured by comparable ideological axes that are far more prominent and essential, or even 'existential', for them than they are for competitors from other party families. For instance, the environment could play the same role for Green parties as the negative identity does for the extreme right; the other extreme right structuring axis, authoritarianism, could be mirrored by the question of social redistribution for social-democratic parties or perhaps public ownership for their Communist counterparts.

The other essential element of our model is that these elements are not simply monolithic values; rather, they represent dimensions regarding which members of a given party family have a certain element of choice, or even a duty to situate themselves vis-à-vis alternative (but not mutually exclusive) dominant conceptions. To reflect further on the proposed examples, social-democratic parties may be identifiable by an emphasis on social justice as well as by the choices they must make to achieve it, for instance by being more or less focused on regulation or taxation. Similarly, attitudes towards the market economy could create an essential dimension on which different social-democratic or socialist parties may take diverging views to achieve similar goals.

If our model is generalisable beyond the confines of the extreme right, the question thus becomes double-barreled:

1. What ideological dimensions structure the ideology of other party families?
2. Which alternative conceptions could become their dominant mode of expression, just as xenophobia, populism, reaction, and repression are for the extreme right?

We would also need to understand whether a structuring dimension is always unique to a party family or if some could be shared between neighbouring party families.

A third aspect of the possible generalisabilty of our model concerns the question of party competition. Although the traditional Downs' model (1957) predicts the convergence of parties towards the median voter, much recent research has found that such convergence fails to occur empirically in the context of two-party systems as well as multiparty systems (see, e.g. Bruter et al., 2010). Could part of the reason for this be that the usual assertion that patterns of competition can be summarised by a unified ideological scale is, indeed, overly simplistic? Could highlighting two or three dimensions that would apply to all competing parties hide the fact that members of given party families may have specific ideological dimensions that are proper to their party family and on which potential voters will specifically judge their stance regardless of their other, more general policy proposals?

In other words, beyond the global world of party competition whereby all existing political parties compete with each other in an election, a multitude of smaller races or internal rivalries take place in an election. The balance of power between the SPD and Die Linke in Germany, the rivalry between the Christian Democrats and the Liberals in Flanders, or the fight between the FPÖ and the BZÖ in Austria represent as many bitter battles that cannot be equated to the overall electoral battle between all parties, simply because in each case a relatively predictable number of votes is at stake and will be attributed to one of each of the pairs of parties, and one of these parties only. In a certain manner, our model adds a story to this second layer of party competition, these intense duels which run in parallel to the main open race.

Obviously, the corollary to these duels resides in the real scope of potential individual-level electoral change. The propensity-to-vote model (van der Eijk & Franklin, 1996) which we use in Chapter 8 allows scholars to establish which parties a given voter realistically expects to vote for in the future. Radical changes beyond those conceived at a given point in time by a specific voter are always possible, but in many cases a number of voters realistically hesitate between two or three political parties competing for their vote and whose ideologies will not be radically opposed. There again, our model suggests that in such a case voters may not look just at the place of these neighbouring rivals on an abstract global left-right scale; the rivals' positioning on some idiosyncratic ideological dimensions may be uniquely relevant to voters situated in a specific sub-part of the ideological spectrum. Thus, someone hesitating between two competing Green parties may be more sensitive to their respective attitudes towards nuclear energy or to their willingness to enter coalitions with other parties in the name of realism' than to the question of whether one is marginally more left wing or right wing than the other.

If this is indeed the case, then this creates a sub-division between multiple types of 'key voters' who may react to different types of stimuli when making their final decision in a given election. As such, this points out an additional reason why we need to understand the specific ideological dimensions that may make any of these switch voters arbitrate between competing neighbouring parties.

Indeed, this perspective would imply a slightly different understanding of the very notion of dealignment whereby dealignment has resulted not in chaos or some randomly floating voters but in individually organised floatation. Every dealigned voter would still be defined by a relatively precise ideological identity card which would also determine a limited set of possible options for every such voter which would be related to his/her individual ideological profile. This subset of possible votes would also immediately be echoed by a set of specific ideological dimensions that would ultimately constitute the basis for the voter's final choice in a given election. It is a little bit as though the ideological universe became multidimensional, and made of a broad number of possible subsets of ideological choice, that is, individual combinations of possible ideological territories with their own individual criteria of electoral choice. In this context, voter A may well evolve in an ideological subset the boundaries of which would encompass social-democracy, green politics, and communism; voter B another subset made of socialism, communism, and the extreme right; and voter C a third yet completely different subset made of conservatism and the extreme right. This could explain why some extreme right parties seem equally to attract some former moderate right-wing voters and some moderate left-wing (or even, at times, extreme left-wing) voters. Indeed, the reactionary pillar could easily be considered shared with conservative parties, but the populist pillar can also be shared with the extreme left or even anarchist movements.

Where does this model leave us? To some extent, assuming the multidimensionality (as opposed to the single location) of any political party's ideology seems to transform an apparently simple situation into a significantly more complex one. This very complexity does not seem all that anomalous when we look at current models of party competition and electoral behaviour. At the end of the day, the two main current reservoirs of vote for the British Liberal-Democrats are elderly people from small southern countryside locations, and a young cosmopolitan and liberal population including students and young active people from large British cities including London and large Northern urban centres. This type of situation simply cannot easily be explained by traditional political sociology models or any possible variation on the Lipset and Rokkan model. If all major parties attract similarly sociologically multi-coloured voters, then we have two choices:

1. Believe that votes are completely random, which does not seem to match what we know about our democracies and individual citizens; or
2. Find a more sophisticated basis for the coherence of voters than some simple sociological trait.

In this context, an ideological mismatch between parties and voters, whether in the context of extreme right parties or of their competitors from all other major party families, ceases to be the exception or the sign of an individual party failure to become a baseline, a rule of the game. There would always be a founding mismatch between a voter and any number of possible parties truly competing for his or her vote, and this mismatch would serve as a basis to understand the kind of voter this citizen is and which ideological or strategic-discursive dimensions will serve as fundamental bases for his or her future electoral decisions. It does not matter whether parties do not understand why Miss X seems to switch from the Liberals to the Greens or the Social-Democrats to the Conservatives, or why Mr Y who supports the Communists never ends up voting for the Socialists, because in their individual cases, the universe of ideological dimensions that matter is more rigid than a single left-right continuum lets us see.

The next question raised by this notion of a mismatch as a founding reality for many citizens' electoral behaviour is its behavioural limit. What are the potential consequences of a mismatch? When do citizens start to get lost along the way for specific parties and for electoral politics in general? Where do abstention, protest, or cynicism and disaffection sit vis-à-vis given ideological dimensions? Are some party families closer to expressing or attracting a form of protest than others, or is there a more general risk that the disequilibrium created by the mismatch between a voter and the parties realistically competing for his or her vote could lead to ever-broader widespread abstention and deeper rooted political protest? On the contrary, is the possibility for parties to move along specific ideological dimensions to refresh their discourse and re-seduce the electorates that they may have lost at one time in their history the best possible provision for the said parties to fight back continuously and avoid losing vast numbers of voters in the long term? What is more, if our model of party competition allows for the survival of multiple parties within a party family as long as they occupy multiple ideological positions within a given universe, then in party systems that institutionally allow for such diversity, such as the Netherlands or Israel, most voters may find some competing forces that will be close enough to their true ideological preference at any given point in time even if this party changes over the years.

A final point has to be made regarding the implications of our model as to the reciprocal effects between the dynamics of electoral change and party competition. In the perpetual fight for parties to adapt their ideological discourse within a bounded territory to maximise their electoral appeal, and the perpetual risk that citizens will prioritise another ideological dimension that also fundamentally matters to them, what is the scope of partisan responsiveness in modern partisan politics? If parties fight parallel fights against internal and external enemies, and look for the best possible ideological location to maximise their reservoir of potential electoral voters, protect them, and gain those of their rivals within the context of a multidimensional model rather than a unidimensional one, then the situation likely to arise will probably fail to provide any equilibrium in the party competition.

Unlike what happens in a traditional Downsian model, the more dimensions that emerge in the ideological universe we depict, the less likely a party will be to have the optimal location from which to fight. In the context of the extreme right, we saw how the subset of potential extreme right voters is rather strictly limited: when looking at propensity-to-vote scores to evaluate which citizens give a non-zero probability that they will vote for one or other of the extreme right parties, such a proportion of non-zeros is relatively small. Within this context, we saw how different parties can end up taking paradoxical positions (again, we may remember the MPF in France, which moved from being a former moderate right-wing movement to becoming the most xenophobic French major extreme right parties). Once again, this context seems to mean that for extreme right parties, more of the competition is internal than external. In the alternative context of parties which would have a much broader subset of potential voters (parties that have a large number of non-zeros), things could be quite different: the stretch between the need to fight internal competition with ideological neighbours, and external competition with more general rivals in the race for institutional power, may become almost impossible to manage. If that is indeed the case, some of the larger parties may ultimately be the most firmly rooted in a situation of crisis and mismatch between the party, its leaders, its members, and its ideological voters; that is, ultimately, they may be the most cursed by ideological mismatch as an existential condition.

Appendix A: Word Lists for the Four Pillars (British Sample)

Negative identity dimension – pillar I: Xenophobic

Throat cutter, Israel, Kosher, Jew, Zion(ist), Enemy, Refugee, Asylum seeker, Islam, Eurabia, Arab, Muslim, Dhimmitude, Hijab, Circumcised, Excision, Integrist, Compatriot, Patriotic, Homeland, Nation, National, Nationals, Belong, Territory, Immigrant, Immigration, Foreign(ers), Others, Outsider, Parasite, Alien, Different, Tribal, Mondialisation, Globalisation, In-group, Out-group, Mixed-blood, Internationalisation, International, Binational, Super State, Colon (in reference to Palestine), USA, American, Bush, White House, NATO, Europe, European, EU, Europhile, Euro-enthusiast, Brussels, European Commission, Eurocrat, Commissioner, EU Treaties (general or specific), Elsewhere, Abroad, Multicultural, Melting Pot, White (race), Black (race), Race, Colonisation, Civilisation, Assimilation, Culture, Cosmopolitan, Identity, Belong, Overseas territories, Mainland, Empire, Isles, Wales, Scotland, Ireland, Emigrant, Leave, Flee, Repatriate, Expatriate, Expulsion, National border, Border, Holocaust, Turkey, Africa, Maghreb, Germany, Saxon, France, Gallic, Birthright, Gypsy, Romanians, Italy, Aggression, Occupation, Minorities, Flood, Invasion, Withdraw(al), Normand, IRA, Foreign terrorists, Foreign Networks, South, East, Eastern Europe, Ethnic, Sovereign(ty), Asia(n), Resettle(ment), Origin, Barbaric, Aboriginal, Invasion, Crowded, Crowding, Federal, Take Over, Community, Immigrants return, Pride, Conflict, Cultural war, War, Secession, England, British, Britons, Monarchy, Kingdom, Fiasco, Terror (meaning 1), Proud, USSR, Moscow, Lenin, Stalin, Hitler, Kaiser, National education, Popular (meaning 1), Abolish, Stealth, Devolution, Interference, Dominated, Servile, Difference, Resist(ance), Break, Supranational, Multinational, Nationalist(ism).

Negative identity dimension – pillar II: Populist

Nonsense, Shambles, Chaos, Contempt, Favouritism, Blind, Apparatchik, Bastards, Devil, Against, Nanny State, Dogma(tic), Thug (elite), Rowdy, Influence, Corrupt, Establishment, Demand, Totalitarian, University, Terror(ism) (meaning 2), Interest, Transnational, Policy, People(s), Siphon, Fact, Mass, Modern, Better, Worse(n), Short Term, Elected, Electoral (system), Unavoidable, Cynic, Regime, Tax, Victim, Tories, Peers, Lords, Squalor, Existing, (Il)legitimate, Anti-, Central(ise), Clean, Referendum, Oppose(-ition), Consensus, Pseudo, Complacency, Block, Restriction, Prevent, Laundering, Work(er), Dictatorial(-ship), Tyranny, Diktat, Fracture, Racket, Arbitrary, Plot, Conspiracy, Media, Journalist, Newspaper, Press, TV, Gang (politicians), Blair, Gordon Brown, Giscard, Thatcher, Other left/ right wing politician, Ruling regime, Larvae, Lie, Paperwork, Responsible, Waste, Elite(-ist), Oligarchy, Cartel, Monopoly, Power(s), Powerless(ness), Parties, Partisan, Government, Minister, Crisis, Politician, Politicised, Isolate, Bureaucracy, Genuine democracy, Administration, Civil Servants, Betray, Traitor, Concession, Concede,

Blackmail, Injustice, Unfair, Inequitable, Inequality, Egalitarianism, Refuse, Reject, Unacceptable, Handcuffs, Imperial, Boycott, Harassment, Expert, Cronies, Cronyism, (Politically) correct, Specific media, Decree, Fall, Collapse, True, Incompetence, System, Independence, Slave, Labour, Marxist, Socialism, Liberal(-ism), Capitalism, Conservative, Rigid, Deregulation, Lobby, Pressure group, Nationalisation, Black market, Confidence, Truth, Genuine, Real, Salvation, Claim, Always, Never, Present, Now, Current, Future, Restore, Advantage, New World Order, Strangulate, Suffocate, Pathology, Sick, Disease, Discriminate, Abuse, Dirty, Survive, Unemployed, Mafia, Dissolution, Inventive, Creative, Solution, Resolve(-ution), Indifferent, Save, Abandon, Free, Above the law, Prejudice, Shame, Suffer, Scandal, Unacceptable, Particracy, Indoctrination, Untrue, Lies, Con, Cajole, Rob, Cheat, Renewal, Innovation, Blood, Union, Right, Left, Treasure, Mistake, Fault, Failings, Catastrophe, Subversion, Fabricate, New, Myths, Tragic, Contagion, Chimera, Illusion, Regret, Average man/ woman

Authoritarianism dimension – pillar I: Reactionary

Tradition, History, Ancient, Ancestor, Generation, Old, Forefathers, Christendom, Christian, Church, Anglican, Catholic, Baptism, Catechism, Sunday School, Bishop, Priest, Feminist, Land, Language, Ownership, Homeland, Freedom Rights, Social Service, Market, Believe, Country (as land or countryside), Reference to historical characters (e.g. Churchill, William), Popular (cultural meaning), Rome, Roman, Agriculture, Farmers, Peasants, Before, Prior, Former, Remain, Stay, Hunting, Fishing, Euthanasia, Cloning, Descendents, Blessed Plot, Wise, Landscape, Past, Rural, Countryside, Father, Mother, Before, Inherit, Heritage, Heir, Family, Depositary, Children, Woman, Daughter, Husband, Wife, Marriage, Abortion, Divorce, Parents, Homosexual, Gay, Lesbian, Same Sex, Habeas Corpus, Magna Carta, Specific historical dates, Land, Village, Homes, Community (local/national), Society (meaning 1), Rebuild, Commit, Nature, Natural, Unnatural, Against Nature, Patrimony, Preserve, Preservation, Man, Men, Humanity, Mankind, Values, Morals, Morality, Respect, Vision, Feudal, Serf, Faith, Organic, Religion, Medieval, Revive, Regenerate, Resuscitate, Return, Folk, Pension(er), Older, Elderly, Farm, Fields, Agriculture, Agricultural, Duty, Professor, School.

Authoritarianism dimension – pillar II: Repressive

To protect, Paedophile, Rape(-ist), Murder(-er), Agitator, Activist, Firm(-ness), Order, Natural order, Disorder, Strength, Struggle, Combat, Fight (meaning 1), Strong, Must, Legal duty, Problem(s), Revolution, State (Stat-al), Citizenship, Subordinate, Crime(inal), Misdemeanour, Delinquent, Delinquency, Justice, Injustice, Life (meaning 1), Death, Combat, Army, Armed, Military, Defence, Soldier, Troops, Police, Severe, Rigour, Rigorous, Punish(-ment), Security, Insecurity, Restoration, Drugs, Specific drugs, Drug addict, Penalise, Consequence, Prison, Penalty, Sentence, Death Penalty, Move(ment), Direct, Right (Legal meaning), Law, Legal, Forbid, Control, Porn, Indecency, Illegal, Outlaw, Authority, Authoritarian, Authorise, Court, Tribunal, Rules, Surveillance, Safe, Violence, Violent, Risk, Impose, Enforce, Essential, Maintain, Reverse, Eliminate, Eradicate, Radical, Remove, Danger, Dangerous, Destruction, Destructive, Exploitation, Prostitution, Master(s), Repression, Repressive, Attack,

Attacker, Uniform, Action, Leadership (meaning 2), Agitate, Agitation, Magistrate, Judge, Barrister, Solicitor, Demolition), Solidarity (meaning 2), Dismantle, Secure, Gang (criminal context), Traffic (criminal context), Lenience, Depenalisation, Unprotected, Anarchic (criminal context), Thug (criminal context), Organised crime, Petty crime.

Appendix B: Interviews of Extreme Right Party Elites: Interview Template

The interviews are semi-structured and consist of two components:

1. An unguided section, whereby respondents will be asked about such things as their main political and policy objectives, what they believe their party stands for and can bring to their country, why they think a number of citizens (a) join them, (b) voter for them, and so on.
2. A guided section, whereby items corresponding to the specific four discursive strategic pillars of the model will be introduced to the respondents, who will be asked how important/relevant they believe they are in the case of their party.

Part I: Spontaneous section

- Brief introduction of interviewer and interviewee.
- Personal story of involvement and aims.
- Any difference between respondent's (R) main priorities, and those of the party as a whole.
- How would (R) describe the party main priorities / objectives / ambitions over the next ten years.
- What can the party bring to the country? What gap does it fill?
- Is there a difference between preferences of party leaders and members? What does (R) think makes someone join the party?
- How about voters? What explains the electoral success of the party?

Part II: Semi-guided

- Main policy issues. How important? Immigration, Europe, crime/law/order, and so on.
- Role of the party leader.
- Relationship to other parties; does the party invalidate other parties; Perceptions of the political/institutional system: is it sustainable, does it imperatively need re-form, what kind?
- Perceptions of other social actors: e.g. bureaucracy, media, education, pressure groups.
- What constitutes the National? Conceptions of identity? Is it compatible with European identity? Sub-national? How/How not?
- Need to restore order? How? Role of the state? Is the state sufficiently respected by all citizens? If not, how can this be remedied?
- Can country problems be sorted out? How? How long would it take? How radical would changes need to be?

Appendix C: Selected Questions from Mass Survey (see Chapter 3): Version United Kingdom- Great Britain

Q7: We have a number of parties in Great Britain, each of which would like to get your vote. How likely is it that you will ever vote for the following parties? Please, answer on a scale from 0 to 10, where 0 means that it is extremely unlikely that you will ever vote for the party mentioned, and 10 means that it is extremely likely that you will vote for that party at some point in the future. [grid 0...10]

1. Conservative
2. Labour
3. British National Party
4. UK Independence Party
5. English Democrats
6. Liberal-Democrats
7. Greens

Q8: Please look carefully at the following statements. Can you please tell us to what extent you agree or disagree with each of them? Please answer on a scale from 0 to 10, where 0 means that you completely disagree with the statement, and 10 means that you completely agree with the statement: [grid 0...10]

REACTIONARY ITEMS

1: Overall, Britain was a better place to live in 20 years ago than it is now.
2: The British values and cultural heritage are not sufficiently respected by the new generations.

REPRESSIVE ITEMS

3: On the whole, in Britain, criminals are not punished severely enough for their crimes.
4: The state should be stronger to guarantee order in our society.

XENOPHOBIC ITEMS

5: On the whole, there are too many foreigners and immigrants who live in Britain.
6: The British culture and traditions are not sufficiently respected by some minorities.

POPULIST

7:   On the whole, politicians in the UK do not tend to care much about the interests of ordinary people.

8:   There is still quite a bit of corruption and dishonesty among the British elite.

Q9: A few days ago, British citizens were invited to elect the Members of the European Parliament. Did you cast your vote and, if so, for which party did you vote?

Chose not to vote
Ineligible to vote
Voted for the Conservative Party
Voted for the Labour Party
Voted for the British National Party
Voted for the UK Independence Party
Voted for the English Democrats
Voted for the Liberal-Democrats
Voted for the Greens
Voted for the Scottish National Party
Voted for Plaid Cymru
Voted for another party (specify):

Q10: And if there was a general election tomorrow, would you cast your vote, and, if so, for which party would you vote?

Would choose not to vote
Would be ineligible to vote
Would vote for the Conservative Party
Would vote for the Labour Party
Would vote for the British National Party
Would vote for the UK Independence Party
Would vote for the English Democrats
Would vote for the Liberal-Democrats
Would vote for the Greens
Would vote for the Scottish National Party
Would vote for Plaid Cymru
Would vote for another party (specify):

Q11: When it comes to politics, people often talk of 'left' and 'right'. Please consider the following scale where 0 means that somebody's ideas are on the far left and 10 means that they are on the far right. Can you please tell us where you would place yourself on this scale?

0 1 2 3 4 5 6 7 8 9 10

Notes

1 Introduction and Research Question

1. Please see Appendix D for a list of abbreviations.
2. Party abbreviations and full names are listed in Appendix D.
3. The group disbanded in November 2007 after members from the Greater Romania Party withdrew from the group following Alessandra Mussolini's comments about Romanian criminals.
4. In Summer 2008 we carried out a pilot study of the text analysis of extreme right party programmes in the United Kingdom. The creation of the conceptual map was thus informed by the pilot study, a thorough reading of the existing literature, and interviews of the extreme right party elite.
5. The data analysed throughout this book is relevant to contemporary extreme right parties, revealing a snapshot in time of the empirical reality., Our findings and the derived conclusions must be read with this caution in mind.

2 Theoretical Framework and Conceptual Map

1. The Sozialistische Reichspartei Deutschlands (Socialist Reich Party of Germany) was a West German political party founded in 1949 in the aftermath of the Second World War as an openly National Socialist and Hitler-admiring split from the German Empire Party. The SRP had about 10,000 members and won 16 seats in the Lower Saxony Landtag election and eight seats in Bremen. It was banned in 1952 by the Federal Constitutional Court of Germany, the only court with the power to do so.
2. Article in *EurActiv*, 17/03/09. See Bibliography for full reference.
3. See Budge et al. (2001); Klingemann et al. (2006).
4. Goebbels, J. (1935) *Wesen und Gestalt des Nationalsozialismus* 12–13 quoted in US Department of State (1943) 'National Socialism' 4.
5. Although the concept of an authoritarian character or personality was first introduced by Abraham Maslow in 1943, Adorno et al. made the term more recognisable in 1950. Their thesis claims to predict one's potential for fascist and anti-democratic behaviour by assessing the 'structure of personality' based on characteristic experiences in early childhood and the pattern of internal, psychic processing. They developed a measure for fascist tendencies known as the F-scale (implicit anti-democratic tendencies and fascist potential), which includes elements of ethnocentrism, anti-Semitism, politico-economic ideology, anti-democratic attitudes, moralistic condemnation, distrust, and punishment.
6. Banton (1983) and Dickens (2000) have documented how, during the nineteenth and the early twentieth century, the concepts of race and racial inequality dominated much of the public discourse. The general belief was that one should 'preserve racial hygiene', races had to be 'maintained' and their purity 'attained', it was seen as legitimate to 'fight for one's race' or to 'awaken racial consciousness'.
7. The concept of identity has become a powerful ideological device wielded as much by academics as political entrepreneurs, social movements, or state institutions (Malesevic, 2006). Until recently, identity was almost unquestioned as a

categorical apparatus of social analysis, as well as in ordinary life, which gives an insight into its omnipotent ideological status. Identity attributes a certain statement of fact, and in this way someone's identity is rarely questioned.

8. Populism shares a notion of opposition but at the same time a high degree of ambiguity. As a political science concept, populism is simultaneously considered to be 1) a 'soft' ideology, 2) a type of regime – particularly salient within the South American context, and 3) a new political stream characterised by its opposition to representative democracy throughout contemporary Europe (Betz, 1994, Kitschelt, 1995). It possesses remarkable multi-dimensionality in its ability to transform into new-populism, national-populism, or video-populism (Taguieff, 1997). Gellner and Ionescu (1969) provided a series of differentiated perspectives of populism based on several case-studies but failed to derive a unified operational concept of populism. Canovan (1981) claimed that populism encompassed such an extreme variety of recognised forms that it made any definitive analysis impossible.

3   Case Selection and Methodology

1. Some countries, such as Norway, Poland, Hungary and Croatia, were not included in the analysis for practical reasons such as lack of availability of manifestos. With these few exceptions, the entire European extreme right landscape is included in this part of the analysis.

2. A difficulty with parties often deemed extreme right by the literature is that some may first seem to be single-issue parties. van der Brug, Fennema, and Tillie talk of anti-immigration parties, but similarly the Belgian Vlaams Belang first constructed its ideological platform around the question of Flemish independence and the Italian Lega Nord around the question of Northern separatism from the corrupt and poor South. More recently, extreme right discourse seems to have merged with another equally important question, that of European integration. Strongly Eurosceptic parties classified as extreme right by much of the literature have emerged in countries like Denmark or the Netherlands, but no better example of the confusion exists than UKIP. In the context of UKIP, the question of European integration seems crucial at every level: programmatic (the core slogan of 'leaving the EU' has long been the party's main trademark), symbolic (the 'pound' symbol of willingness to fight till death for the pound against the adoption of the Euro in the UK) and organisational, with European Parliament elections traditionally being the main rendezvous of UKIP and its voters. The strong Eurosceptic identity of UKIP must considered when assessing their electoral success in second-order elections such as European Parliament elections. Supporters of classifying UKIP as extreme right suggest UKIP's Euroscepticism as an issue variation on its extreme right identity in the same way the Vlaams Belang and Lega Nord twisted the separatist theme to anchor a more global extreme right identity. They point out that UKIP now runs in all major elections and has largely diversified its manifesto despite its apparent origins as a single-issue party (with proposals on the economy, social welfare, migration, crime etc.). They also point to personal and intellectual 'routes' with other extreme right parties, as embodied by UKIP's choice of partners in the European Parliament and recent claims that some UKIP members were being approached by organisers of the English Defence League (Taylor, 2010 in *Guardian*). Some authors go further and look at voter preferences. For instance John et al. (2004) use evidence from exit polls of the 2004 European and London elections, and a national survey, to examine likelihood of voting for the major and minor parties, and explore

second preferences in the London elections. They argue that the electorate perceives a linkage between the British National party and the UK Independence Party in their concern about migration from Central Europe. This suggests UKIP voters have embraced the broader extremist appeal of UKIP, not only its Eurosceptic discourse. Finally, in the context of our model, Euroscepticism can be alternatively phrased in civic populist or cultural xenophobic ways. One can resent European integration as a perceived foreign threat to British identity, or even as the horse of Troy of globalisation. These arguments would fully fit our definition of the xenophobic pillar; however, one could instead criticise European integration as a model of bureaucracy, state-like intrusiveness, and technocracy, thereby fully echoing our conception of the populist pillar. Thus, the argument about keeping UKIP within the territory of this investigation does not in any way suggest that UKIP was always of the extreme right or that its extreme right identity preceded or superseded its Eurosceptic one, but is simply an acknowledgement that in terms of its current ideological breadth as well as its electoral appeal, it is de facto competing within the territory of extreme right electoral politics. Moreover, UKIP, because of its choice of Europe as its core issue, faces in a particularly fascinating way the dilemma of the negative identity dimension that our model portrays. Because we have a unique opportunity here to gain a better understanding of the party's ideological discourse, we decided to include it in our analysis to settle the debate of whether it should be in or out of the party family. Much of the same argument could be made about the inclusion of the French MPF and many other parties included in our analysis.

3. UKIP: 28, BNP: 24, FN: 21, MPF: 19.
4. In semi-structured interviews, questions or themes are normally specified before the interview according to specific hypotheses but the interviewer is freer to probe beyond the answers in a manner which would appear prejudicial to the aims of standardisation and comparability. This structure encourages the interviewer to change the structure of the interview pragmatically as necessary by developing open-ended questions. This technique is by far the most commonly applied in elite interviewing.
5. Rather than interviewing leaders of extreme right and non extreme right parties and then comparing their responses, we focused only on interviewing extreme right party leaders about their strategic-discursive preferences. We acknowledge that interviews of the extreme right party elite should not be taken at face value and the findings should be regarded with due caution, but believe these interviews provide valuable insight into the hearts and minds of the elite we otherwise would know little about.
6. In other aspects of our research, we analyse a variety of textual data that includes party-directed press releases, campaign material and posters, and information on party websites.
7. Borg, 1966:97
8. Contemporary parties of the extreme right party family often rely upon the Internet as the natural medium for their communication. As a consequence, their websites are often interactive and professional. The BNP has recently revamped its website and now includes an interactive forum where members and the general public alike can join discussion groups, watch BNP TV, buy merchandise from T-shirts to mugs, listen to music by extremist bands, or, indeed, read press releases and commentary on news or forthcoming BNP events.
9. We also tested the specificity of the word categories we assigned to the coding framework of the extreme right parties by running a comparative text analysis on the main right-wing and main left-wing parties within some party systems.

10. Words and word categories across parties and countries were conceived to be equivalent rather than a mere translation. For example, 'Saxons' in the British case was treated as equivalent to 'Gaulois' in the French context, while 'Wales' was balanced out by 'Corsica'.
11. This project entitled 'Feeling European? Citizens' European Identity and Parties' Vision on the Future of EU Citizenship' was financed by the Economic and Social Research Council, Grant reference number RES-062–23-1838.
12. See for example the European Commission FP7-funded PIREDEU project.

4 The Conceptual Map and Extreme Right Elites

1. The importance of studying the discourse contained within party manifestos and conducting the interviews with leaders and members of the parties in question is underlined when significant differences become apparent between what the voters are voting for and what the members think and believe in. Klandermans and Mayer's study of extreme right activists (2006) confirms this disparity between the preferences of voters of the AN and the ideological frames of the militants. Gianfranco Fini may have seduced voters from the centre right since the party's *aggorniamento* in the Congress of Fiuggi (Ivaldi, 2001), but many AN party members at the local level are still completely impregnated by the fascist tradition (Klandermans & Mayer, 2006).
2. The fieldwork involved in conducting the interviews was funded by small grants from the ESRC and STICERD.

5 Capturing the Ideological Identities of Extreme Right Parties

1. Results are statistically significant at the 0.01 and 0.10 level, respectively, which is convincing considering the small n of 25 parties, and were calculated using the PCW to control for manifesto-length variations. Negative correlations are also found in the press releases of each party between the xenophobic and populist pillars, and of all parties except the Dansk folkeparti between the reactionary and repressive pillars.

6 Exploring the Extreme Right Universe: Patterns of Internal Party Competition

1. The study is available at http://www.bsk.utwente.nl/skon.

7 How Stable Is the Discourse of Extreme Right Parties over Time? Analysis of the Press Releases of Five European Extreme Right Parties

1. We use quarters as a unit of measurement to avoid picking up too much random short-term variation, which would arguably be the case if we aggregated press releases each month. All press releases available have been included in the analysis without exception.
2. Unfortunately, four quarterly periods of BNP press releases were not available. We coded press releases before and after this brief period.

25

8 Match or Mismatch? Investigating the Match between Extreme Right Parties' Ideological Positions and the Ideological Preferences of Voters

1. As highlighted before in terms of studying the discourse of extreme right parties, the Comparative Manifestos Project (Budge et al., 2002) focuses on the relatively prominent and successful parties and excludes most of the other parties belonging to the extreme right party family.
2. See footnote 24.
3. Low = men, high = women. Note: there is obviously some debate about the best way to evaluate the correlation between continuous and dichotomous variables, with the dominant answer the use of biserial correlation, which is just a form of Pearson moment correlation.
4. The higher the ideological pillar scores, the higher the likeliness to vote for extreme right parties. Because of the nature of the variables, for ease of presentation we use voting level as the fixed category in Tables 8.13 and 8.14 and Figure 8.1. This format does not affect the results but simply allows us to use 3- and 4-point categories as opposed to 10 points, which streamlines the presentation.
5. As is always the case with nearly any social science model, the notion of exogeneity is relative. One could of course argue that the other parties' candidates, campaigns, and records could in the long run fuel or lower citizens' adhesion to populist ideological statements. From a 'modelling tradition' perspective, it is certainly sufficiently exogenous not to be included as a control in the equation, which would simply artificially inflate our R^2.

References

Abedi, A. (2002) 'Challenges to Established Parties: The Effects of Party System Features on the Electoral Fortunes of Anti-Political Establishment Parties' *European Journal of Political Research* 41: 551–83.

Aberbach, J.D., Chesney, J.D., & Rockman, B.A (1975) 'Exploring Elite Political Attitudes: Some Methodological Lessons' *Political Methodology* 2.1–27.

Adams, J.F, Merrill, S., & Grofman, B. (2005) *A Unified Theory of Party Competition: A Cross National Analysis Integrating Spatial and Behavioural Factors* (Cambridge, Cambridge University Press).

Adorno, T.W., Frenkel-Brunswik, E., Levinson, D.J., & Sanford, R.N. (1950) *The Authoritarian Personality* (New York, Harper and Row).

Aldrich, J. (1983) 'A Downsian Spatial Model with Party Activists' *American Political Science Review* 77(4): 765–91.

Allport, G. (1994) *The Nature of Prejudice* (Cambridge, Addison-Wesley).

Allum, N. (1998) A social representations approach to the comparison of three textual corpora using Alceste. Dissertation, London School of Economics and Political Science.

Andersen, R. & Evans, J. (2004) *Social-Political Context and Authoritarian Attitudes: Evidence from Seven European Countries* (Glasgow, CREST Working Paper No. 104).

Andersen, R. & Evans, J.A.J. (2003) 'Values, Cleavages and Party Choice in France, 1988–1995' *French Politics* 1.1: 83–114.

Andersen, J.G. & Bjorklund, T. (2000) 'Radical Right-Wing Populism in Scandinavia: From Tax Revolt to Neo-Liberalism and Xenophobia' in Hainsworth, P. (ed.), *The Politics of the Extreme Right: From the Margins to the Mainstream* (London, Pinter): 193–223.

Anderson, C. (1996) 'Economics, Politics and Foreigners: Populist Party Support in Denmark and Norway' *Electoral Studies* 15: 497–511.

Arendt, H. (1958) *The Origins of Totalitarianism* (London, Allen and Unwin).

Art, D. (2006) *The Politics of the Nazi Past in Germany and Austria* (Cambridge, Cambridge University Press).

Arter, D. (1992) 'Black Faces in the Blond Crowd: Populist Racism in Scandinavia' *Parliamentary Affairs* 45.3: 357–72.

Arzheimer, K. & Carter, E. (2006) 'Political Opportunity Structures and Right-Wing Extremist Party Success' *European Journal of Political Research* 37(1): 103–13.

Arzheimer, K. & Klein, M. (1997) 'Die Wähler der REP und der PDS in West-und Ostdeutschland' in Backes, U. & Jesse, E. (eds.), *Jahrbuch Extremismus and Demokratie 9* (Baden-Baden, Nomos).

Backer, S. (2000) 'Right-Wing Extremism in Unified Germany in Hainsworth, P. (ed.) *The Politics of the Extreme Right* (London and New York, Pinter).

Backes, U. & Mudde, C. (2000) 'Germany: Extremism without Successful Parties' *Parliamentary Affairs* 53.3: 457–68.

Backes, U. & Moreau, P. (1994) *Die Extreme Rechte in Deutschland* (München, Akademischer Verlag).

Backes, U. & Jesse, E. (1993) *Politischer Extremismus in der Bundesrepublik Deutschland* (Bonn, Bundeszentrale für Politischer Bildung).

Backes, U. (1990) 'The West German Republikaner: Profile of a Nationalist Populist Party of Protest' *Patterns of Prejudice* 24.1: 3–18.

Bale, T. (2003) 'Cinderella and Her Ugly Sisters: the Mainstream and Extreme Right in Europe's Bipolarising Party Systems' *West European Politics* 26.3: 67–90.

Banton, M., (1983) *Racial and Ethnic Competition* (Cambridge, Cambridge University Press).

Bardi, L. (2003) 'Parties and Party Systems in the European Union — National and Supranational Dimensions' in Luther, K.R & Müller-Rommel, F. (eds.) *Political Parties in the New Europe: Political and Analytical Challenges* (Oxford, Oxford University Press).

Bastow, S. (2000) 'Le Mouvement National Républicain: Moderate Right-Wing Party or Party of the Extreme Right?' *Patterns of Prejudice* 34.2: 3–18.

Bauer, M.W. (2000) 'Classical Content Analysis' in Bauer, M.W. & Gaskell, G. (eds.), *Qualitative Researching with Text, Image and Sound* (London, Sage).

Benoit, K. & Laver, M. (2003) 'Extracting Policy Positions from Political Texts Using Words as Data' *American Political Science Review* 97: 311–31.

Betz, H.G. (2002) 'Rechtspopulismus und Rechtsradikalismus in Europa' *Österreichische Zeitschrift für Politikwissenschaft*: 251–64.

Betz, H.G & Immerfall, S. (1998) *The New Politics of the Right: Neo-Populist Parties and Movements in Established Democracies* (New York, St. Martin's Press).

Betz, H.G. (1994) *Radical Right-Wing Populism in Western Europe* (Basingstoke, Macmillan).

Betz, H.G. (1993) 'The New Politics of Resentment: Radical Right-Wing Populist Parties in Western Europe' *Comparative Politics* 25.4 413–27.

Betz, H and Immerfall, S (eds) (*1998*) *The New Politics of the Right: Neo-populist Parties and Movements in Established Democracies* (Basingstoke: Macmillan).

Billiet, J. & De Witte, H. (1995) 'Attitudinal Dispositions to Vote for "New" Extreme Right Wing Parties: A Case of the Vlaamsblok' *European Journal of Political Research* 27: 181–202.

Billig, M. (1979) *Fascists: A Social Psychological View of the National Front* (London, Academic Press).

Borg, O. (1966) 'Basic Dimensions of Finnish Party Ideologies: a Factor Analytical Study'. *Scandinavian Political Studies* 1: 94–117.

Breakwell, G. (2004) 'Identity Change in the Context of the Growing Influence of European Union Institutions' in Herrman, R., Risse, T., and Brewer M. (eds.) *Transnational Identities:* 25–39.

Brechon, P. & Kumar Mitra, S. (1992) 'The National Front in France: The Emergence of an Extreme Right Protest Movement' *Comparative Politics* 25.1: 63–82.

Brinegar, A. & Jolly, S. (2005) 'Location, Location, Location: National Contextual Factors and Public Support for European Integration' *European Union Politics* 6.2: 155–80.

Brubaker, R. (2009) 'Ethnicity, Race, and Nationalism' *Annual Review of Sociology* 35: 21–42.

Brubaker, R. (2004) *Ethnicity without Groups* (Cambridge, Harvard University Press).

Brubaker, R. (1992) *Citizenship and Nationhood in France and Germany* (Cambridge, Harvard University Press).

Bruter, M., Erikson, R. & Strauss, A. (2010) 'Uncertain Candidates, Valence, and the Dynamics of Candidate Position-Taking' *Public Choice* 144–1/2: 153–68.

Bruter, M. & Harrison, S. (2009) *The Future of our Democracies? Young Party Members in Europe* (London, Palgrave Macmillan).

Bruter, M. (2009) 'Time Bomb? The Dynamic Effect of News and Symbols on the Political Identity of European Citizens' *Comparative Political Studies* 42.12: 1498–1536.

Bruter, M. (2005) *Citizens of Europe? The Emergence of a Mass European Identity* (London, Palgrave Macmillan).

Bruter, M. (2003) 'Winning Hearts and Minds for Europe? News, Symbols and European Identity' *Comparative Political Studies* 36(10): 1148–79.

Bruter, M. & Harrison, S. (forthcoming article) 'Cocktail Politics? The Discursive Strategies of the Extreme Right in Europe'.

Bryman, A. (2001) *Social Research Methods* (Oxford, Oxford University Press).

Bryman, A. & Cramer, D. (1990) *Quantitative Date Analysis for Social Scientists* (London, Routledge).

Budge, I., Klingemann, H.D, Volkens, A., Bara, J., & Tanenbaum, E., with Fording, R.C., Hearl, D.J., Kim, H.M., McDonald, M.D., & Mendez, S. (2001) *Mapping Policy Preferences: Estimates for Parties, Electors, and Governments 1945–1998.* (Oxford, Oxford University Press).

Budge, I. (2000) 'Expert Judgements of Party Policy Positions. Uses and Limitations in Political Research' *European Journal of Political Research* 37(1): 103–13.

Budge, I. & Keman, H. (1990) *Parties and Democracy: Coalition Formation and Government Functioning in Twenty States* (Oxford, Oxford University Press).

Budge, I. & Laver, M. (1986) 'Office Seeking and Policy Pursuit in Coalition Theory' *Legislative Studies Quarterly* 4: 485–506.

Bull, A.C. & Gilbert, M. (2001) *The Lega Nord and the Northern Question In Italian Politics* (Basingstoke, Palgrave Macmillan).

Burgess, P. (2000) *Europeanisation and Multiple Identities:* Conference at the European Union Institute, Florence 9–10 June.

Campbell, A., Converse, P.E., Miller, W.E., & Stokes, D.E. (1960) *The American Voter* (Chicago, University of Chicago Press).

Carter, E. (2005) *The Extreme Right in Western Europe* (Manchester, Manchester University Press).

Carter, E. (2002) 'Proportional Representation and the Fortunes of Right-Wing Extremist Parties' *West European Politics* 25: 125–46.

Cheles, L., Ferguson, R., & Vaughan, M. (1991) *Neo-Fascism in Europe* (London, Longman).

Coffé, H. (2005) 'Do Individual Factors Explain the Different Success of the Two Belgian Extreme Right Parties' *Acta Politica* 40.1: 74–93.

Cole, A. (2005) 'Old Right Versus New Right? The Ideological Positioning of Parties of the Far Right' *European Journal of Political Research* 44.2: 203–30.

De Lange, S. (2007) 'A New Winning Formula? The Programmatic Appeal of the Radical Right' *Party Politics* 13: 411–35.

Delanty, G. (1996) 'The Frontier and Identities of Exclusion in European History.' *History of European Ideas* 22.2: 93–103.

Deloye, Y. & Bruter, M. (2007) *Encyclopaedia of European Elections* (London, Palgrave).

Dexter, L. (1970) *Elite and Specialised Interviewing* (Evanston, Northwestern University Press).

DiGusto, G. & Jolly, S. (2008) *French Xenophobia and the Radical Right: Public Attitudes toward Immigration,* paper presented at Annual Meeting of MPSA Conference, Chicago.

Downs, W. (2002) 'How Effective Is the Cordon Sanitaire? Lessons from efforts to contain the far right in Belgium, France, Denmark, and Norway' *Journal für Konflikt-und Gewaltforschung* 4, 32.

Downs, A. (1957) *An Economic Theory of Democracy* (Harper, New York).

Druwe, U. & Mantino, S. (1996) 'Rechtsextremismus'. Methodologische Bemerkungen zu einem politikwissenschaftlichen Begriff' in Falter, J.W., Jaschke, G., & Winkler, J.R. *Rechtsextremismus: Ergebnisse und Perspektiven der Forschung* (Westdeutscher Verlag).

Dülmer, H. & Klein, M. (2005) 'Extreme right-wing voting in Germany in a multi-level perspective: a rejoinder to Lubbers and Scheepers', *European Journal of Political Research*, (44), 243–63

Duverger, M. (1951) *Political Parties* (London, Methuen).

Eatwell, R. & Mudde, C. (eds) (2004) *Democracy and the New Extreme Right Challenge* (Routledge, London).

Eatwell, R. (2003) 'Ten Theories of the Extreme Right' in Merkl, P.H. & L. Weinberg, L. (eds), *Right-Wing Extremism in the Twenty-First Century* (London, Frank Cass): 47–73.

Eatwell, R. (2002) 'The Rebirth of Right-Wing Charisma? The Cases of Jean-Marie Le Pen and Vladimir Zhirinovsky' *Totalitarian Movements and Political Religions* 3.3: 1–24.

Eatwell, R. (2000) 'The Rebirth of the 'Extreme Right' in Western Europe?' *Parliamentary Affairs* 53.3: 407–25.

Eatwell, R. (1997) 'Toward a New Model of the Rise of the Extreme Right'. *German Politics* 6.3: 166–184.

Eatwell, R. (1996) 'On Defining the Fascist Minimum: The Centrality of Ideology' *Journal of Political Ideologies* 3.1: 303–19.

Eatwell, R. & Sullivan, N (eds) (1992) *The Nature of the Right: European and American Politics and Political Thought since 1789* (London, Continuum International Publisher Group)

Eatwell, R. (1989) 'The Nature of the Right: the Right as a Variety of Styles of Thought' in Eatwell, R. & O'Sullivan, N. (eds) *The Nature of the Right: European and American Political Thought since 1789* (London, Pinter): 62–76.

van der Eijk, C., Franklin, M.N., & Marsh, M. (1996) `What voters teach us about Europe-wide elections : what Europe-wide elections teach us about voters', *Electoral Studies*, 15: 149–166.

Erikson, R.S. (1978) 'Constituency Opinion and Congressional Behavior: A Reexamination of the Miller-Stokes Representation Data' *American Journal of Political Science* 22.3: 511–35.

Esping-Andersen, G. (1985) *Politics against Markets: The Social Democratic Road* (Princeton, Princeton University Press).

Evans, J.A.J. (2005) 'The Dynamics of Social Change in Radical Right-Wing Populist Party Support' *Comparative European Politics* 3.1: 76–101.

Evans, J. A.J., Arzheimer, K., Baldini, G., Bjørkland, T. et al. (2001) 'Comparative Mapping of Extreme Right Electoral Dynamics: An Overview of EREPS (Extreme Right Electorates and Party Success)' *European Political Science* 1.1.

Evans, J. A.J. & Ivaldi, G. (2002) 'Les Dynamiques Électorales de l'Extrême Droite Européenne' *Revue Politique et Parlementaire* 104.1019: 67–83.

Evans, G., Heath, A., & Lalljee, M. (1996) 'Measuring Left-Right and Libertarian Authoritarian Values in the British Electorate' *The British Journal of Sociology* 47: 93–112.

Falter, J.W. (1994) *Wer wählt rechts? Die Wähler and Anhänger rechtsextremistischer Parteien im vereinigten Deutschland* (München, Beck).

Falter, J.W. & Schuman, S. (1988) 'Affinity Towards Right-Wing Extremism in Western Europe' *West European Politics* 11.3.

Feld, Scott L. and Bernard Grofman. 2001. 'Issue Salience and Electoral Success: The Paradox of Nonmonotonicity.' Presented at the Annual Meetings of the Public Choice Society. March. San Antonio, TX.

Fennema, M. (1997) 'Some Conceptual Issues and Problems in the Comparison of Anti-Immigrant Parties in Western Europe' *Party Politics* 3: 473–92.

Ferrara, F. & Weishaupt, T. (2004) 'Get Your Act Together' Party Performance in European Parliament Elections' *European Union Politics* 5.3: 283–306.

Fiorina, M.P. (1981) *Retrospective Voting in American National Elections* (New Haven, Yale University Press).

Fischer, S. (1980) 'The "Decline" of Parties Thesis and the Role of Minor Parties' in Merkl, P. (ed.) *Western European Party Systems* (New York, The Free Press).

Flanagan, S. (1987) 'Value Change in Industrial Society' *American Political Science Review* 81.4: 1303–19.

Fleck, C. & Müller, A. (1998) 'Front-Stage and Back-Stage: the Problem of Measuring Post-Nazi Anti-Semitism in Austria' in Larsen, S.U. (ed.) Modern *Europe after Fascism 1943–1980s* (Boulder, Social Science Monographs): 436–54.

Flick, J. (2002) *An Introduction to Qualitative Research, 2nd ed.* (London, Sage).

Flohr, H. (1968) *Parteiprogramme in der Demokratie: ein Beitrag zur Theorie der Rationalen Politik* (Göttingen, Schwartz).

Forbes, H.D (1997) *Ethnic Conflict: Commerce, Culture, and the Contact Hypothesis* (New Haven, Yale University Press).

Franklin, M. N. (1992) 'The Decline of Cleavage Politics' in Franklin, M.N, Mackie, T.T., Valen, H. et al. (ed.) *Electoral Change: Responses to Evolving Social and Attitudinal Structures in Western Countries* (Cambridge, Cambridge University Press).

Franzosi, R. (1999) *From Words to Numbers: Narrative, Data, and Social Science* (Cambridge, Cambridge University Press).

Gabel, M.J. & Huber, J.D. (2000) 'Putting Parties in their Place: Inferring Party Left-Right Ideological Positions from Party Manifestos Data' *American Journal of Political Science* 44.1: 94–103.

Gallagher, T. (2000) 'Exit from the Ghetto: The Italian Far Right in the 1990s' in Hainsworth, P. (ed.) *The Politics of the Extreme Right: From the Margins to the Mainstream* (London and New York, Pinter).

Gallagher, M., Laver, M., & Mair, P. (1995) *Representative Government in Modern Europe* 2nd ed. (New York, McGraw-Hill).

Gardberg, A. (1993) *Against the Stranger, the Gangster, and the Establishment: A Comparative Study of the Ideologies of the Swedish Ny Demokrati, the German Republikaner, the French Front National and the Belgium Vlaams Block* (Helsinki, Universitetetstryckeriet).

Givens, T. E. (2005) *Voting Radical Right in Western Europe* (Cambridge, Cambridge University Press).

Givens, T.E. (2002) 'The Role of Socio-Economic Factors in the Success of Extreme Right Parties' in Schain, M., Zolberg, A., & Hossay, P. (eds) *Shadows over Europe: The Development and Impact of the Extreme Right in Western Europe* (New York, Palgrave).

Golder, M. (2003) 'Electoral Institutions, Unemployment, and Extreme Right Parties: A Correction' *British Journal of Political Science* 33: 525–34.

Golder, M. (2003) 'Explaining Variation in the Success of Extreme Right Parties in Western Europe' *Comparative Political Studies* 36.4: 432–66.

Goodwin, B. & Taylor, K. (2009) *Politics of Utopia* (New York, Peter Lang Publishing).

Goul Andersen, J. & Bjørklund, T. (2000) 'Radical Right-Wing Populism in Scandinavia: From tax revolt to neo-liberalism and xenophobia' in Hainsworth, P. (ed.) *The Politics of the Extreme Right: From the Margin to the Mainstream* (London and New York, Pinter).

Goul Andersen, J. & Bjørklund, T. (1992) 'Denmark: The Progress Party — Populist Neo-Liberalism and Welfare State Chauvinism' in Hainsworth, P. (ed.) *The Extreme Right in Europe and the USA* (London, Pinter).

Griffin, R. (1998) *International Fascism: Theories, Causes, and the New Consensus* (London, Arnold).

Griffin, R. (1991) *The Nature of Fascism* (London, Pinter Publishers).

Guiraudon, Virginie and Martin A. Schain, 2002, 'The French Political "Earthquake" and extreme Right in Europe,' *European Studies Newsletter*, 5: 1–5.

Hainsworth, P. (2000) *Politics of the Extreme Right: From the Margins to the Mainstream*, (Pinter, Frances Publishers Ltd).

Hainsworth, P. (ed.) (1992) *The Extreme Right in Europe and the USA* (London, Pinter).

Harmel, R. & Gibson, R.K. (2007) 'Right-Libertarian Parties and the "New Values": A Re-examination' *Scandinavian Political Studies* 18.2: 97–118.

Harris, G.T. (1997) *Dark Side of Europe: The Extreme Right Today* (Edinburgh, Edinburgh University Press).

Harrison, S. (2007) 'Extreme Right' in Deloye, Y. & Bruter, M. (eds) *Encyclopaedia of European Elections* (Basingstoke, Palgrave Macmillan).

Harrison, S. (2003) *Ideological (mis)match: Mapping Extreme Right Ideological Discourse and Voters' Preferences*, unpublished doctoral thesis.

Harrison, S. (2004) 'Un Fauteuil pour Deux? The Extreme Right and The Extreme Left in the European Parliament Elections' 2004 Conference paper presented at the AFSP/GSPE European Parliament (Strasbourg 18–19 November 2004).

Hassenteufel, P. (1991), 'Structures de représentation et "appel au peuple" – Le populisme en Autriche', *Politix*, 14, 95–101.

Heitmeyer, W. (1994) *Das Gewalt-Dilemma: Gesellschaftliche Reaktionen auf fremdenfeindliche Gewalt und Rechtsextremismus* (Fischer, Frankfurt am Main).

Heitmeyer, W. (1993) 'Hostility and Violence towards Foreigners in Germany' in Björgo, T. & Wiite, R. (eds) *Racist Violence in Europe* (New York, St. Martin's Press).

Holzer, W. I. (1981) 'Zur wissenschaftlichen Propädeutik des polititischen Begriffs Rechtsextremismus' in Dokumentationsarchiv des österreichischen Widerstandses (ed.) *Rechtsextremismus in Österreich nach 1945* (Vienna, Österreichischer Bundesvarlag): 13–50.

Hooghe, L., Marks, G., & Wilson, (2002) 'Does Left/Right Structure Party Positions on European Integration' *Comparative Political Studies* 35.8: 965–89.

Hooghe, L. & Marks, G. (1999) 'The Making of a Polity: The Struggle over European Integration' in Kitschelt, H., Lange, P., Marks, G., & Stephens, J.D. (eds) *Continuity and Change in Contemporary Capitalism* (Cambridge, Cambridge University Press): 70–100.

Hoogerwerf, A. (1971) 'The Netherlands: From Politics to Administration' in Rejai, M. (ed.) *Decline of Ideology?* (Chicago, Aldine, Atherton): 140–59.

Ignazi, P. (2003) *Extreme Right Parties in Western Europe* (Oxford University Press, Oxford).

Ignazi, P. (2002) 'The Extreme Right: Defining the Object and Assessing the Causes' in Schain, M., Zolberg, A., & Hossay, R. (eds,) *Shadows over Europe: The Development and Impact of the Extreme Right in Western Europe* (Basingstoke, Palgrave Macmillan).

Ignazi, P. (1997) 'The Extreme Right in Europe: A Survey' in Merkl, P. & Weinberg, L. (eds) *The Revival of Right-Wing Extremism in the Nineties* (London and Portland, Frank Cass).

Ignazi, P. (1992) 'The Silent Counter-Revolution Hypotheses on the Emergence of Extreme Right-Wing Parties in Europe' *European Journal of Political Research* 22: 3–34.

Ignazi, P. & Ysmal, C. (1992) 'New and old extreme right parties' *European Journal of Political Research* 22.1: 101–21.

Inglehart, R. (1977) *The Silent Revolution Changing Values and Political Styles among Western Publics* (Princeton, Princeton University Press).

Ivarsflaten, E. (2008) 'What Unites Right-wing Populist in Western Europe?: Re-examining Grievance Mobilization Models in Seven Successful Cases' *Comparative Political Studies* 41.1: 3–23.

Ivarsflaten, E. (2005) 'The Vulnerable Populist Right Parties: No Economic Realignment Fuelling their Electoral Success' *European Journal of Political Research* 44.3: 465–92.

Ivaldi, G. (2001) 'L'Analyse Comparée des Soutiens Électoraux du National-Populisme en Europe Occidentale. Apports et limites des grands programmes d'enquêtes transnationales' in Perrineau, P. (ed.) *Les croisés de la société fermée. L'Europe des extrême droites* (Tour d'Aigues, Edition de l'Aube) : 147–162.

Jackman, R. & Volpert, K. (1996) 'Conditions Favouring Parties of the Extreme Right in Western Europe' *British Journal of Political Science* 26.4: 501–21.

John, P., Margetts, H., & Weir, S. (2005) 'One in Five Britons Could Vote Far Right' *New Statesman* 134, 24 January.

Kedourie, E. (1994) *Nationalism* 4th expanded edition (London, Blackwell Publishers).

Katz, R.S. & Mair, P. (1994) 'How Parties Organise: Change and Adaptation in Party Organisations in Western Democracies' *Comparative Politics* 11.

Katz, R.S. (1980) *A Theory of Parties and Electoral Systems* (Baltimore, Johns Hopkins University Press).

King, G., Keohane, R.O., & Verba, S. (1994) *Designing Social Inquiry* (Princeton, Princeton University Press).

Kitschelt, H. (2007) 'Growth and Persistence of the Radical Right in Post-Industrial Democracies. Advances and challenges in comparative research' *West European Politics* 30.5: 1176–1206.

Kitschelt, H. (1996) 'European Party Systems: Continuity and Change' in Rhodes, M. et al. (eds) *Developments in West European Politics* (Basingstoke, Macmillan): 131–150.

Kitschelt, H. & McGann, A.J. (1995) *The Radical Right in Western European Comparative Analysis* (Ann Arbor, University of Michigan Press).

Klandermans, B. & Mayer, N. (eds) (2006) *Extreme Right Activists in Europe. Through the Magnifying Glass* (London and New York, Routledge).

Klandermans, B. (1997) *The Social Psychology of Protest* (Cambridge, MA, Blackwell).

Klein, L. & Simon, B. (2006) 'Doing it for Germany. A Study of Die Republikaner and Junge Freiheit' in Klandermans, B. & Mayer, N. (eds.) *Extreme Right Activists in Europe: Through the Magnifying Glass* (London and New York, Routledge).

Klein, L. & Simon, B. (2006a) 'Identity in German Right-Wing Extremism. Levels, Functions and Processes' in Klandermans, B. & Mayer, N. (eds) *Extreme Right Activists in Europe. Through the Magnifying Glass* (London and New York, Routledge).

Klingemann, H.D., Volkens, A., Bara, J., Budge, I., & Macdonald, M. (2006) *Mapping Policy Preference II: Estimates for Parties, Electors and Governments in Eastern Europe, the European Union and the OECD, 1990–2003* (Oxford, Oxford University Press).

Knigge, P. (1998) 'The Ecological Correlates of Right-Wing Extremism in Western Europe' *European Journal of Political Research* 34: 249–79.

Koopmans, R., Statham, P., Giugni, M., & Passy, F. (2005) *Contested Citizenship: Political Contention over Migration and Ethnic Relations in Western Europe* (Minneapolis, University of Minnesota Press).

Koopmans, R. & Kriesi, H. (1997) 'Citoyenneté, Identité Nationale et Mobilisationde l'Extrême Droite: Une Comparaison entre la France, l'Allemagne, les Pays-Bas et la Suisse' Birnbaum, P. (ed.) *Sociologie des Nationalismes* (Paris, Presses Universitaires de France): 295–324.

Koopmans, R. (1996) 'Explaining the Rise of Racist and Extreme Right Violence in Western Europe: Grievances and Opportunities' *European Journal of Political Research* 30: 185–216.

Kriesi, H. (1999) 'Movements of the Left, Movements of the Right: Putting the Mobilization of Two New Types of Social Movements into Political Context' in Kitschelt, H., Lange, P., Marks, G., & Stephens, J.D. (eds). *Continuity and Change in Contemporary Capitalism* (Cambridge, Cambridge University Press): 398–425.

Kriesi, H., Koopmans, R., Duyvendak, J.W., & Giugni, M. (1995) *New Social Movements in Western Europe* (Minneapolis, University of Minnesota Press).

Laver, M. (2005) 'Policy and the Dynamics of Party Competition' *American Political Science Review* 99.2: 263–82.

Laver, M., Benoit, K., & Garry, J. (2003) 'Extracting Policy Positions from Political Texts Using Words as Data' *American Political Science Review* 97: 311–31.

Laver, M., Benoit, K., & Garry, J. (2002) *Placing Political Parties in Policy Spaces* (Dublin, Trinity College Press).

Laver, M. & Garry, J. (2000) 'Estimating Policy Positions from Political Texts' *American Journal of Political Science* 44.3: 619–34.

Laver, M., & Schofield, N. (1990) *Multi-party Government: The Politics of Coalition in Europe* (Oxford, Oxford University Press).

Lawson, K. (1976) *The Comparative Study of Political Parties* (New York, St. Martin's Press).

Lewis-Beck, M. & Mitchell, G. (1993) 'French Electoral Theory: The National Front Test' *Electoral Studies* 12: 112–127.

Lijphart, A. (1984) *Democracies: Patterns of Majoritarian & Consensus Government in Twenty-one Countries* (New Haven, Yale University Press).

Lipset, S.M. & Rokkan, S. (1967) *Party Systems and Voter Alignments: Cross National Perspectives* (New York, The Free Press).

Lubbers, M. & Scheepers, P. (2001) 'Explaining the Trend in Extreme Right-Wing Voting: Germany 1989–1998' *European Journal of Political Research* 17.4: 431–46.

Lubbers, M., Scheepers, P., & Billiet, J. (2000) 'Multi-level Modelling of Vlaams Blok Voting' *Acta Politica* 35: 363–98.

Lubbers, M. & Scheepers, P. (2000) 'Individual and Contextual Characteristics of the German Extreme Right Vote in the 1990s' *European Journal of Political Research* 38.1: 63–94.

Lucardie, P. (2000) 'Prophets, Purifiers and Prolocutors: Towards a Theory on the Emergence of New Parties' *Party Politics* 6.2: 175–86.

Luebbert, G.M. (1986) *Comparative Democracy: Policymaking and Governing Coalitions in Europe and Israel* (New York, Columbia University Press).

Malesevic, S. (2006) *Identity as Ideology: Understanding Ethnicity and Nationalism* (New York, Palgrave Macmillan).

Mannheim, K. (1960) *Ideology and Utopia: an Introduction to the Sociology of Knowledge* (London, Routledge & Kegan Paul).

Martin, L. & Vanberg, G. (2008) 'A Robust Transformation Procedure for Interpreting Political Text' *Political Analysis* 16.1: 93–100.

May, J. (1973) 'Opinion Structure of Political Parties: The Special Law of Curvilinear Disparity' *Political Studies* 21.2: 135–51.

May, T. (2001) *Social Research, Issues, Methods and Process* (Buckingham, Open University Press).

Mayer, N. (2005) *Radical Right Populism in France: How Much of the 2002 Le Pen Votes Does Populism Explain?* working paper, The Centre for the Study of European Politics and Society.

Mayer, N. & Sineau, M. (2002) 'France: The Front National' in Amesberger, H. & Halbayr, B. (eds) *Rechtsextreme Parteien — eine mögliche Heimat für Frauen?* (Opladen, Leske and Budrich): 61–112.

Mayer, N. (1998) 'The French National Front' in Betz, H.G & Immerfall, S. (eds) *The New Politics of the Right: Neo-Populist Parties and Movements in Established Democracies* (Basingstoke, Palgrave Macmillan).

Mayer, N. (1995) 'Ethnocentrism and the Front National Vote in the 1988 French Presidential Election' in Hargreaves, A. & Leaman, J. (eds) *Racism, Ethnicity and Politics in Contemporary Europe* (Brookfield, Edward Elgar).

Mayer, N. & Perrineau, P. (1992) 'Why Do They Vote for Le Pen?' *European Journal of Political Research* 22: 123–41.

Mayer, N. & Perrineau, P. (eds) (1989) *Le Front National à Decouvert* (Paris, Presses de la Fondation Nationale des Sciences Politiques).

Macdonald, S.E., Listhaug, O., & Rabinowitz, G. (1991). 'Issues and Party Support in Multiparty Systems' *American Political Science Review* 85: 1107–31.

McGann, A.J. & Kitschelt, H. (2002). Right-wing Politics in the Alps: The Dynamics of Electoral Support and Strategic Party Interaction in Switzerland and Austria. Paper prepared for the Council of European Studies 2002 Conference of Europeanists, Chicago, 14–17 March.

McGann, A. J. & Kitschelt, H. (2005) 'The Radical Right in the Alps: Evolution of Support for the Swiss SVP and Austrian FPÖ' *Party Politics* 11.2: 147–72.

Meinhof, U. (2003) 'Migrating Borders: An Introduction to European Identity Construction in Process' in Bordering Identities Special Issue of *Journal of Ethnic and Migration Studies* 29.5: 781–96.

Meinhof, U. (2002) *Living (with) Borders: Identity Discourses on East-West Borders in Europe* (Aldershot, Ashgate).

Mény, Y. & Surel, Y. (2002) *Democracies and the Populist Challenge* (New York, Palgrave).

Merkl, P.H. & and Weinberg, L. (eds.), 1997. *The Revival of Right-Wing extremism in the Nineties* (London, Frank Cass).

Merkl, P. & Weinberg, L. (eds) (2003) *Right-Wing Extremism in the Twenty-First Century* (London, Frank Cass).

Merkl, P. & Weinberg, L. (eds) (1993) *Encounters with the Contemporary Radical Right* (Boulder, Westview Press).

Michels, R. (1911) *Zur Soziologie des Parteiwesens in der modernen Demokratie: Untersuchungen über die oligarchischen Tendenzen des Gruppenlebens* (Klinkhardt, Leipzig).

Middentorp, C.P. & Meloen, J.D. (1990) 'The Authoritarianism of the Working Class Revisited' *European Journal of Political Research* 24.2: 211–28.

Miller, W.E. & Stokes, D.E. (1963) 'Constituency Influence in Congress' *American Political Science Review* 6.

Minkenberg, M. (2006) 'Repression and Reaction: Militant Democracy and the Radical Right in Germany and France' *Patterns of Prejudice* 40.2: 25–44.

Minkenberg, M. (1998) *Die neue radikale Rechte im Vergleich* (Opladen, Westdeutscher Verlag).

Minkenberg, M. (1998) 'Context and Consequence: The Impact of the New Radical Right on the Political Process in France and Germany' *German Politics and Society* 16.3.

Minkenberg, M. (1994) 'German Unification and the Continuity of Discontinuities: Cultural Change and the Far Right In East and West' *German Politics* 3.2: 169–92.

Moyser, G. (1987) *Research Methods for Elite Studies* (Winchester, Allen and Unwin).

Mudde, C. (2004) 'The Populist Zeitgeist' *Government and Opposition* 39.3: 541–63.

Mudde, C. (2007) *Populist Radical Right Parties in Europe* (Cambridge, Cambridge University Press).

Mudde, C. (2000) *Ideology of the Extreme Right* (Manchester, Manchester University Press).

Mudde, C. (1999) 'The Single-Issue Party Thesis: Extreme Right Parties and the Immigration Issue' *West European Politics*, 22.3: 182–97.

Mudde, C. (1996) 'The War of Words defining the Extreme Right Party Family' *West European Politics* 19.2: 225–48.

Mudde, C. (1995) 'Right Wing Extremism Analysed: A Comparative Analysis of the Ideologies of Three Alleged Right-Wing Extremist Parties (NPD, NDP, CP 1986)' *European Journal of Political Research* 27.2: 203–44.

Müller, L.A. (1989) *Republikaner, NPD, DVU, Liste D...* (Göttingen, Lamuv).

Mummendey, A. & Waldus, S. (2004). 'National Differences and European Plurality: Discrimination and Tolerance Between European Countries.' in Herrman, R., Risse, T., & Brewer, M. (eds) *Transnational Identities* (New York, Rowmann and Littlefield): 59–74.

Nagle, J.D. (1970) *The National Democratic Party: Right Radicalism in the Federal Republic of Germany* (Berkeley, University of California).

Netjes, C. (2004) *'Sleeping Giant or Much Ado About Nothing? Examining the role of attitudes towards European integration on national vote choice in Denmark'* Paper presented at the AFSP/GSPE Conference (Strasbourg, France, 18–19 November 2004).

Norris, P. (2005) *Radical Right: Voters and Parties in the Electoral Market* (Cambridge, Cambridge University Press).

Nielsen, H. (1976) 'The Uncivic Culture: Attitudes the Political System in Denmark and Vote for the Progress Party: 1973–75' *Scandinavian Political Studies* 11: 147–16.

Page, E.C. & Wright, V. (1995) *Bureaucratic Elites in Western European States* (Oxford, Oxford University Press).

Panebianco, A. (1988) *Political Parties: Organisation and Power* (Cambridge, Cambridge University Press).

Pedahzur, A. & Avarham, B. (2001) 'The Institutionalisation of Extreme Right-Wing Charismatic Parties: A Paradox?' *Party Politics* 8.1–31.

Pedersen, M. (1982), 'Towards a New Typology of Party Lifespans and Minor Parties' *Scandinavian Political Studies* 5.1: 1–16.

Pelinka, A. (1998) *Austria: Out of the Shadow of the Past* (Boulder, Westview Press).

Perrineau, P. (1985) 'Le Front National: Un Électocrat Authoritaire' *Revue Politique et Parlementaire* 964 : 24–31.

Petrocik, J.R. (1996) 'Issue Ownership in Presidential Elections, with a 1980 Case Study' *American Journal of Political Science* 40.3: 825–50.

Poguntke, Thomas (2001) Parties Without Firm Social Roots? Party Organizational Linkage. Working Paper 13, Keele European Parties Research Unit, Keele University.

Rabinowitz, G. & Macdonald, S. (1989) 'A Directional Theory of Issue Voting' *American Political Science Review* 83: 93–121.

Reif, K. & Schmitt, H. (1980) 'Nine Second-Order National Elections. A Conceptual Framework for the Analysis of European Election Results' *European Journal of Political Research* 8: 3–44.

Reisigl, M. & Wodak, R. (2000) *The Semiotics of Racism: Approaches in Critical Discourse Analysis* (Vienna, Passagen-Verlag).

Renan, E. (1882) *Qu'est-ce qu'une nation?* (Lecture delivered 11 March 1882 at the Sorbonne).

Richards, D. (1996) 'Elite Interviewing: Approaches and Pitfalls' *Politics* 16.3: 199–204.

Riedlsperger, M. (1998) 'The Freedom Party of Austria: From Protest to Radical Right Populism' in Betz, H.G. & Immerfall, S. (eds), *The New Politics of the Right: Neo-Populist Parties and Movements in Established Democracies* (Basingstoke, Palgrave Macmillan): 27–44.

Risse, T. (2001) 'A European Identity? Europeanization and the Evolution of Nation-State Identities' in Cowles, M.G, Caparaso, J., & Risse, T. (eds) *Transforming Europe: Europeanization and Domestic Change* (Ithaca, New York).

Rohrschneider, R. (1996) 'Institutional Learning versus Value Diffusion: The Evolution of Democratic Values among Parliamentarians in Eastern and Western Germany' *The Journal of Politics* 58.2: 442–46.

Rose, R. & Mackie, T.T. (1988) 'Do Parties Persist or Fail? The Big Trade-off Facing Organizations' in Lawson, K. & Merkl, P. (eds) *When Parties Fail: Emerging Alternative Organizations* (Princeton, Princeton University Press): 533–58.

Rose, R. (1991) 'Comparing Forms of Comparative Analysis' *Political Studies* 39.3: 446–62.

Roskos-Ewoldsen, D., Roskos-Ewoldsen, B., & Dillman-Carpenter, F. (2002) 'Media Priming: A Synthesis' in Bryant, J. & Zillmann, D. (eds) *Media effects: Advances in Theory and Research'* (Mahwah, NJ: Erlbaum): 97–120.

Ross, M.H. (1998) 'Review: Ethnic Conflict: Commerce, Culture, and the Contact Thesis by H.D Forbes' *Canadian Journal of Political Science* 31.2: 393–5.

Rydgren, J. (2008) 'Immigration Sceptics, Xenophobes or Racists? Radical Right-Wing Voting in Six West European Countries' *European Journal of Political Research* 47. 6: 737–765.

Rydgren, J. (2006) *From Tax Populism to Ethnic Nationalism: Radical Right-Wing Populism in Sweden* (Oxford, Berghahn Books).

Rydgren, J. (2005) *Movements of Exclusion: Radical Right-Wing Populism in the Western World* (New York, Nova Publishers).

Rydgren, J. (2004) *The Populist Challenge: Political Protest and Ethno-Nationalist Mobilization in France* (New York, Berghahn Books).

Rydgren, J. (2004) 'Explaining the Emergence of Radical Right-Wing Populist Parties: The Case of Denmark' *West European Politics* 27.3: 474–502.

Rydgren, J. (2003) 'Meso-Level Reasons for Racism and Xenophobia: Some Converging and Diverging Effects of Radical Right Populism in France and Sweden' *European Journal of Social Theory* 6.1: 45–68.

Rydgren, J. (2002) 'Radical Right Populism in Sweden: Still a Failure, but for How Long?' *Scandinavian Political Studies* 25.1: 27–56.

Safran, W. (1993) 'The National Front in France: From Lunatic Fringe to Limited Respectability' in Merkl, P. & Weinberg, L. (eds) *Encounters with the Contemporary Radical Right* (Oxford, Westview Press).

Sainsbury, D. (1980) *Swedish Social Democratic Ideology and Electoral Politics 1944–1948 A study of the Functions of Party Ideology* (Stockholm, Almqvist & Wicksell).

Sartori, G. (1994) *Comparative Constitutional Engineering: An Inquiry into Structures, Incentives and Outcomes* (New York, SUNY Press).

Sartori, G. (1987) *The Theory of Democracy Revisited* (New York, Chatham House).

Sartori, G. (1976) *Parties and Party Systems* (Cambridge, Cambridge University Press).

Sartori, G. (1968) 'The Sociology of Parties: A Critical Review' in Stammer, O. (ed.) *Party Systems, Party Organisations, and the Politics of New Masses* (Berlin, Free University of Berlin).

Scarrow, S. (1996) 'Politicians of Parties: Anti-Party Arguments as Weapons for Change in Germany' *European Journal of Political Research* 29: 297–317.

Schain, M., Zolberg, A., & Hossay, R. (eds) (2002) *Shadows over Europe: The Development and Impact of the Extreme Right in Western Europe* (Basingstoke, Palgrave Macmillan).

Schain, M. (1990) 'Immigration and Politics' in Hall, P.A., Hayward, J., & Machin, H. (eds) *Developments in French Politics* (London, Macmillan).

Schattschneider, E. (1957) 'Intensity, Visibility, Direction and Scope' *American Political Science Review* 51(4) (December 1957).

Scheuch, Erwin K. unter Mitarbeit von Hans Dieter Klingemann (1967) *Theorie des rechtsradikalismus in westlichen Industriegesellschaft.* In: Hamburger Jahrbuch Für Wirtschafts – und Sozialpolitik (12), S. 11–19.

Schonhardt-Bailey, C. (2005) '*Measuring Ideas More Effectively: An Analysis of Bush and Kerry's National Security Speeches*' (Political Studies, PSonline).

Shapiro, R.Y. & Mahajan, H. (1986) 'Gender Differences in Policy Preferences: A Summary of Trends from the 1960s to the 1980s' *Public Opinion Quarterly* 50: 42–61.

Shepsle, K.A. (1991) *Models of Multiparty Electoral Competition* (London, Harwood).

Simon, A.F. & Iyengar, S. (1996) 'Toward Theory-Based Research in Political Communication' *Political Science and Politics* 29.1: 29–33.

Steenbergen, M. & Scott, D.J. (2004) 'Contesting Europe? The Salience of European Integration as a Party Issue' in Marks, G. & Steenbergen, M. (eds) *European Integration and Political Conflict* (Cambridge, Cambridge University Press).

Stemler, S. (2001) 'An overview of content analysis' *Practical Assessment, Research & Evaluation*, 7(17).

Stenner, K. (2005) *The Authoritarian Dynamic* (Cambridge, Cambridge University Press).

Stöss, R. (1988) 'The Problem of Right-Wing Extremism in Western Germany' *Western European Politics* 2: 34–36.

Sudman, S. & Bradburn, N.M (1982) *Asking Questions: A Practical Guide to Questionnaire Construction* (San Francisco, Jossey-Bass).

Svåsand, Lars. 1998. 'Scandinavian Right-Wing Radicalism' In Hans-Georg Betz and Stefan Immerfall, eds., *The New Politics of the Right: Neo-populist Parties and Movements in Established Democracies.* New York, NY: St. Martin's Press.

Swank, D., & Betz, H.-G. (1996). Internationalization and right-wing populism in Western Europe. Paper presented at the Conference on Globalization and Labor Markets, Workshop on Political Economy, University of California, Los Angeles.

Swank, D. & Betz, H.G. (2003) 'Globalization, the Welfare State and Right-Wing Populism in Western Europe' *Socio-Economic Review* 1.2: 215–45.

Swyngedouw, M. (2001) 'The Subjective Cognitive and Affective Map of Extreme Right Voters: Using Open-Ended Questions in Exit Polls' *Electoral Studies* 20: 217–241.

Swyngedouw, M. & Ivaldi, G. (2001) 'The Extreme Right Utopia in Belgium and France: The Ideology of the Flemish Vlaams Blok and the French Front National' *West European Politics* 24.3: 1–22.

Swyngedouw, M. (1998) 'The Extreme Right in Belgium: Of an Non-Existent Front National and an Omnipresent Vlaams Blok' in Betz, H.G. & Immerfall, S. (eds) *The New Politics of the Right. Neo-Populist Parties and Movements in Established Democracies* (New York, St Martin's): 59–75.

Svåsand, L. (2003) 'Scandinavian Right-Wing Radicalism' in Betz, H.G. & Immerfall, S. (eds) *The New Politics of the Right: Neo-Populist Parties and Movements in Established Democracies* (New York, St. Martin's Press).

Taggart, P. (1996) *The New Populism and the New Politics: New Protest Parties in Sweden and in Comparative Perspective* (New York, St. Martin's).

Tarchi, M. (2003) 'The Political Culture of the Alleanza Nazionale: An Analysis of the Party's Programmatic Documents (1995–2002)' *Journal of Modern Italian Studies* 8:2: 135–81.

Tauber, K.P. (1967) *Beyond Eagle and Swastika: German Nationalism Since 1945* (Middletown, Weslayan University Press).

Tilly, C. (2003) *The Politics of Collective Violence* (Cambridge, Cambridge University Press).

van der Brug, W. & van der Eijk, C. with Schmitt, H., Marsh, M., Thomassen, M., Franklin, M., & Bartolini, S. (2007) 'The Future of European Elections: 2004 and Beyond' in van der Brug, W. & van der Eijk, C. (eds), *European Elections and Domestic Politics: Lessons from the Past and Scenarios for the Future* (Indiana, University of Notre Dame Press).

van der Brug, W. & Fennema, M. (2007) 'What Causes People to Vote for a Radical Right Party? A Review of Recent Work' *International Journal of Public Opinion Research* 19.4: 474–487.

van der Brug, W. & Mughan, A. (2007) 'Charisma, Leader Effects and Support for Right-Wing Populist Parties' *Party Politics* 13.1: 29–51.

van der Brug, W., Fennema, M., & Tillie, J. (2005) 'Why Some Anti-Immigrant Parties Fail and Others Succeed. A Two Step model of Aggregate Electoral Support' *Comparative Political Studies* 38.5: 537–73.

van der Brug, W. (2004) 'Issue Ownership and Party Choice' *Electoral Studies* 23.2: 209–233.

van der Brug, W. & Fennema, M. (2003) 'Protest or Mainstream? How the European Anti-Immigrant Parties Developed into Two Separate Groups by 1999' *European Journal of Political Research* 42: 55–76.

van der Brug, W., Fennema, M. & Tillie, J. (2000) 'Anti-Immigrant Parties in Europe: Ideological or Protest Vote' *European Journal of Political Research* 37: 77–102.

van der Eijk, C., van der Brug, W., Kroh, M., & Franklin, M. (2006) 'Rethinking the Dependent Variable in Electoral Behaviour — on the Measurement and Analysis of Utilities' *Electoral Studies* 25.3: 424–447.

van der Eijk, C., Franklin, M., & van der Brug, W. (1999) ,Policy Preferences and Party Choice' in Schmitt, H. & Thomassen, J. (eds) *Political Representation and Legitimacy in the European Union* (Oxford, Oxford University Press).

van der Eijk, C. & Franklin, M. (eds. (1996) *Choosing Europe?* (Ann Arbor, University of Michigan Press).

van Holsteyn, J.M. & Irwin, G.A. (2003) 'Never a Dull Moment: Pim Fortuyn and the Dutch Parliamentary Election of 2002' *West European Politics* 26.2: 41–66.

van Kersbergen, K. (1995) *Social Capitalism: A Study of Christian Democracy and the Welfare State* (London, Routledge).

van Spanje, J. & van der Brug, W. (2007). 'The Party as Pariah — Ostracism of Anti-Immigration Parties and its Effect on their Ideological Positions' *West European Politics* 30.5: 1022–40.

Voerman, G. & Lucardie, P. (1992) 'The Extreme Right in the Netherlands: The Centrists and Their Radical Rivals' *European Journal of Political Research* 22: 35–54.

Veugelers, J. & Magnan, A. (2005) 'Conditions for Far-Right Strength in Contemporary Western Europe: An Application of Kitschelt's Theory' *European Journal of Political Research* 44.7: 837–60.

Veugelers, J. (1997) 'Social Cleavage and the Revival of Far Right Parties: The Case of France's National Front' *Acta Sociologica* 40.1: 31–49.

von Beyme, K. (1988) 'Right-Wing Extremism in Post-War Europe' in von Beyme, K. (ed.) *Right-Wing Extremism in Western Europe* (London, Frank Cass).

von Beyme, K. (1985) *Political Parties in Western Democracies* (Aldershot, Gower): 1–10.

von Beyme, K. (1984) *Politischer Parteien in WestEuropa* (Munich, Piper).

Weaver, K.R. & Rockman, B.A. (1993) *Do Institutions Matter? Government Capabilities in the United States and Abroad* (Washington D.C., Brookings Institution Press).

Weber, M. (1964) *The Theory of Social and Economic Organisation* (New York, Collier Macmillan).

Wittgenstein, L. (1953) *Philosophical Investigations* (London, Blackwell Publishing).

Wodak, R. & Krzyzanowski, M. (2008) *Qualitative Discourse Analysis in the Social Sciences* (New York, Macmillan).

Wodak, R., de Cillia, R., Reisigl, M., & Liebhart, K. (1999) *The Discursive Construction of National Identity* (Edinburgh, Edinburgh University Press).

Wodak, R. (1996) *Disorders of Discourse* (London, Longman).

Internet downloads

Arzheimer, K. & Carter, E. (2003) 'Explaining Variation in the Extreme Right Vote: The Individual and the Political Environment', Working Paper 19, http://www.politik.uni-mainz.de/kai.arzheimer/extreme-right-vote/Explaining-Variation-in-the-Extreme-Right-Vote.html (accessed on 05 April 2005).

Baldini, G. (2001) 'The Extreme Right Parties in Italy: An Overview', *University Mainz*, http://www.politik.unimainz.de/ereps/download/italy_overview.pdf (accessed on 5 April 2005).

BBC News (14 June 2004) 'Kilroy: We'll Wreck EU Parliament', http://news.bbc.co.uk/1/hi/uk_politics/3803599.stm.

BBC News (17 April 2006) 'More "considering voting for BNP"', http://news.bbc.co.uk/go/pr/fr/-/1/hi/uk_politics/4915096.stm .

Berry, J. M. 'Validity and Reliability Issues in Elite Interviewing', http://ase.tufts.edu/polsci/faculty/berry/paper-validity.asp.

Election World, http://www.electionworld.org/europeanunion.htm (source used for European election results, accessed on 30 March 2005).

Election World, http://www.electionworld.org/unitedkingdom.htm (source used for 2001 United Kingdom election—BNP electoral score, accessed on 30 March 2005).

EurActive (17 March 2009) http://www.euractiv.com/en/opinion/extreme-right-seeks-european-unity/article-186842.

European Commission, http://www.europa.eu.int/comm/eurostat/Public/datashop (source used for statistical data concerning unemployment, accessed on 20 March 2005).

Guiraudon, V. & Schain, M.A. (2002) 'The French Political "Earthquake" and Extreme Right' in *Europe Council for European Studies*, http://www.ces.columbia.edu/pub/Guiraudon-Schain_sep02.html (accessed on 10 December 2008).

Ivaldi, G. (2002) 'The Front National split: party system change and electoral prospects', Manchester University Press, http://hal-unice.archives-ouvertes.fr/docs/00/09/00/97/PDF/Ivaldi-The_Front_National_split_party_system_change_and_electoral_prospects.pdf (accessed on 12 July 2010).

Lilliker, D.G. 'Interviewing the Political Elite: Navigating a Potential Minefield', http://www.blackwellsynergy.com/servlet/useragent?func=synergy&synergyActio n=showFullText&doi=10.1111/14679256.00198&area=production&prevSearch=au thorsfield percent3A percent28Lilleker percent2CDG percent29.

London School of Economics and Political Science, 'Notes on elite interviewing EPIC workshop', http://www.lse.ac.uk/collections/EPIC/events/Interviewing.pdf.

Margetts, H., John, P., & Weir, S. (2004) 'The Latent Support for the Far Right in British Politics: The BNP and UKIP in the 2004 European and London Elections', *http://www.ipeg.org.uk/papers/latentsupport210405b.pdf (accessed on 30 May 2010)*.

Mayer, N. & Sineau, M. (2002) http://www.elections2002.sciences-po.fr/Enjeux/pdf/FN percent20- percent20VD percent202001.pdf (article on the FN in France).

Poguntke, T. (2001) 'The German Party System: Eternal Crisis?' *Keele European Parties Research Unit (KEPRU)* Working Paper 2, http://www.keele.ac.uk/depts/spire/research/KEPRU/Working_Papers/KEPRU%20Paper2.pdf (accessed on 12 July 2010).

Parties and Elections (database), http://www.parties-and-elections.de/france.html (source for 2002 French national election-FN electoral score, accessed 30 March 2005).

Parties and Elections (database), http://www.parties-and-elections.de/italy.html (source for electoral scores of Italian extreme right party Lega Nord, accessed on 5 April 2005).

Pennsylvania State University, http://www.personal.psu.edu/users/s/m/smy122/Thesis/Chapter percent20Two.doc (student thesis, author unknown).

http://www.politik.unimainz.de/ereps/electoral_results.htm (extreme right electoral scores in Western Europe, accessed on 30 March 2005).

profil online, 'Schwarz-Blau: Haiders zweiter Frühling', http://www.profil.at (Austrian current affairs magazine article reporting on Haider's re-election in Carinthia, accessed on 5 April 2005).

Smith, S. (2004) 'What they said about... Haider's return', *The Guardian*, http://www.guardian.co.uk/editor/story/0,12900,1165774,00.html (source for Haider victory in Carinthia, accessed on 5 April 2005).

Stemler, S. (2001) 'An Overview of Content Analysis', http://pareonline.net/getvn.asp?v=7&n=17.

Taylor, M. (2010) 'English Defence League: new wave of extremists plotting summer of unrest', http://www.guardian.co.uk/uk/2010/may/28/english-defence-league-protest-bnp (accessed on 29 May 2010).

University of South Florida (2005) 'Teacher's Guide to the Holocaust: The Rise of the Nazi Party' (timeline), http://fcit.coedu.usf.edu/holocaust/timeline/nazirise.htm

(source for details of economic context leading to the rise of the NSDAP, accessed on 20 March 2004).

Urbanti, N. (1999) 'Rhetoric and Representation: The Politics of Advocacy', http://ptw.uchicago.edu/urbinati99.pdf, (paper presented at the University of Chicago, 11 October 1999).

Verfassungsschutz, http://www.verfassungsschutz.de (source used for German Federal Court for the Protection of the Constitution, accessed on 21 March 2005).

Index

American (anti-, Americanisation, etc),
   5, 74, 81–82, 86, 97
Anti-Federalist League, 123
Anti-Globalisation, 3
Anti-Semitism (ic), 4, 39, 97, 213

Baoso (JM), 86
Bayrou (F), 135
Berlusconi (S), 7, 31, 41, 42
Bolkestein (F), 129
Bossi (U), 41
Boulanger (-ism), 119, 123
BRD, 42
Brussels, 98, 99

Centruum, 129
Chirac (J), 42, 89, 128, 135, 158, 199
Conservative Party (Tory), 28, 77, 130
Cordon sanitaire, 139
Couteaux (PM), 120

Debré Law, 128
De Gaulle, 83
De Villiers (P), 9, 78, 120

Electoral system, 11–12, 53–54, 95
ESRC, 54, 64, 209, 216
Ethnocentric (-ism), 5, 43, 213
European Parliament, 7–11, 27–28, 52,
   55–56, 60, 64–65, 69, 88, 91, 118,
   123, 125, 137, 141, 151–153, 165,
   179, 187–191, 195, 200, 214
European Union, 15, 17, 64, 73, 85, 86,
   90–91, 97, 99, 118, 123, 143, 165
Europe of Freedom and Democracy
   Group (EP), 9
Eurosceptic (-ism), 8, 120–123, 138, 186,
   189–190, 193, 214–215

Fascism (ist), 3, 4, 26, 28, 30, 125, 213, 216
Fini (GF), 39, 216
Fortuyn (P) (and List Pim Fortuyn), 4, 6,
   39, 66, 129, 181
Forza Italia, 9, 31

Frey (G), 126

Gaullist, 120, 186
Gemeinshaftswesen, 38, 78
German Reich Party, 125, 188
Globalisation, 63, 84, 86, 87, 215
Goebbels, 38
Gollnisch (B), 28, 136
Griffin (N), 28, 78

Haider (J), 10, 15, 39
Hitler (A), 91, 213

Identity Tradition and Sovereignty
   Group (EP), 8, 28
Internationalism (ist), 89, 90
Islam (ic, ist, ization), 82–83, 85, 97, 129
Israel, 86, 206

Janmaat, 129
Jew (ish, Judaism), 40, 61

Karatzaferis, 9
Kjaersgaard (P), 7

Le Pen (JM), 7, 10, 17, 39, 41, 42, 73, 76,
   78, 119, 128, 129, 135, 136, 138,
   155, 158, 185
Le Pen (M), 10, 120, 136
Liberal Democrats (UK), 205
Libertas, 9
Linke (Die), 203
Lisbon Treaty, 9

Maastricht Treaty, 120
Mégret (B), 119, 185
Merkel (A), 86
Mitterrand (F), 89
Muslim, 61, 81, 97
Mussolini (A), 9, 213

National Front (UK), 123, 129, 189, 190
Nationalism (-ist), 2, 4, 5, 33, 40, 41, 42,
   78, 91, 137, 165

Nazi (-ism), 20, 26, 39, 53
Neo-Fascist, 4, 20, 30, 125
NSDAP, 3, 12, 38

ÖVP, 7, 15

Parti Socialiste, 128
Pasqua (C), 120, 128, 186
Patriotism (-ic), 72, 75, 100, 101
Poujade (-ism), 119, 123
Proportional representation, 8, 11, 12,
   119, 128

Racism (-ist), 4, 5, 26, 39–41, 67, 80, 81,
   85, 97, 139, 165
Radicalism, 2, 5, 31, 38, 115
Regionalist, 5
Royal (S), 135
RPR, 128

Sarkozy (N), 86, 89, 135, 199

Schönhuber (F), 28
Second-order elections, 8, 12, 179, 214
Second World War, 119, 213
Separatism (-ist), 5, 138, 214
SPD, 203
SPÖ, 15
STICERD, 216
Strasbourg, 98

Tchador, 82
Thatcher, 129
Threshold (electoral), 6, 10, 11, 27, 53,
   126, 154, 183

UDF, 128

Verfassungsschutz, 12
Vichy, 53, 119, 123
VVD, 129

Wilders (G), 8